A YEAR IN A
Scots Kitchen

CELEBRATING SUMMER'S END TO
WORSHIPPING ITS BEGINNING

CATHERINE BROWN

NEIL WILSON PUBLISHING, GLASGOW, SCOTLAND

First published in 1996 by Neil Wilson Publishing Ltd
303a The Pentagon Centre
36 Washington Street
GLASGOW
G3 8AZ

Tel: 0141-221 1117
Fax: 0141-221 5363
E-mail: nwp@cqm.co.uk
http://www.nwp.co.uk/

A catalogue record for this book is available from the British Library.

ISBN 1-897784-79-1

1   3   5   7   9   10   8   6   4   2

Designed by Mark Blackadder
Typeset in 11/14pt Perpetua
Printed by Cromwell Press

Contents

PART ONE: WINTER AND SPRING

With thanks

The editor had an idea for a new column, could we meet for lunch? The Penguin Café perched above Glasgow's Princes Square, as I remember, was the venue and I arrived feeling pleasantly expectant at the prospect of a new challenge. So what was the subject? Scottish food. Knowing how much I had already written on the subject, he thought there was an angle in exploring the past and the present, side by side. An old-established traditional method beside a modern, updated style. I could do a potted history of the tradition, some investigative interviews with the artisans and craftspeople in the food world, and we would call the column Great Scottish Food.

Without this push, in the early 1990s, back into a subject which I had decided held no more mileage for me, the seed for this book would not have been planted. To Arnold Kemp, Editor of *The Herald* (1980–1994) my sincere thanks. To *The Herald*'s Chief Assistant Editor, Anne Simpson, who fed, watered and nursed it with immense skill and enthusiasm during the first year of its life, also my sincere thanks.

Besides the weekly-column idea, there was also the suggestion that if I managed 1,000 words a week on Scottish food for 52 weeks, at the end of the year there would be enough material for a book. And so there was. But by this time the seed had grown into a tree with too many shooting branches. To produce fruit it had to be pruned and shaped into the right form. From 1992-95 a number of different pruned and reshaped versions hit a considerable number of publishing editors desks in the UK, every one accompanied by Fiona Taylor's illustrations from the Great Scottish Food series, and every one rejected. Then, just as it seemed as though its death was imminent, one helpful London publisher (Anne Dolamore at Grub Street) suggested I send it to Neil Wilson Publishing (previously of Lochar). He might be interested. To Neil Wilson my sincere thanks for having the courage to take on this book.

While Arnold, Anne and Neil are the key people who made this book possible, a great many others have fed, watered, pruned and shaped it throughout its growing life.

Iseabail Macleod, Editorial Director of the Scottish National Dictionary Association, has edited it with great skill, enthusiasm and encouragement. Robert Stewart has acted as my agent in Scotland providing more enthusiasm, encouragement and advice. Fiona Wilson, Neil Wilson's Production Manager, has skillfully and sensitively cared for the practical making of the book. A great many artisans and craftspeople throughout the food industry — the guardians of our culinary treasures — have given it much of its colour and character. Many academics with specialist knowledge, as well as food industry experts have freely provided me with valuable information. Esther and Ailie (my daughters) have been my toughest critics.

To you all, my sincere thanks. The harvest is yours. Enjoy it.

Measures

M-day (30 October, 1995) was the first phase of metrication, when pre-packaged food and drink (except for pints of beer and cider in pubs, and pints of milk in glass bottles) changed.

Loose, over-the-counter sales, have a reprieve, but only until 1 January, 2000, when selling lbs and pints in any form becomes illegal.

The march of metrication, of course, is about standardization in Europe. Whether you've joined the Imperial Measurements Preservation Society, or not, metric units are not aliens from outer space. They're simple, easy measures, and they are already all around us in existing food and drink. Children in school have been taught metric measures since 1974. The easiest way to learn is from the packaging you're already buying. If you get wise to the proportional differences, you become a free-thinker with a dual choice.

For a rough guide to buying foods sold loose in metric the proportional differences are:

Imperial	Metric
¼lb	100g (slightly less)
½lb	250g (slightly more)
1lb	500g (slightly more)
2lb	1 kilo (a little more)
1 pint	500ml (slightly less)

Dual thinking on a proportional basis in recipes works more or less the same way *:

Imperial	Metric
1oz	25g (slightly less)
4oz	125g (slightly more)
8oz	250g (slightly more)
1lb	500g (slightly more)
4fl oz	125ml (slightly more)
5fl oz (¼ pint)	150ml (almost the same)
8fl oz	250ml (slightly more) — 1 US cup
10fl oz (½ pint)	300ml (almost the same)
20fl oz (1 pint)	500ml (slightly less)
40fl oz (2 pints)	1 litre (a little less)

Despite several attempts to standardize with Europe, the US has resisted metrication and continues to measure both liquids and solids in their convenient cups based on proportions of 8fl oz (½ US pint) which is almost 250ml.

Sets of US cup measures are very convenient measures, and wherever possible, I have used them in the recipes. An 8fl oz cup can be used instead of the measure though they are now usually available in cookshops and some supermarkets.

A tablespoon is 15ml; a dessertspoon, 10ml and a teaspoon 5ml.

Only in baking recipes is it necessary sometimes to make more exact conversions.

The Scots Gard'ner:
published for the climate of Scotland
by John Reid, Gard'ner, 1655-1723

To Reid, whose *Gard'ner's Calendar* and list of *Garden Dishes, and Drinks in Season* is reproduced at the end of each month, we owe a particular thanks for his work as a pioneering gardener. Many pleasure gardens attached to historic houses were influenced by his skill in garden layout — a new phenomenon in the late 17th century as the need for fortified homes diminished. But besides this talent, Reid's interest extended beyond the formal lawns and be-flowered borders to the kitchen garden where his vigorous enthusiasm for growing fruits, vegetables and herbs, as well as tending his hives of bees, is especially valued.

Reid left Scotland in 1683 at the age of 28 (the same year that *The Scots Gard'ner* was published) to begin a new life in New Jersey, encouraged by reports of the good climate and fertile land, but also to join a community of fellow Quakers seeking freedom from religious intolerance in Scotland. He was the first Scot to write a gardening book with Scottish conditions in mind. He was the second professional gardener to write a *Gard'ners Calendar*, the English John Evelyn, being the first. Reid's gardening message may be 300 years old, but Scots must still find practical solutions to the 'cold, chilled, barren, rugged-natur'd ground', as he describes it. The temptation may be to say — it can't be done. Asparagus and artichokes in Scotland? If Reid could do it, then why not in modern times.

He not only challenges us to garden adventurously, he also reminds us of the changing seasons. Yes, we may need reminding of that too. The late 20th century's global market brings us year-round supplies of fresh produce, so that the seasons are in danger of running together like colours in the wash. Will we, by the 21st century have lost sight of what's fresh and seasonal in our own country? In the heart of pea-growing Angus, the greengrocery shelves, mid-winter, have supplies of peas from Kenya. The late 20th century pea-growing Angus farmer complains that it is no longer commercial for him to grow peas since he can't compete with the low wages paid by Kenyan pea growers.

Reid's *Scots Gard'ner* was free from such political food issues — a timely reminder?

Dividing the Year

ACCORDING TO NATURE

The great seasonal festivals of the year have their origins in the rhythm of the earth and the primitive religion of people whose natural instincts were for self-preservation and racial survival. Before science explained nature, mysteriously the seasons brought food for life's survival. But equally difficult to understand was why one year there was plenty and the next year not enough. So they kindled a symbolic bonfire in the hope that it would please the life-giving sun. They offered sacrifices of thanksgiving, and performed many symbolic acts which they hoped would encourage nature to treat them kindly. When it did, they believed that their actions had been correct. Superstition, sacrifice, myth, magic and folklore, relating to nature, was their religion.

Though they were simple nature-worshippers, indulging in what are now regarded as naive practices, their motivation was entirely logical, and their emotions about nature extremely powerful. They were not just happy when winter ended and spring began, or sad when summer faded into autumn, they worshipped this progress of the yearly cycle. It was a cause of adoration and reverence, that life should be followed by death, followed by rebirth. The yearly cycle of life, death and resurrection gave them their faith. Each group of peoples took a consensus on what seemed to be the most effective rites and ceremonies which then became their distinctive beliefs and dogmas.

Living on the islands which now make up the UK, there was an amalgam of racial strains of primitive peoples in different permutations, and in different proportions, which eventually created four distinct nations within a comparatively small area. In Scotland, the predominant racial strain was Celtic. There was also a strong mixture of Scandinavian blood from the Norse colonies in Caithness, Orkney and Shetland plus a few 'pirate nests' in the Hebrides and along the coasts. Though there were other racial strains (Northern English, Flemish and Norman) there were no wholesale conquests in this primitive period of Scottish history, and so the great festivals of the ancient Celtic and Norse people in Scotland became firmly established and nationally distinct.

While the Norse sea reivers followed the movements of the sun and the moon, celebrating their festivals according to the solstices and equinoxes, the romantic, mystical, poetical Celts divided their year according to the movement of flocks from lowland pasture to highland pasture and vice versa. In the Celtic calendar, Beltane (1 May) was the beginning of summer while Samhuinn (31 October) was the beginning of winter; 1 November was the end of the old year and the beginning of the new. The Celtic New Year began at sunset on 31 October.

It's a variation in the division of the year which continues to this day, with the Scottish Quarter days occurring in February, May, August and November while in England they are in March, June, September and December.

Among the ancient Celts, the most influential nature worshippers were the Druids, though they were by no means the only cult. Christian missionaries discovered several others, as well as many popular superstitions and magical practices which pre-dated the Druids. But compared with the early beliefs of other primitive peoples, Druidism was a sophisticated, civilizing force, practising divine worship and involving priests who were regarded as philosophers and theologians. They had a powerful esoteric attraction and practised secret priestly rites. They took on the management of order in the community, educating children as well as taking responsibility for settling disputes and deciding rewards and penalties. Unlike non-Celtic Europe, which had polytheistic systems, the mystical nature-worship of the Celtic Druids proved to be much more compatible with the new Christian faith which arrived in Scotland with St Ninian at the Isle of Whithorn (fourth century) and St Columba on Iona (sixth century).

In the first century, the Christian church celebrated only Sundays, Easter and Pentecost. In the second century, Lent was initiated and in the fourth century there was the institution of Saints' days. Though the Nativity of Christ is mentioned in the second century, it was not until the sixth century that it became a universal celebration.

During the early days of Christian mission, the priests had great difficulty converting the people from sun worshipping to worshipping a God of love and forgiveness who had nothing to do with the practical needs of day-to-day self-preservation. Of course the church failed, and the people continued to carry on with the old familiar rites and ceremonies. Which is hardly surprising, considering that these customs had been regarded as vital to their survival since the beginnings of existence. The solution for the Christian church was to accept defeat. The times of the nature festivals would be preserved, some of the less barbaric rites and ceremonies of the nature-worshippers could continue, but they would all be given a Christian significance. Yule, the northern nature-worshippers' midwinter festival and the Roman Saturnalia, would become a celebration of the Nativity of Christ, while Midsummer's Day would celebrate the life of St John the Baptist instead of the radiant sun god, the Norse Baldur.

In Scotland, the celebration of the Celtic spring goddess Bride, would become Candlemas Eve, the eve of the Purification of the Virgin; the Beltane rites in May of summer's beginning, would be dedicated to the Holy Cross; Lammas in August would continue to celebrate the grain harvest but with Christian rites in churches with loaves of bread and the end of summer, Samhuinn, the most deeply significant festival of the Celtic nature-worshippers, would become a night when all the Christian saints would be hallowed.

The Festivals

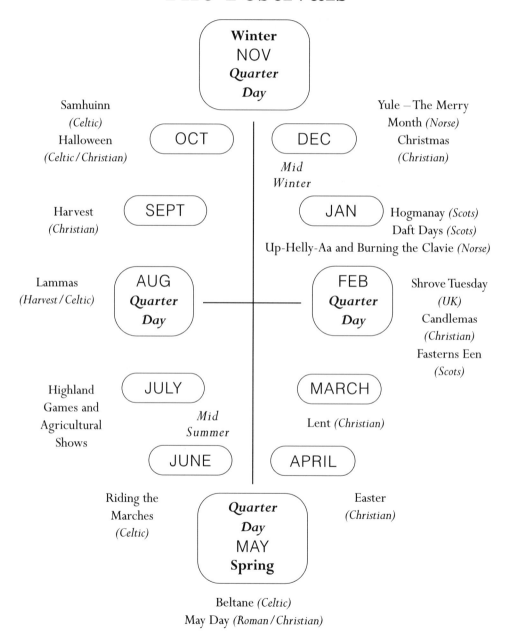

Winter
NOV
Quarter Day

OCT

DEC

Samhuinn *(Celtic)*
Halloween *(Celtic / Christian)*

Yule – The Merry Month *(Norse)*
Christmas *(Christian)*

Mid Winter

SEPT

JAN

Harvest *(Christian)*

Hogmanay *(Scots)*
Daft Days *(Scots)*
Up-Helly-Aa and Burning the Clavie *(Norse)*

AUG
Quarter Day

FEB
Quarter Day

Lammas *(Harvest / Celtic)*

Shrove Tuesday *(UK)*
Candlemas *(Christian)*
Fasterns Een *(Scots)*

JULY

MARCH

Highland Games and Agricultural Shows

Mid Summer

Lent *(Christian)*

JUNE

APRIL

Riding the Marches *(Celtic)*

Easter *(Christian)*

Quarter Day
MAY
Spring

Beltane *(Celtic)*
May Day *(Roman / Christian)*

Winter and Spring

Celebrating Summer's End

Samhuinn, The Celtic New Year, Halloween

Samhuinn, and the spring festival of Beltane (1 May), were the most important feasting periods for the early Celts who divided their year, simply, in half. The two festivals marked out winter and summer symbolizing darkness and light, the ebb and flow of the tides, the death and resurrection of nature. While Beltane was celebrated at first light, with fires lit at sunrise on hilltops, Samhuinn, summer's end, marked the beginning of the Celtic year and was celebrated in the dark, with fires lit at sundown on sacred sites of standing stones or graveyards. Today, guising, bonfires, fireworks and communal partying at this time of the year are first and foremost good fun, especially when they hit that scary nerve, but their roots go deep into ancient rites which celebrated the natural rhythm of life and death on earth.

At the beginning of November nature was disturbed, the earth decaying and the sun dying away in the sky. Of course there was cause for thanksgiving in the recently gathered harvest of crops, but it was believed that on this night of seasonal change the sleeping spirits of good and evil were awakened. For a night only, they came alive and the powers of darkness were in the ascendant. Good spirits came back to visit their relatives, while those with less honourable intentions — witches, ghoulies, ghaisties, warlocks, bogles, kelpies, gnomes and trolls — the whole unhallowed clamjamfrie of the netherworld, came back to do as much harm as they could.

Lighting a bonfire was a means of burning the evil spirits which hovered above the flames, since fire was a cleanser and purifier. Burning an effigy of a witch on the bonfire became a symbolic attempt to destroy all agents of malevolence (hence the burning of Guy Fawkes). While there was panic and terror in their minds, and though this was essentially a festival of the Cult of the Dead, their festivities involved a great deal of fun and frolicking. Communal celebration meant letting off steam, while at a deeper level there was the joyful belief in the immortality of the soul.

Halloween guising continues as one of the frolics of this festival. It's thought to have originated in the folk-memory of Druidic feasts when a mask was used to avoid being recognized by the spirits of the dead. They also believed that the hazel tree (The Golden Bough) was imbued with magic, because wizards considered it the root and symbol of wisdom, and that the apple tree (The Silver Bough) was the talisman which admitted favoured mortals into the Otherworld, giving them the power to foretell the future.

Today, the apple rite of dooking for apples is linked to the Ordeal by Water. To get to the land of the Silver Bough you had to pass first through water and then fire. Obsolete in its original form, but still enduring in suspended treacly scones, the ordeal by fire entailed fixing an apple and a lighted candle to either end of a rod. The rod was then hung from a height and twirled, while participants attempted to grab a bite of the fruit without being burnt by the candle.

On the magic front, many customs and superstitions have been handed on from one generation to the next. Magic continues to fascinate. Simple lucky charms whether worn on bracelets or in pouches all have their origins in primitive nature-worship, as do the ring, thimble, button and silver coins which are put into cakes or dumplings as 'surprises' for children. In Scotland, a variety of eating traditions developed in connection with lucky charms at Halloween.

In some parts the lucky charms were buried in a large pot of champit tatties (mashed potatoes) while in others they were put into a clootie dumpling (a spicy fruit pudding boiled in a cloth). In the Highlands, the hiding-mixture was whipped cream with oatmeal known in Gaelic as fuarag (Scots crowdie). The young people (sometimes blindfolded) sat in a circle round the pot, each with a spoon, supping until it was empty. Part of the fun was the supping, but there was even greater hilarity when everyone disclosed what their fortunes were to be. Who finds the most valued ring will be the first to marry; a silver coin, will be wealthy; the button or thimble, will not marry; the wishbone, will have their heart's desire; the horseshoe, will have good luck.

Today, children are the most enthusiastic revellers at Halloween as they continue — despite the attractions of more sophisticated entertainment — to catch the spirit of its spooky merriment. Helped by enthusiastic adults the tradition is still handed on from one generation to the next, though there are subtle changes.

While my children's Halloween consisted of guising, making turnip lanterns, dooking for apples and catching be-treacled scones, they also introduced other ideas which were never part of my childhood. For a few years, while they were still young teenagers, they liked to celebrate with a whole night of Halloween partying. Guising still continued on the 31st, but the thing was to have a weekend special Halloween fancy-dress party, when they could stay up late into the night.

Their idea of a good night's fun-and-games involved preparing in advance a tape recording of ghostly howls and shrieks. The house would be arranged so that it was almost totally dark except for a few turnip lanterns. Then they would play wild games like Hunt the Witch, when one of the mob was sent off to hide. 'Hunt the witch!' they shrieked, as frightening noises echoed round the darkened house. Then they would end up, exhausted, in the kitchen for calming drinks and a basin of swirling water and apples as they took their turn at dooking their heads into the water to catch an apple. Those with painted faces were allowed to hang over the back of a chair with a fork in their mouths, dropping the fork into basin in the hope of catching an apple.

The next bout of hilarity involved putting hands behind their backs, and trying to bite into be-treacled scones and pancakes which hung from a string tied to the kitchen pulley.

We never did lucky-charm tatties, or Highland fuarag, but the charms went into clootie dumplings or a fancy Halloween cake. Other eating concoctions were their own inventions: Worm Soup, made with spaghetti; Witch's Spider Trifle, when a spider's web was piped in chocolate icing on top of the cream, a spider was a black grape with bootlace-liquorice for legs and dead flies (currants) were scattered about the web; Skull and Crossbones biscuits were shaped out of shortbread; Dead Fly's Jelly was orange jelly with currants while a Poison Pie was made with a mushroom, onion and hard boiled egg filling covered with a puff pastry lid, decorated with more skull and crossbones.

This fiendishly got-up crowd of late 20th-century teenagers brought their night's hilarity to an appropriately ghoulish end when Count Dracula murdered everyone, one by one. Lying in a heap on the floor dead (beat) was the best place to be after their wild night of scary fun.

EARLY TWENTIETH CENTURY

HALLOWEEN STAPAG ALSO KNOWN AS FUARAG

'Good thick cream was put in a basin and well beaten up. While the cream was being stirred round and round oatmeal was gradually added till the whole got as thick as porridge. Then all the members of the household gathered round, each armed with a spoon, and partook of the stapag. On Hallowe'en stapag was always made, and, as milk would just be beginning to get scarce then a considerable amount of saving up used to be gone thro' in connection with the cream. Into this stapag a ring, a thimble and a button along with some silver coins used to be added. Each had to dip his or her spoon to the very bottom of the dish but no scraping was allowed. People did not always keep their Sunday manners about them on Hallowe'en, and tho' only one spoon was supposed to be in the dish at one time yet by some means a dozen or so might be seen scraping about.'

M M Banks, *British Calendar Customs, Scotland, Vol III, (June to December)*, 1941.

LATE TWENTIETH CENTURY

HALLOWEEN CAKE WITH CHARMS

Heavy with fresh autumnal fruits, its mellow flavour and moist texture contrasts with a crust of burnished nuts and fruit.

The method makes use of very fine, easy-to-mix 'cake' flour which makes a velvety, fine textured sponge without the labour of lengthy creaming.

INGREDIENTS

250g (8oz) castor sugar
250g (8oz) fine self-raising, cake flour
250g (8oz) butter
4 medium eggs
3 tablespoons milk
1kg (2lbs) fresh ripe autumn fruits peeled and chopped
roughly into one-inch chunks (apples, pears and plums etc)
50g (2oz) hazelnuts or walnuts
50g (2oz) undyed glace cherries
1 eating apple sliced thinly

Topping:
2 egg yolks
50g (2oz) softened unsalted butter
2 desertspoons honey

METHOD

Pre-heat the oven to gas mark 4, 180C/350F. Line a 20-23cm/8-9in round or square cake tin. Wrap charms (button, thimble, coins, horseshoe, wishbone) tightly in greaseproof paper.

To aerate the flour and sugar, sift both into a bowl and whisk with an electric beater for about 30 seconds. Soften the butter slightly, but do not melt (20-30 seconds in the microwave).

Whisk the eggs and milk together in a bowl. Put the butter and three-quarters of the egg and milk mixture into the flour. Beat for about 60 seconds, to aerate and build up the structure of the cake. Add the rest of the egg mixture and beat for another 20 seconds. Dust fruit with flour to prevent it sinking. Add the fruit and charms and mix through.

Pour into the cake tin. Cover the top with hazelnuts/walnuts, cherries and sliced apple and bake for 60-90 minutes or until a skewer comes out clean.

For the top:

Fifteen minutes before the end of the baking time, mix the butter, yolks and honey to a runny paste, remove the cake from the oven, and spread over the cake. Return to the oven to set the crust. It should be lightly browned. Best served warm from the oven.

Warming Restoratives Toasting St Andrew

Cock-a-Leekie, Porridge and Brose, Tatties, Neeps and Kail, Clapshot, Stovies

Curing winter's ills

Matched against the visual charms of green olives and deeply red sun-dried tomatoes, stodgy grey porridge and creamy brown stovies might signal a gastronomic bore. Unless, of course, the less visually attractive foods also have flavour punch. Then colour matters not. Restoring warmth and curing ills is the thing. And northern people who practice the healing art when winter bites are the ones to be celebrated. People like our Mary, a perky little woman in her fifties with a slight figure which belied her capacity for hard work. She cleaned, tirelessly, in the college in Elgin where I worked and lived alone in a flat just a few doors from my bedsit. One day, during my first disabling winter in this Arctic (north-east) shoulder of Scotland, when I didn't turn up for work, she appeared inquiring about my health and clutching a deep enamel bowl with a plate on top.

'I've brought you some broth.'

Mary's broths, it turned out, were a legend in the neighbourhood. She had made potfuls all her life, and when her large family left home, she had continued making enough to feed herself, and many more besides. The leftovers were put into a large bowl and taken to whoever needed restoring.

She had an inventive way with broths, making them with anything which was available, though her method varied little. The meat or poultry went in first — for a long slow simmer along with barley, lentils, dried peas and robust vegetables — then the more delicate greens and herbs were added nearer the end of the cooking. Rice went with chicken, barley with beef, lentils with ham.

Though several decades have passed since she turned up on my doorstep that night with her broth, I still remember it vividly. Hens for her broth were mature matrons which had spent many years scratching the farmyard. Tough, maybe, but they had chicken flavour with kick. At the bottom of the bowl, buried amongst the rice, was a chunk of breast attached to a bone. On top, was the clear golden broth with green leeks floating in it.

I swear it cured me of my ills.

COCK-A-LEEKIE

EARLY EIGHTEENTH CENTURY

The first written mention of this colourful Scottish broth appears in the *Ochtertyre House Book* (1737) when dinner included 'cockie leekie fowlls in it.'

But this is the earliest recipe, from Meg Dods' *Cook and Housewives Manual*, the early 19th-century Scottish Mrs Beeton:

'Boil from four to six pounds of good shin-beef, well broken, till the liquor is very good. Strain it, and put to it a capon, or large fowl, trussed for boiling, and when it boils, half the quantity of blanched leeks intended to be used, well cleaned, and cut in inch-lengths, or longer. Skim this carefully. In a half-hour add the remaining part of the leeks and a seasoning of pepper and salt. The soup must be very thick of leeks, and the first part of them must be boiled down into the soup till it becomes a green lubricious compound. Sometimes the capon is served in the tureen with the cock-a-leekie ... Some people thicken cock-a-leekie with the fine part of oatmeal. Those who dislike so much of the leeks may substitute shred greens, or spinage and parsley, for one half of them. Reject the coarse green part of the leeks. Prunes and raisins used to be put in this soup.'

TWENTIETH CENTURY

Attempting a modern cock-a-leekie with an immature battery chicken is akin to attempting cassoulet without confit. Mature birds with flavour are sometimes available from farm shops where they have genuine free-range hens, or sometimes from fishmongers or butchers. Failing that, from 1 October (until the end of February) there is always the possibility of a more flavourful pheasant or other game bird — cock or hen — which has roamed freely.

Of course, the broth's success depends as much on the leeks as the poultry. Because of its sweeter, more delicate flavour, compared with onions, the leek is often described as king of the soup onions. Small to medium sized leeks have the sweetest flavour. The chicken and leeks marriage is thought to have developed its national reputation as a classic dish of the 18th-century Edinburgh tavern. It developed largely as a result of the very fine leeks from market gardens along the fertile Lothian coast, which supplied Edinburgh with vegetables and fruits.

A variety of the Common Long Winter Leek, raised in this area, and possessing a long, thick stem and broad leaves, is described as a 'Poireau de Musselbourgh' by William Robinson in *The Vegetable Garden* (1885) when he says that 'the fine qualities of this vegetable are much better known to the Welsh, Scotch and French than to the English or Irish.'

Scots leeks continue to be distinguished from other leeks, particularly by their long leaf (green flag) and short blanch (white). The large amount of green is required to give broths a good green colour. A traditional Scottish leek will have almost as much green as white, while 'long blanched' leeks with only a very short green flag are more typically English.

Though the Musselburgh leek, which was grown for winter hardiness and which was most probably the original variety in cock-a-leekie, is no longer grown commercially it continues to be grown by some amateur gardeners.

Leeks are now grown commercially from September to April starting with the early varieties of Perlina, Verina, Tilina, Argenta, Startrack, Pancho, Jolant. Mid-season varieties: Prelina, Verina, Tilina, Startrack, Proibleu, Wintra, Cortina, Porino. Late varieties: Cobra, Porino, Kajak, Pinola, Derrick.

In 1995, 230 hectares of commercial leeks were grown on around 106 farms.

COCK-A-LEEKIE WITH SAUSAGES

To make two meals, first roast the chicken or game birds and then make the remains into a broth, with sausages.

In the broth, potatoes are used instead of rice, and instead of onions a fennel-bulb adds its fresh, aniseed tang. Prunes add sweetness, balancing any bitterness in mature leeks.

INGREDIENTS

To roast the chicken or game birds:
1 x 2kg (4lb) chicken or game birds
4 tablespoons olive oil
salt

To make the broth:
sprigs of fresh herbs, parsley, thyme and bay leaf (tied together)
water to cover
4 medium or 8 small Maris Piper or other similar
all-purpose, not too floury potatoes, peeled
500g (1lb) leeks, split and washed
1 fennel bulb, very finely sliced
500g (1lb) pork sausages
salt and pepper
2 tablespoons chopped parsley
50g (2oz) small bite-sized, ready-to-eat 'breakfast' prunes

METHOD

Cooking the chicken/game birds:

Rub oil over the skin and season with salt. Roast in a hot oven, Gas Mark 8/230C/450F, turning every 20 minutes. For chicken, allow 20 minutes per 500g (1lb), game birds 15 minutes.

Making the broth:

Remove the bird from the oven and serve. Reserve the remaining roasting juices and put into a large pot. Remove all the edible meat and chop coarsely. Reserve.

Put the carcass into the pot with the juices, cover with cold water and bring to simmering point. Add the herbs, and simmer for about an hour. Add the potatoes and simmer for another twenty minutes or until they are just soft. Strain. Remove the potatoes. Press all the juices through the sieve and discard debris.

Return the broth to the pan and add the fennel, cook for five minutes. Add the remaining meat, the leeks and parsley. Simmer for two minutes. Season.

Meantime, grill the sausages until crisp and well-browned.

To serve as a main course in deep (1 litre/2 pint) Japanese noodle bowls or equivalent: put a potato and two sausages into each bowl along with a few prunes and some chopped parsley. Ladle over the hot broth. Serve with crusty bread.

COMMUNAL PORRIDGE AND BOTHY BROSE

EIGHTEENTH CENTURY

A black iron pot hangs on the swey over the farmhouse fire, its contents heaving and plopping gently until it's lifted over to the table. Then the family stand round, each holding a wooden bowl filled with freshly-skimmed cream, for dunking, and the horn spoon which they use to dip into the pot for spoonfuls of their morning *parritch*. Once everyone has had 'them' and before 'they' cool, 'they' are poured into the porridge drawer to set (in the same way that Italians pour polenta onto a board to set). Also like polenta, 'they' will be cut up and reheated for another meal later.

But meantime out in the bothy the farm labourers have been up since five o'clock, feeding and grooming the horses. They return to a cold fireside but the farmer has supplied them with a week's rations of oatmeal. The farmer's wife gives them a kettle of boiling water and they pour the hot water over the oatmeal in their wooden bowls. They also get their billy cans filled with milk to drink with their morning brose.

EARLY TWENTIETH CENTURY PORRIDGE

'Allow for each person one breakfast cupful of water, a handful of oatmeal (about an ounce and a quarter), and a small saltspoonful of salt. Use fresh spring water and be particular about the quality of the oatmeal. Midlothian oats are unsurpassed the world over.

Bring the water to the boil and as soon as it reaches boiling-point add the oatmeal, letting it fall in a steady rain from the left hand and stirring it briskly the while with the right, sunwise, or the right-hand turn for luck — and convenience. A porridge-stick, called a spurtle, and in some parts a theevil, or, as in Shetland, a gruel-tree, is used for this purpose. Be careful to avoid lumps, unless the children clamour for them. When the porridge is boiling steadily, draw the mixture to the side and put on the lid. Let it cook for from twenty to thirty minutes according to the quality of the oatmeal, and do not add the salt, which has a tendency to harden the meal and prevent its swelling, until it has cooked for at least ten minutes. On the other hand, never cook porridge without salt. Ladle straight into porringers or soup-plates and serve with small individual bowls of cream, or milk, or buttermilk. Each spoonful of porridge, which should be very hot, is dipped into the cream or milk, which should be quite cold, before it is conveyed to the mouth.'

F M McNeill, *The Scots Kitchen*, 1929.

LATE TWENTIETH CENTURY PORRIDGE AND BROSE

Though millions of pounds are spent annually in Britain on the breakfast cereal market, not all Scots have abandoned porridge and brose for more sophisticated alternatives. For the generation who grew up in a more frugal environment — deprived of Coco Pops and Frosties — *halesome parritch* and *bothy brose* remains a staple part of their diet. Plain as parritch it may be, but it has a warm inner glow and the capacity to last well into the day. While there are those who eat either porridge or brose all year round, others change with the seasons, eating porridge in winter and brose in summer. Some, have passed on the tradition entirely intact to the next generation.

While I grew up supporting the breakfast cereal market, my children have taken a different tack. What appeals to them is the versatility of porridge, morning, noon and night, whenever the pangs of hunger strike. They reach for oatmeal to make sustaining and comforting bowlfuls, often in the microwave. Not oatmeal porridge 'the only way' but with handfuls of nuts and raisins or chopped fresh fruits which is often stuck together with sweet ingredients such as syrup, honey or a favourite jam and lubricated with tangy yogurt, crème fraîche, soured cream, some passion fruit or lemon juice. Their late 20th-century porridge is a rich source of innovation with many highly personal permutations.

Signs of creative porridge developments can also be found on some restaurant menus. The delicious raspberry porridge which is served at The Village Bakery, Penrith with honey and thick cream, the raspberries beaten through the hot porridge till it takes on a pink colour; the sensational porridge which is served with port-soaked prunes plus soaking liquor at a plush Edinburgh B&B; the phenomenal porridge devised by Tony Wignall of Inver Cottage Restaurant in Argyll, which he serves in a large, wide Scottish soup plate, making a well-like shape in the middle of the porridge which he fills with Lagavulin malt whisky, sprinkling demerara sugar round the sides of the porridge and serving it with a bowl of double cream.

Oatmeal cuts for porridge and brose (see p.140)

Of the variety of cuts of oatmeal, pinhead will give the coarsest result, fine oatmeal 'flour' producing something akin to a custard which is useful for invalids and babies. At one time 'oat flour' was sold by millers and there are still a few who continue to mill it.

To make a fine flour for oatmeal porridge/custard, useful for babies and invalids, grind a medium or fine oatmeal in a coffee grinder and then sieve out the coarsest grains.

The most popular 'cut', however, is medium, but to add a coarser texture, some pinhead can be added. Unless you are intent on making a pot of wallpaper paste, porridge does not benefit from lengthy cooking on a low heat, but is at its best when cooked and served fairly speedily.

PORRIDGE

INGREDIENTS

For 1 serving:
1 cup (250ml/8fl oz) milk or water
2 heaped tablespoons oatmeal, fine, medium or
coarse or a mixture according to taste
pinch of salt

METHOD

Put the water into a non-stick pan or large bowl which will go into the microwave. Add the oatmeal, stir in and leave for at least an hour, preferably overnight for the oatmeal to soften and swell.

To cook in a pan:

Heat up in the pan until it reaches boiling point, stir with a spurtle till it thickens. Remove. Stir in a little raw meal for a coarser texture and mealier flavour, season with salt and serve immediately.

To cook in the microwave:

Stir before putting in, cook on high for 5-10 minutes. Stir once during the cooking. Season, add more meal (optional) and serve.

MIXED-GRAIN PORRIDGE/BROSE MIX

A German mountaineer friend makes up this mix and goes off into the hills for several weeks, surviving on little else. His individual touch is to mix in sweetened drinking chocolate. Margaret Mackenzie at Brin Herb Garden (see page 99) adds lemon verbena to the mix she sells at the garden shop.

INGREDIENTS

Grain mix:

To make 1.5kg (3lb) basic mix

250g (8oz) rolled wheat flakes, plain or toasted

250g (8oz) oatmeal

250g (8oz) pearl barley

250g (8oz) sunflower seeds

250g (8oz) rolled rye flakes

250g (8oz) raisins

150ml (4fl oz) dried milk powder (optional)

Seed and nut mix:

1 cup (250ml/8fl oz) sesame seeds

1 cup (250ml/8fl oz) pumpkin seeds

1 cup (250ml/8fl oz) chopped, mixed nuts

To sweeten:

fresh fruits, honey, syrup, jam, treacle, drinking chocolate

METHOD

Mix all the ingredients in the grain mix together and store in a jar with a tight-fitting lid.

Mix all the ingredients in the seed and nut mix and store in another jar with a tight-fitting lid.

To make:

For every cup of grain mix add two cups of water or milk. Put into a bowl and leave overnight to soak. It may be eaten cooked or uncooked. To cook, heat through in a pan or the microwave until it thickens. Sweeten with honey, syrup, jam, treacle or drinking chocolate to taste. Sprinkle over the mixed seed and nut mix and serve with live yogurt or milk.

To make girdle scones with leftover cooked porridge mix:
To one cup of cooked porridge add: 1 egg; 2 tablespoons of oil; 250g (8oz) self-raising 'cake' flour and a pinch of salt. Mix with milk to a soft but thick dropping consistency. Heat and grease girdle or frying pan. Drop spoonfuls onto the hot surface, sprinkle with some of the seed and nut mix. Turn when bubbles begin to show, brown on the other side. Serve buttered while hot for breakfast with bacon.

TATTIES, NEEPS AND KAIL

To make a dinner

Like the impoverished Irish peasant, many Scots lived chiefly on tatties, and an ingenious collection of meatless dishes which grew up around this convenient root vegetable, unharmed by rain or wind. In Orkney, tatties were mixed with neeps or kail and called *clapshot*. In the North-East, *kailkenny* was a dish of tatties, cabbage and cream. In the Borders they made *rumbledethumps*, which had more or less the same ingredients but like Irish *colcannon* and *champ*, was made with butter instead of cream. *Stovies*, on the other hand, were universal, as were *chappit tatties* and *tattie soup*.

Tatties

There was a gradual, if reluctant, acceptance of the potato in Scotland throughout the 18th century, as a useful food supply. During this time, in the more remote Highlands and Islands, where land for growing grain was scarce, people subsisted on potatoes for nine months of the year, while in Lowland areas, where the climate and soil were better, the diet was less dominated by them. One estimate judged that in the Lowlands they made up only about a third of the daily diet.

Traditionally, the Scots have always preferred a drier floury or mealier potato with a stronger, more dominant flavour, specializing in potato varieties such as Golden Wonder, Kerr's Pinks, Duke of York and King Edward, which have a high dry content compared with other wetter potatoes. In the 19th century a common sight in city streets, were farmers' carts selling 'Mealy tatties', which were simply dry floury potatoes boiled in salted water.

In the last fifty years, however, potato growers in Scotland have taken a different tack with breeding programs preoccupied with maximizing yields, and going for varieties which produce larger, more uniformly shaped, but often less-flavourful potatoes. So the balance has changed. Before World War II, unevenly shaped, deep-eyed, mealy potatoes with low water content, high dry matter and more flavour accounted for three-quarters of the potato acreage in Scotland. Today, they make up between five and ten per cent.

The most popular modern mealy potato is Maris Piper which was first raised in 1963. Old variety mealy potatoes are now described as 'Scottish Quality Varieties', joining a niche sector of the potato market which along with Salad Potatoes and Baking Potatoes command a premium price because of their superior taste and low yield per acre.

According to Alan Wilson in *The Story of the Potato* (1993), the first mealy, low-yielding potato was Duke of York (1891), raised by W Sim of Aberdeenshire. It reached its peak in the UK market in the 1940s. But due to low yields compared with its rivals, it fought a losing battle and retreated to Scotland, eventually to be grown only by specialist allotment holders or home gardeners. Now it's being revived as a commercial crop with the development of potatoes for specialist purposes. Duke of York is a first early, yellow-fleshed potato with an outstanding flavour which is best when young. As maturity is reached the dry matter increases, the flavour is less intense and it becomes difficult to boil without breaking down into soup, though it continues to make a good mealy baked potato.

For the first half of the 20th century, the maincrop King Edward (1902) was one of the UK's most popular potato varieties. It was raised in Lincolnshire by an unknown breeder and has a pale yellow flesh, an aromatic flavour, and is best roasted or baked. It was abandoned by many growers, not because of its low yield, but because it's a fussy potato to grow, requiring good irrigation and a strong soil with plenty of organic matter, doing badly on heavy, acidic, or sandy soils.

In 1906, the Golden Wonder was raised by John Brown near Arbroath. A late maincrop potato with a distinctive flavour and unusually thick, brown, rough skin, it tops the scale in dry-matter content, making it the premium mealy potato in Scotland and Ireland. Never popular in England, because of its extreme mealiness, it remains an exclusively Scottish and Irish potato.

Vying with Golden Wonder for the mealy market are Kerr's Pinks (1907). It was raised by J Henry of Banff and first named Henry's Seedling. But in 1916 it won the Lord Derby Gold Medal and Henry sold all the seed to a Banff seedsman (Mr Kerr) who renamed it and launched it on the market in 1917 as Kerr's Pinks. For almost 50 years it was, along with King Edward, among the top ten UK varieties. It's easier to grow than King Edward, being less fussy about soil type, and has the advantage of higher yields than the Golden Wonder. In Ireland it has dominated the national acreage since its introduction, and today accounts for 28 per cent of the potato crop.

One of the problems with the revival of these old 'quality varieties' on the commercial market is that the cooking qualities are less well known. They should be used for baked jacket potatoes or chips. If boiled they should not be peeled because of their deep 'eyes'. Take a thin slice from both ends which will remove the woody part which joined-up with the runner from the old potato, or take a single peeling round the potato from north to south pole, simmer slowly and keep checking, or they will easily go into the bree (cooking water).

Neeps

Linking up with mealy potatoes in native dishes is the neep (Swedish turnip, or Swede, or rutabaga, from the Swedish dialect name 'rotbagga'). Though the name 'turnip' is generally used in England for the white turnip (Fr *navet*) the Scots (and some Northern English) have adopted the word 'turnip' for their entirely different, but more commonly grown Swede.

While the Romans were responsible for introducing the English white turnip, *Brassica rapa*, the yellow turnip, *Brassica campestris*, came to Scotland in the late 18th century. It was around this time that the pioneers of English agriculture were growing crops of turnips for feeding to cattle during the winter, thus allowing them the opportunity of building up breeding herds when previously most of the animals had to be killed in the autumn.

The Scots took to the yellow turnip as a vegetable for human consumption more enthusiastically than the English, who appear to have regarded it first and foremost as cattle fodder. Only in some parts of Northern England was it eaten with any enthusiasm, while the Scots created something of a gastronomic treat out of it. 'Our club [The Cleikum gastronomic club],' says Meg Dods (1826), 'put a little powdered gineger [sic] to their mashed turnips, which were studiously chosen of the yellow, sweet, juicy sort, for which Scotland is celebrated.'

In time, mashed turnips or bashed neeps as they were known, became the traditional accompaniment to Haggis at Burns Suppers, along with chappit tatties (mashed potatoes).

Kail

Also mixed with potatoes was kail, the old vegetable (carved in jade by the Ancient Greeks to line the sarcophagus of Akhenaton's tomb) which has a record of 45 different listings in the Scottish National Dictionary.

In Scotland the 'kailyaird' (kitchen garden) was to the Lowland Scot, what the potato-plot was to the Irish peasant. Kail became synonymous with eating, the midday meal known as 'kail' was taken when the kail-bells of St Giles Cathedral in Edinburgh chimed at dinner-time (in the 18th century at 2 o'clock). Scotland is frequently referred to as 'The Land o Kail' and 'kailyaird' has been applied to a school of early 20th-century fiction which included J M Barrie and S R Crockett, depicting a couthy style of Scottish village life.

Originally a staple green winter vegetable, kail survives well in the harsh Scottish winter, since it has the rare quality in a vegetable of benefiting from periods of hard frost. It has no heart but grows on a long stem with curled, finely dented leaves. Its flavour changes from mild to a more intensely spicy astringent flavour after it has been frosted, when some of the starch is converted to sugar. Like parsley, it provides depth of flavour alongside sweeter vegetables like carrots and turnips. It's also happy with spices such as cinnamon (which the Danes use in their kail soup) and it marries well in a stir-fry with ginger and garlic or nuts and raisins.

While Scots originally used the spelling kail coming from the generic name *cole*, a name for all kinds of cabbage, today it's known throughout the UK as kale. Scots continue to use it in broths, or as a vegetable in its own right, while in England it's largely used as winter feeding for cattle. In Shetland, a variety is grown which is thought to have ancient Scandinavian origins. Over the years it has been adapted to suit the soil and climate, and unlike other varieties Shetland kail forms a head.

Kail's demise as a common vegetable in Scotland has been largely due to EC regulations which have put an end to the small market gardeners who were the main source of supply. In the last few years, however, several varieties (Buffalo, Moosebor and Winterbor) have been grown commercially on a large scale in Perthshire and Fife, using Danish seed. Often described as a cabbage which will not grow up, its leaves are picked from the stalk as it continues to grow upwards during the season which lasts from October through to March. The leaves picked should be fairly young and tender. If they are left too long on the stalk they will become tough and woody.

KAIL WITH GINGER AND GARLIC

A quick-and-easy stir-fry method flavouring the peppery kail with equally robust flavours. For a gentler flavour use butter and omit the garlic and ginger.

INGREDIENTS

For 4 servings:
2 tablespoons olive oil
2-3 cloves of garlic, crushed
50g (2oz) fresh unpeeled ginger, grated
375g (12oz) washed kail
50g (2oz) large Californian raisins

METHOD

Remove the centre core from the kail and chop leaves finely. This can be done in the food processor but it should not be cut too fine.

Heat a wok and add the oil. When hot add the garlic and ginger. Stir for a few seconds until the aroma is released, then add the kail. Stir quickly over a strong heat until it just wilts. Add raisins and serve.

CLAPSHOT

NINETEENTH CENTURY ORKNEY DAILY FARE

Hooked on the end of the chain which hangs from the rafters over the peat fire is a pot of boiling potatoes. For breakfast the potatoes are skinned, put back into the pot with some oatmeal and salt and then mashed. They are eaten communally from the pot with horn spoons and milk or buttermilk.

For dinner at midday, the second boiling of potatoes is couped (tipped) onto the table and a bowl of melted butter or dripping used for dunking. No knives or forks are used. For supper, kail or neeps are cooked and added to peeled cooked potatoes, then mashed together, seasoned with salt and pepper and eaten with bere (barley) bannocks.

'This vegetarian dish,' says John Frith, author of *Reminiscences of an Orkney Parish* (late 19th century), 'bore the curious name of "clapshot".'

A hundred years ago, vegetables were it. Clapshot was your dinner.

LATE TWENTIETH CENTURY

CLAPSHOT WITH BURNT ONIONS

Many modern writers (including the Orcadian writer and poet, the late George Mackay Brown) have included an onion in clapshot, though there is no sign of it in Frith's early description. The onion is usually boiled with the turnip and potatoes, but another modern variation is to cook a panful of 'burnt' onions. The dark caramelized onions are sprinkled over the top of the dish, adding colour, texture as well as a striking contrast of flavours with peppery turnip. It's a method used by chef-proprietor Ronnie Clydesdale, at Glasgow's Ubiquitous Chip Restaurant where he has taken an innovative approach to this and many other traditional Scottish foods based, largely, on taste memories of his grandmother's cooking.

For traditional clapshot, omit the onions.

INGREDIENTS

For 4 servings:
500g (1lb) floury potatoes, Golden Wonder, King
Edward, Kerr's Pink, peeled
500g (1lb) yellow turnip (swede) peeled and diced
25g (1oz) butter
125g (4oz) washed kail
salt and freshly ground black pepper

Burnt onions:
1 large Spanish onion, thinly sliced
1 tablespoon extra virgin olive oil
1 tablespoon granulated sugar

METHOD

Making the clapshot:

Put the turnip into a pot, just cover with water and simmer for about ten minutes before adding the potatoes. Cut the potatoes in half and put into the pot with the turnip.

Because they are floury and also peeled, it is important not to overcook or they will disintegrate into potato soup. They can be steamed in a steamer on top of the turnip.

To cook the kail, remove the central stalks and chop the leaves finely. Add to the potato and turnip for two minutes when they are ready. Drain, and reserve the liquid for soups. Dry off a little over a low heat before mashing with butter, taste and season. Put into serving dish.

Making the burnt onions:

While the potatoes and turnip are cooking, heat up the oil in a pan and add the onions. Cook slowly for about 15 minutes, driving off as much moisture as possible. They should be crisp and golden brown. Sprinkle over the sugar and stir continuously for another five minutes while the sugar caramelizes and the onions darken.

Serve on top of the clapshot. When in Orkney eat with beremeal bannocks, alternatively, a wheaten soda bread and Orkney farmhouse cheese or a mature creamy Dunlop.

STOVIES

EARLY NINETEENTH CENTURY

COMMUNAL STOVIES (IN KINROSS AND FIFE)

'Then we ha' stove tatas. That's when they're pet in the pot wi' out water, wi' a bit suet, some sibes an' a pickle salt.'

Scottish National Dictionary

LATE NINETEENTH CENTURY

BUTTERED STOVIES

'Choose potatoes of a good quality and put them into a pot with a very little water — just enough to cover the bottom and prevent burning. Sprinkle with salt, and add tiny bits of butter here and there. Cover closely, and simmer very gently till soft and melted.'

Lady Clark of Tillypronie (1841-1897)

LATE TWENTIETH CENTURY

Over the years, the Scots have interpreted stewed potatoes in a number of different ways. Aberdonians make them with potatoes, onions, fat and a little water and serve them with oatcakes and a bowl of milk. They also make oven stovies, which are not unlike the French way with Dauphinoise potatoes, minus the garlic, but with milk or cream. Harvest stovies are with grated cheese. Bacon stovies use bacon fat. In Glasgow stovies with meat were known as 'high heelers', without meat 'Barefit'. They can be made in a round cake shape in the frying pan or microwave; they can be made with new potatoes and carrots, flavoured with lemon and cumin, with leeks and kail … There is no end to the innovation.

TRADITIONAL STOVIES ON THE STOVE

This is made with *stovie stock*, the leftover gravy and dripping from a roast which can be bought from traditional butchers in small plastic pots, the layer of beef dripping on top of the gravy from their roast beef. For vegetarians, one tablespoonful of miso is a useful alternative flavouring.

INGREDIENTS

For 4-6 servings:
50g (2oz) oil, dripping, or butter

3 medium onions, roughly chopped
1kg (2lb) floury potatoes, main crop or new
125ml (4fl oz) meat stock or gravy
125-250g (4-8oz) cooked meat
2-3 tablespoons finely chopped parsley, chives or
spring onions
Seasoning: salt, freshly ground black pepper,
allspice or grated nutmeg

METHOD

You will need a large heavy-base pan with a tight-fitting lid. Heat the fat in the pan and add the onions. Cook until lightly brown. Peel potatoes, if they are main crop, but leave the skin on new potatoes. Slice about 5mm (¼in) thick. Or slice roughly in different thicknesses so that the thin go into a mush, while the others stay whole. Add them to the pan with the onions and stir well, coating all sides with fat.

Put the lid on the pan, and leave on a low heat for about ten minutes, stirring a couple of times. Then add the gravy or water. Cover and cook over a very low heat stirring once or twice, until the potatoes are cooked. Add the meat, mix through, and turn up the heat to brown a little.

Taste for seasoning. Mix in some freshly chopped parsley or chives or spring onions and serve with oatcakes and a glass of milk.

STOVIES IN THE OVEN

Baked in a straight-sided soufflé dish this can be left in its dish or turned out for serving.

INGREDIENTS

For 4-6 servings:
3 tablespoons sunflower oil
3 medium onions, halved and finely sliced
1kg (2lb) potatoes, washed
2 cloves garlic, crushed
2 tablespoons olive oil
125g (4oz) cooked leftover meat or bacon, finely
chopped, or grated Cheddar cheese (optional)
salt, freshly ground white pepper

METHOD

Preheat the oven to gas mark 4/180C/350F. Layer the ingredients in 19-20cm (7½-8in) round soufflé dish. Heat the oil in the pan and add the onions. Cook gently, driving off the moisture, till they are a light golden brown and quite crisp. Slice potatoes wafer thin (on a mandolin, if available). There is no need to peel them if the skins are thin.

Put a thin layer of onions in the dish. Put a layer of potatoes on top of the onions. Season with garlic, salt and pepper. Dribble a little oil over. Continue in layers adding meat/cheese etc with the onions. End with a layer of potatoes covered with more oil.

To bake in oven:
Cover with a layer of foil and/or a lid, making sure that there is no escaping steam. Bake for 50-60 minutes.

To cook in microwave:
Cover and cook on high for 15 minutes checking after ten minutes.

To serve:
When ready to serve remove the lid, press down on the foil to make really firm. Remove foil. Place serving plate on top of dish and invert. If some of the onions have stuck, scrape off and place back on top. Serve with oatcakes and a glass of milk.

STOVIES WITH CARROTS

These spicy stovies can be adjusted according to taste, or the spice element can be left out entirely.

INGREDIENTS

For 4 servings:
500g (1lb) carrots, peeled
1 tablespoon virgin olive oil
1 teaspoon ground cumin
1-2 teaspoons mild curry paste
1 onion, finely sliced
500g (1lb) floury potatoes, peeled
salt
juice of 1 lemon
water

freshly ground white pepper
2 tablespoons chopped coriander or parsley

METHOD

Slice the carrots and potatoes wafer thin, on a mandolin if available. Heat the oil in a pan and add the cumin and curry paste. Add the onions and sauté until soft but not browned. Then add the carrots and toss. Put on the lid and leave for about five minutes, stirring occasionally.

Add potatoes, salt, lemon juice and stir well. Leave for another five minutes with the lid on, stirring occasionally to prevent sticking.

Add about 1cm (½in) of water. Cover and simmer very slowly, stirring every now and again. Cook until the carrots and potatoes are tender. By this time the liquid should have reduced to almost nothing. Add more water if it goes dry before they are cooked. Taste for seasoning. Add parsley or coriander and serve.

TOASTING ST ANDREW

The patron saint first of Pictland and eventually of all Scotland is honoured every 30 November at St Andrew's Night dinners when the toast is: 'To the memory of St Andrew, and Scotland Yet!'

Andrew was a doer-behind-the-scenes. A quiet, self-effacing apostle who went off and found the loaves and fishes for the gathering on the shores of the sea of Galilee. He was martyred on a cross decussate, X-shaped rather than the usual T-shaped cross, which eventually became recognized as the Scottish national emblem first appearing on the royal seal in 1290.

Sanct Andra's Day, *Andyr's Day* or *Andermas* is celebrated as a patriotic festival at home and abroad by expatriate Scots. Dinner menus usually contain a selection of national dishes, though not always a haggis.

There was no haggis on the menu at the Parklands Hotel in St Andrews when St Andrews University launched their Scottish Studies Institute in 1993, with a gathering from *a' the airts*. Scottish poets, Liz Lochead, Edwin Morgan and Don Paterson, along with Communicado Theatre and Lammas band, performed with a night of poetry readings, drama and music, while Scottish chef, Brian Maclennan, orchestrated a special dinner for the event.

The doer-behind-the-scenes had gathered donations of food from his local suppliers. There was Finnan haddock from Kerracher's of St Andrews, gigot of Angus lamb from Kennedy's of Carnousite while the cheeses were from Howgate of Dundee.

The meal began with potted hough, which he had made the day before. Two slices on a white plate with crimson red slices of baked beetroot and a bunch of delicate green lamb's lettuce, the well-seasoned, thick, meaty jelly providing a light start to the meal. Then there was contrast in the intense richness of a creamy fish-flavoured sauce coating a small portion of Finnan haddock. The gigot of lamb was roasted and served with tureens of Scottish winter vegetables and a dish of potatoes and crunchy oatmeal skirlie.

If this seems like a gastronomic overload, it has to be said that the portions were not large, and the streets outside were covered with snow — calories were not a worry but a priority. The penultimate course of brown-burnished, spicily aromatic clootie dumpling was served with a Drambuie flavoured whipped cream, followed by Howgate cheeses and dumpling-maker Pat Russell's oatcakes.

Dinner to celebrate the launch of
St Andrews University's Scottish Studies Institute,
30 November 1993

POTTED HOUGH
with beetroot and lamb's lettuce

*

FINNAN HADDOCK

*

ROAST GIGOT of ANGUS LAMB
with Roast Root Vegetables

FLOURY POTATOES
with Skirlie

*

CLOOTIE DUMPLING
and Drambuie Cream

*

SCOTTISH CHEESE
and Oatcakes

NOVEMBER.

Contrive or forecaft where, and what you are to fow and plant. Trench and fallow all your vacant grounds. Prepare and mix foils and compofts throughly: mifs not high-way Earth, cleanfings of ftreets; make compofitions of dungs, foils, and lyme.

Lay bair Roots of Trees that need, and dung fuch as require it. Plant all fruit Trees, Forreft-trees, and fhrubs that lofe the leaf, alfo prune fuch. Plant cabbage. Sow hafties for early peas in warme grounds but truft not to them.

Gather the feeds of holly, yew, afh, &c. Ordering them as in Chap: 3. furnifh your nurferies with ftocks.

Shelter tender evergreen feedlings. Houfe your Cabbag, Carrots, Turneeps: and any time e're hard frofts your Skirrets, Potatoes, Parfneeps, &c. Cover Afparagus, Artichocks, as in the laft moneth. Sow bairs-ears, plant Tulips, &c. Shut the confervatory. Preferve your Choiceft Flowers. Sweep and cleanfe the walks of leaves, &c. Stop your bees clofe fo that you leave breathing vents.

Garden Difhes and Drinks in Seafon, are.

Cabbage, Coleflower, Onions, Leeks, Shallot, &c. Blanched Sellery, Succory, Pickled Afparagus, Purflain, &c. Frefh Parfneeps, Skirrets, Potatoes, Carrots, Turneeps, Beet-rave, Scorzonera, parfly and fennell Roots.

Aples, Pears, &c.

Cyder, Perry, wine of Cherries, Rafps, Currans, Goosberries, Liquorifh, Hony, &c.

John Reid, *The Scots Gard'ner*, (1683)

Revelling in the Daft Days

The Hogmanay Sideboard, Black Bun or Clootie
Dumpling, Shortbread, Steak Pie and Trifle,
Shetland Yule Breakfast

Many festivals, one spirit

The winter solstice celebrations in Scotland begin on Christmas Eve and carry through to
Hogmanay and into the first days of January. A week to ten days of festivities, when eat-
drink-and-be-merry prevails. Not many employers expect much work to be done, and
some close down and give everyone a holiday. For what has happened in the late 20th
century festive calendar is a revival — with some modern alterations — of the old *Daft
Days*. Originally styled on the French *Fête des Fous,* they were the time when the celebration
of the winter solstice started (pre-Reformation) with a religious Christ's mass of
thanksgiving in the church followed by a gathered-family festive meal at home. It then
overflowed into secular revels, satirical plays and community gatherings in the streets
when *drouthy neebors neebors meet*.

It looked for a while as though the TV screen would become a substitute for the
street, but the failure of the box to replace the live experience appears to have saved the
old festival from extinction. Now there has been a return to the old Hogmanay traditions
of secular, social, public-in-the-street partying and first-footing round the neighbours,
most notably in Edinburgh, where people street-party around the centre of the town in
what is reputedly the largest communal New Year gathering in Europe.

It also looked, in the first half of the 20th century, as though Scots might continue
to reject popish Christmas because of its unacceptable Church of Rome connections, plus
its habit of heavy feasting which was out of line with the ethics of ascetic Presbyterians of
the Reformed Scottish Church. Before World War II, most Scots still worked on Christmas
Day, shops stayed open, life went on as normal. A miserly two days holiday were given at
Hogmanay. Throughout the 1920s and 30s my Dundonian father, and his six brothers and
sisters, hung up their stockings for Santa's presents on Hogmanay, not Christmas Eve and
their father opened his shop and worked on Christmas Day.

It has been, ironically, the power of secular, commercialized Christmas, and not the
church, which has revived Christmas in Scotland, and provided Scots with an opportunity,

once again, to link up the two festivities. Now the festive season has been stretched into a more satisfying period of midwinter feasting. A large chunk of time taken out of cold northern winters for relaxing, revelling in special luxury eating and drinking, having fun with family and friends, as well as expressing goodwill among the wider community. Two days will not do. It takes a week, preferably a fortnight, to unwind, to celebrate vigorously, to recover, to start all over again … to catch again the old spirit of the Daft Days.

For Northerners, the midwinter habit of celebrating has very deep roots. Throughout the Middle Ages, as the Christian church in Scotland took over 25 December, it also took over Twelfth Night or 6 January, known as *Uphalieday*, the feast of Epiphany. Throughout a long period of Catholic Scotland before the Reformation, Epiphany was a great court festival with plays, pageantries, guising and revels involving much parody and mocking of the authorities such as the 16th-century play *Ane Satyr of the Thrie Estatis*, which has been revived several times at the Edinburgh Festival.

Though it exposed the corruption of both the monarchy and the church, it was originally performed on Epiphany before the King and Queen at Linlithgow. It was the Scots in an irreverent, jokey mood, when relaxed hilarity and goodwill took the stage — at least for a night.

For most of Scotland, however, the Reformation meant the loss of both religious dedication at Christmas as well as satirical fun and games of the twelve Daft Days which went with it. In 1649, a century after *The Thrie Estatis* was performed before the king and church, the church's General Assembly banned Christmas and the Daft Days. Abolishing this annual (and only) holiday in the year, church ministers were advised to make checks on their congregations, with special house visits, to make sure everyone was working, and no one cooking up something festive on the stove.

Hogmanay

Of course, the people continued to celebrate, prohibition being a powerful incentive to rebel, and there are stories of those who hid the roast goose under the bed when the minister called. Attention moved, though, to the 'hinner end o' Yule' and to New Year's Night, untainted by the Church of Rome therefore religiously more acceptable to the narrow-minded church hierarchy. What happened was an amalgam of the old festivities of Christmas, Yule and Twelfth Night or Epiphany into what has now become known as Hogmanay. From its early beginnings, and up to the early 20th century, it brought together the forbidden customs from older festivals, and the new celebration took a strong grip on the emotions of the Scottish people, which shows little sign of abating.

A possible derivation of the name, according to the *Scottish National Dictionary*, is from the French *aguillanneuf*, a street cry for gifts on New Year's Day. It appears to have come into the language from early Franco-Scottish connections, the cry altering and changing from the 17th century onwards until it was eventually modified into a cry of children and beggars who knocked on doors looking for a gift of food, such as an oatmeal bannock or some money. The transfer of the word to the communal celebrations lasting several days, appears to have developed during the 18th and 19th centuries with people celebrating at stone circles or mercat crosses as the New Year was welcomed in.

Though now a universal celebration throughout the country (except in Shetland), in its early days Hogmanay was most enthusiastically celebrated in the strongly Protestant areas of the country, such as the Covenanting South-West, and least observed in the Catholic 'belt' beyond the Grampians and in Aberdeenshire and the North-East, where Episcopalian influences were strong and Christmas was still an acceptable time to feast.

While townspeople will gather at a clock in the town centre, the rural tradition is to 'see in the bells' at home before taking off first-footing and partying in houses. In the Highlands and Islands, where the *ceilidh* tradition survives, there are several nights of all-night entertainment plus drinking and eating, as the ceilidh moves each night round neighbouring communities.

In the area of Wester Ross where I've spent most Hogmanays in the last 35 years, the spirit of Hogmanay past still survives, some of it in a different form as one generation takes over from another. The singing is less in Gaelic now, and there are no longer enough old men to stand in a circle, clasping their arms round one another's shoulders, their head's bowed, singing and swaying to the rhythm of haunting Gaelic songs relating the tragic effects of the Clearances, still deeply felt.

The first-foots do not carry a piece of fuel for the fire, an orange, some shortbread or some cake, but none are without a bottle of whisky. They are welcomed, all through the night, in every house where a light continues to burn. The old tradition continues of using a small communal 'dram' glass, a remnant of the days when a Highland crofter was unlikely to have owned more than one glass. It's filled by each first-foot from his or her own bottle, and they go round the gathered company refilling the glass and wishing each person — *Slàinte, Bliadhna Mhath Ùr* (good health, happy new year). It's not necessary to drink the whole glass, and some will only let it touch their lips. The skill is to drink slowly, and last the night … and the next night …

A sideboard of cold meats, oatcakes, cheese, shortbread, pancakes, soda scones and clootie dumplings are among the most usual fare for the night. Favourite meats are a cold haunch of venison or leg of mature mutton, a thick slice placed on a crisp oatcake. While this is the kind of fare on the West Coast, I have also been to Hogmanays in the more arctic North-East where festive food was a hot choice of stovies from a huge pot, served with pickled beetroot and oatcakes. In some houses the hot bowlful was of Scotch broth, served with hot butteries. Compared with a sit-down, gargantuan Christmas feast, Hogmanay fare is modest. Nothing is over-rich, nothing obligatory. Huge amounts of energy are burnt walking from house to house, often a distance apart, in the cold so that food is welcome sustenance and never the cause of over-eating.

Up-Helly-Aa and Burning the Clavie

While Hogmanay remains the strongest communal celebration in mainland Scotland, in the remote Shetland islands, more deeply Norse in their ancestry than any other part of Scotland, the Lerwick fire festival of Up-Helly-Aa marks the end of the 24 days of Yule.

For 500 years (9th-13th century) during their occupation of a large part of Scotland, the Vikings feasted, danced, joined hands and whirled in a circle round symbolic, fire-worshipping bonfires. Though they were eventually defeated at the battle of Largs in 1263, and converted by the Celts to the Christian church, the spirit of the Viking Yule remains strong on the islands where its roots are deepest. In the 19th century, and for some time into the 20th, Yule day in Shetland continued to be celebrated not on 25 December but on 6 January, which was according to the old calendar, changed in 1752.

Auld Yule was a period of a whole month — the Merry Month — which began seven days before Yule, and ended 24 days after, on Up-Helly-Aa day, the last Tuesday in January. The Yule day itself was traditionally a time for feasting and vigorous exercise, a practical and healthy means of keeping warm when men played a game of traditional football with a specially made Yule Ba. The remnants of this activity remain in the game of Uppies and Doonies, now played on New Year's Day in the main street of Kirkwall in Orkney when the two teams, relating to the top and the bottom of the town, engage in a heaving mass of disorderly scrum, as the ball goes either up or down the street.

But Lerwick's Up-Helly-Aa in Shetland is a more organized event developed from an old festive midwinter custom of burning tar barrels. In 1881 the tar barrels became torches and a committee was formed to run the festival. By 1889 the idea had developed of burning a longship and creating a pageant for a day in the town.

It's a community festival which has grown in the last hundred years into one of the largest winter fire-festivals in Europe. It begins in the morning with a pageant of a full-sized Norse galley with a dragon's head and a fish's tail and is accompanied by Guizers dressed as Norsemen. The galley spends the day in the town while the Guizers visit hospitals, schools and homes for the elderly. In the early evening they take part in the spectacular torchlit procession of several thousand people to a playing field where their torches are thrown into the galley, igniting it, and sending the whole ship blazing up into the night air.

The merrymaking continues throughout the night in halls and hotels, with Guizers turning up to provide entertainment and receive hospitality. During the day the halls have been organized by hosts and hostesses who sell tickets for their hall and who provide food and entertainment, often until dawn. To sustain the revelry, gallons of soup are made, the best is flavoured with reestit mutton (see p.159). In addition there are large quantities of home-baking as well as home-made toffee for children. It's 24 hours of fire, frolic and feasting based on myth, history and innovation which has become firmly established, and greatly loved by the people.

Another survivor of the Auld Yule fires of Norse ancestry, which at one time blazed all along Scotland's northern and eastern coasts, is the fire festival at Burghead on the Moray coast where the community gathers each year on 11 January to burn *The Clavie*. The word appears to be a corruption of the Gaelic *cliabh* pronounced 'clee-av', meaning the basket which is used for carrying the fire. While the Shetlanders converted their blazing tar barrels into a longship, the people of this small fishing village continue with the older tradition and a half barrel is fixed to a stake and filled with tar-soaked wood which is set alight with a live peat. When it is well alight it is carried through the town by the Clavie King and his followers until it reaches the doorie, a large grassy knoll reputed to be a centre of Druidic fire worship, where it is fixed to a pillar with a spoke.

The fire is revived with more tar, poured onto the glowing mass and there is a tremendous cheer as the flames shoot up into the black night, throwing their glow onto the crowd of up-turned faces. When it has died down, the clavie is dismantled and there is a mad scramble for a piece of what's left of the barrel, an ember from a sacred Druidic fire bringing good luck for the rest of the year.

THE HOGMANAY SIDEBOARD

Black Bun or Clootie Dumpling

In the Highlands and Islands festive dumplings-in-a-cloth cooked in a pot, are more likely to be made for Hogmanay than black-with-spices buns. These are more common in the Lowands, where originally a brick oven was available for baking and they also had easier access to spices. All of which has contributed to the fact that it was the bakers of Edinburgh, and not those in Stornoway, who became known as the masters of the black bun, exporting them in sizes '4, 8, 10, 12, 16 and more pounds' to England, Ireland and Wales in the early 19th century.

The bun appears to have been a later version of a festive cake baked for the pre-Reformation revelry at Twelfth Night or Epiphany and containing a dried pea, entitling the person who found it to become queen or king for the night's fun. When R L Stevenson declared it '… a black substance inimical to life', the description stuck, and 'black' it has remained.

EARLY EIGHTEENTH CENTURY

The main spices used in the forerunner of the 'black bun' were cinnamon, nutmeg, cloves, and caraway. These were used along with currants, lemon and orange peel and almonds with French brandy as additional flavouring. In the 19th century raisins were added along with the currants, and ginger was used instead of caraway. One recipe uses ginger but also adds Jamaica pepper (allspice) and black pepper but omits the nutmeg. All Scottish bakers who make the bun have their own spice mix and flavours vary enormously from the strong peppery versions to milder cinnamon flavoured buns. Black treacle is a modern addition and does not appear in early recipes.

PLUM CAKE

'Take a peck of flour and two pound of butter; rub the butter among the flour, till it be like flour again; take 12 eggs, a lb of sugar, beat them well together; then take a mutchkin of sweet barm, half a mutchkin of brandy, then your flour with the beaten eggs and sugar, and put in the barm and brandy and work all well together; then take ten lb of currants, 2 lb cordecidron [lemon peel], 2 lb of orange peel, 2 lb blanched almonds, cut, half an ounce of cinnamon, half an ounce of nutmeg and cloves, half an ounce of carvey-seed [caraway]; take off the fourth part of the leaven for a cover, and work the fruits and spices among the rest, then put on the cover, and send it to the oven.'

Mrs McLintock, 1736

LATE TWENTIETH CENTURY

BLACK BUN

This is a pastry crust bun with a dense, moist filling which can be used immediately or left for a month or two to develop the flavour.

INGREDIENTS

For the bun mixture:
1. 25 kg (2lb 8ozs) raisins and currants
half a bottle brandy, or more

25g (1oz) freshly ground cinnamon

25g (1oz) freshly ground caraway seed or ground ginger

1-2 grated nutmegs

1 teaspoonful freshly ground cloves

50g (2oz) ground almonds

50g (2oz) whole almonds, blanched

2 tablespoons black treacle

2 very sharp cooking apples, grated

125g (4oz) plain flour

Pastry:

300g (11oz) plain flour

125ml (4fl oz) boiling water

175g (6oz) unsalted butter

50g (2oz) lard

1 egg yolk

1 tablespoon sugar

zest of 1 lemon, grated

1 egg yolk for brushing

METHOD

Soaking the spices and fruit:

Put the dried fruit and spices into a pan and pour over the brandy. Heat gently for a few minutes until the fruit begins to swell, do not boil. Cover and leave for a day, or up to seven days if you wish, turning the fruit occasionally. Then add remainder of the ingredients.

To make the pastry:

Pre-heat the oven to gas mark 3/170C/325F. Grease two 1.5 litre (3 pint) loaf tins or one 23cm (9in) square cake tin.

Put the butter and lard into a bowl. Cut up roughly. Pour over boiling water and mix with a whisk till all the butter has melted and the water and fat are mixed. Add the egg and beat in. Sift the flour on top, add the sugar and lemon rind. Mix to a soft dough. Wrap in foil and put in the fridge to harden for a couple of hours. Roll out and line the tins, leaving enough dough to make a top.

To finish the bun:

Pack in the bun mixture. Turn in the edges and moisten. Roll out the remaining pastry to make a lid and press on tightly. Make a number of slits with a knife or skewer. Brush with egg.

Bake for two to three hours, depending on its size. If in a larger tin, it can be removed from its tin three-quarters of the way through the baking and continued upside down to ensure that the base is properly cooked. Test with a skewer, which should come out clean.

The pastry should be a deep golden when cooked. Leave to cool. Wrap tightly and store in a cool place. Serve in thin fingers with whisky. Can be tightly wrapped and kept for a year.

LATE TWENTIETH CENTURY

CLOOTIE DUMPLING

There is a sustaining warmth and weightiness in a suet dumpling which comes from the unique combination of spices and suet.

Butter makes a lighter, more fragile dumpling, which may split as it dries out in the oven.

INGREDIENTS

125g (4oz) self-raising flour

175g (6oz) fine white breadcrumbs

125g (4oz) beef suet or butter

2 teaspoons baking powder

2 teaspoons each, freshly ground cinnamon, ginger and nutmeg

175g (6oz) sultanas

175g (6oz) Californian raisins

2 tablespoons golden syrup

2 tablespoons black treacle

2 eggs

1 large cooking apple, grated

1 large carrot, grated

zest of 2 oranges

freshly squeezed orange juice or mild ale to mix

Cotton or linen cloth — 55cm (22in) square

Silver coins, wrapped in greaseproof paper, for children

METHOD

Preparing the pot and cloth:
Fill a large pot with water, place a metal grid or upside-down saucer in the base. Bring to

the boil and put in cloth for a few minutes. Lift out with tongs and spread out on table. Sprinkle with plain flour, shake off excess.

Making the mixture:
Put all the ingredients into a large bowl (add silver coins wrapped in greaseproof paper for children) and mix to a fairly stiff consistency with orange juice. Put in the centre of the cloth, bring up edges and tie with string, leaving space for expansion. Hold up the tied ends and pat the dumpling into a good round shape.

Cooking:
Place in the simmering water which should come about halfway up the dumpling, and simmer gently for four hours, checking water level every so often.

Finishing and serving:
Fill a large bowl with cold water. Lift out the dumpling and plunge into the cold water. Keep submerged for 60 seconds to release the cloth from the pudding skin. Put into a bowl about the same size as the dumpling, untie the string, open out the cloth, place the serving-dish on top and reverse. Peel off the cloth and dry out the skin in a warm place. Serve with sweetened double cream or whipcol (see p.41).

Alternative microwave method:
Grease a 3-pint pudding-bowl, dust with flour and put in mixture (omit coins). Cover with a plate, leaving room for expansion and microwave on high for eight minutes. Leave to rest for ten minutes in the microwave and microwave again on high for another eight minutes when it should be cooked through. Test with a skewer and turn out.

SHORTBREAD

No common biscuit

The British Empire may have had it, but there are no signs of decay in the empire which has grown this century around Scottish shortbread. Sold in millions of tons around the world, its fame is largely due to the talents of Scottish bakers and their determination that shortbread should remain shortbread and not be classed as a common biscuit. An issue which is related in the history of the Scottish Association of Master Bakers when a government tax tried to claim it as a biscuit. But it has a long and distinguished ancestry as a 'speciality item of flour confectionery', argued the bakers, winning their case and saving the shortbread.

Its life began as a decorated and flavoured confection. Caraway seeds, preserved lemon, orange peel, and nuts were festive additions which gave it its status as 'flour confectionery'. Shortbread or short-bread cake, in its original form, was made by adding melted butter to an every-day bread dough, making it something more akin to a butterized version of an English lardy cake. The result might have been called a *short cake* or *buttery cake*, but it took a more original name, and like black bun, captured an important export market.

Old festive shortbreads made by the rural communities were shaped into large round bannocks or rectangles, not cut neatly into squares or wedges, but broken up into uneven chunks for serving. Recipes today have abandoned the yeast leavening, but two of the old festive bannocks survive in the Pitcaithly Bannock with nuts, caraway and preserved lemon and orange peel and in the Yetholm Bannock with crystallized ginger.

Around the early 19th century, the more genteel 'petticoat tails' appeared on elegant afternoon tea stands, though confusion about the origin of the name revolved around the question of whether it was another Scottish borrowing from the French. Was it a corruption of 'petites gatelles' (Meg Dods, 1849 edition), or a simple shape analogy, with the bell-hoop petticoats once worn by court ladies. The petticoat theory prevails.

LATE TWENTIETH CENTURY

SHORTBREAD RECIPES

It's texture is a matter of taste, adjusted by varying the coarseness of the flour (using ground rice for grittiness), cornflour and icing sugar for a more melting texture. The flavour of the butter is crucial.

INGREDIENTS

For a 'gritty' granular texture:
125g (5oz) plain soft flour
25g (1oz) rice flour
100g (4 oz) butter
50g (2oz) caster sugar

For a fine but crunchy texture:
100g (4oz) plain soft flour
25g (1oz) rice flour
25g (1oz) cornflour
100g (4oz) butter
25g (1oz) caster sugar
25g (1oz) icing sugar

For a smooth 'melting' texture:
100g (4oz) plain soft flour
50g (2oz) cornflour
100g (4oz) butter
50g (2oz) icing sugar

METHOD

Traditional:

Put the butter onto a work surface, knead the sugar into it, then the flour etc gradually until it becomes a firm, not too soft and not too firm ball of dough.

In food processor:

Pulse butter and sugar till creamy, add flour and pulse until smooth. Remove and knead, adding more flour if necessary.

To bake:

Either press into a greased 270 x 175mm (10¾ x 7in) swiss-roll tin and prick with a fork, or use a special shortbread mould, or roll into a cylinder shape and coat in granulated sugar, chill and slice into thin round biscuit shapes.

Bake slowly at gas mark 3/170/325F until an even golden brown.

With almond and caraway (Pitcaithly Bannock):

Add: 1 tablespoon flaked almonds; 1 tablespoon caraway seeds; 1 tablespoon crystallized orange, finely chopped. Roll out to a large round shape about 2cm (¾in) thick. Prick the top with a fork or skewer. Sprinkle with 1 tablespoon flaked almonds and press in lightly. Pinch the edge with finger and thumb to decorate and bake for 1-1½ hours till a pale golden brown throughout.

With stem ginger (Yetholm Bannock):

Add: 2 tablespoons stem ginger, finely chopped and decorate on top with thin slices of stem ginger. Bake as for Pitcaithly Bannock.

With marmalade:

Roll mixture into golf ball shapes. Make a deep impression in the middle and fill each one with ½ teaspoon marmalade. Close up, reshape and put on baking tin. Press down slightly and bake 30 minutes. Dust with icing sugar and serve warm.

NEW YEAR'S DAY DINNER: STEAK PIE AND TRIFLE

The Jack House Test

In a long life of dining out, the late Jack House used a steak pie as his test of a good restaurant.

'Can they make a real steak pie?' he would enquire when you recommended a new restaurant to him. 'If it turns out to be a sort of casserole steak with a square of pastry sitting on top, then watch out!'

The love of his life was Glasgow, where he worked as a journalist and author, and for a time wrote an Eating Out column in the *Scottish Field*, though he claimed no association with professional gourmets. To his mind they were a suspect race who chattered too self-indulgently for his liking.

There were no flights of fancy in his column, no pretentious gastronomic pronouncements. He dealt with the facts, the good, the bad, the old, the new, the gossip, the comfort, the service, or the lack of it. He was happy that people called him a bon viveur, and often laughed about 'living the life of Riley', but his favourite description of himself was an aristologist.

'What, you don't know what an aristologist is? According to my dictionary, aristology is the art of dining.'

In Jack's post-World War II eating-out heyday, sophisticated Glasgow restaurants included the Mal Maison, the One-o-One and Ferrari's, but he thought that the best steak pie was at the Boulevard Hotel in unfashionable Clydebank and he went back so many times — as he did to many other restaurants which passed his test — that they kept a table which became known as 'Mr House's Table'.

Straightforward reporting was his discipline, but he drew the line at writing recipes. 'I can hardly boil an egg,' he would say. 'How can you expect me to write a recipe?' So we will never know more of the steak pie at the Boulevard Hotel, except that to pass the House Test it must have been properly made, no squares of loose pastry, no skimping on ingredients.

MID TWENTIETH CENTURY

STEAK PIE

The steak pie for New Year which my Glasgow grandmother served up in her city-centre tenement flat was a from a butcher's oven though it began its life in her pot. A stew cooked first with steak and sometimes cheaper sausages to eke out the more expensive meat, which was poured into a large white enamel pie ashet. Taken, when cool, to the butcher, he put the puff pastry on top, and baked it.

Though she had an oven attached to her kitchen range it was never used for baking, just reheating or keeping pies and fish suppers hot. On New Year's Day the reheated steak pie was followed by the dumpling— the brown steaming mound of dried fruits and spices which had been put into the oven to give it a good 'skin'. The butcher may have helped with the pie, but she needed no assistance with the clootie.

LATE TWENTIETH CENTURY

A layer of mushrooms are steamed on top of the meat, removing the need for a pie funnel to hold up the pastry and also keeping the pastry dry and free from sogginess.

INGREDIENTS

For 4-6 servings:
2 tablespoons beef dripping, or oil
1 large onion, finely chopped
500g (1lb) rump steak
250g (8oz) ox kidney or beef sausages or both
1 tablespoon plain flour, seasoned with salt and pepper
water or stock
½ teaspoon ground cloves
1 tablespoon parsley, chopped
1 tablespoon marjoram, chopped
bay leaf
250g (8oz) medium-sized mushrooms (optional)
1 litre (2 pint) pie-dish and pie funnel or cup
200g (6oz) puff pastry

METHOD

Making the filling:
Heat the oil and brown the onions until dark, but not burnt. Brown the sausages. Skin, split, core and cut up kidney. Using a rolling-pin, or meat-bat, beat out the rump steak till thin. Cut into long strips. Coat the meat with the seasoned flour. Cut sausages in half. Roll meat round either the sausages or the kidney.

Put into the base of the pie-dish, end on. Cover with onions. Pile whole mushrooms on top, so that they come up high above the rim to hold up the pastry. Pour over enough water to come three-quarters of the way up the filling.

Baking the pie:

Pre-heat the oven to gas mark 8/230C/450F. Roll out the pastry an inch or so larger than the pie, cut round pie to fit. Wet rim of pie-dish. Cut a thin strip from the leftover pastry and place round rim, wet edge, and place on pastry lid. Seal down well. Use leftover pastry to make pastry leaves. Brush top and leaves with beaten egg, place on leaves, make two holes for steam to escape. Bake for about 30 minutes in the hot oven until the pastry is risen and browned. Reduce the heat to gas mark 4/180C/350F and bake for another hour until the meat is cooked. If the pastry is browning too much, cover with foil. Fill up the pie with hot water or stock before serving.

TRIFLE

A farmhouse legend

East Balhallgardy is a sturdy granite farmhouse, down muddy lanes just out of Inverurie where Aberdeen Angus cattle graze on farmlands which have been in the Maitland family since the 18th century. At Christmas and New Year the farmer's wife, Aileen Maitland, cooks the festive meal for her extended family. It's normally the only time she makes a festive trifle, but today her niece, Fiona Taylor, has brought me to sample the trifle which has become a legend.

We stand, warming up round the Raeburn in the farm kitchen, and Aunt Aileen protests that there is nothing very grand, or even special about it. 'Farming people like good basic food, you know, the trifle is really very plain, no fruit or jelly,' she says. 'I hope you won't be disappointed. The recipe's from my mother-in-law, and it's more or less exactly how she made it when I came here to live when I got married. I just copied her.

'We'd two milking cows, and for dinner every day at noon, when all the workers ate their main meal of the day, there were always big puddings. When fruit was in season there would be rhubarb crumbles and apple pies, but for the rest of the year it was milk puddings, rice, semolina and custard. I used to take in a huge jug of fresh cream every day from the dairy. Lashings of it were poured over the puddings — and no one died of a heart attack.

'The trifle was a very special festive pudding. Afterwards, the children would come into the kitchen looking for a scrape of the leftovers in the dish. Is the trifle all eaten? Och aye.'

There are no milking cows on the farm now, but Aunt Aileen has turned the old dairy, adjoining the house into a shop to sell her own freshly picked fruit and jams during the summer. The trifle begins with a pot of this strawberry jam, emptied into a pan and warmed slightly. The home-made light egg sponge which she has made the previous day is chopped up roughly and put into the huge crystal bowl. When the jam is warm and runny it's poured over the sponge and left to soak for a few hours.

Her farm hens are not laying for the moment, so eggs for the custard — which goes on top — have been bought, not from the local supermarket, but from another farm where the hens run wild in woods.

'For a good egg,' she says, 'you need a healthy hen'. She uses six eggs from Rhode Island Red hens to a pint of milk.

The custard is made. A delicate operation, eggs and milk heated slowly — without the aid of a double saucepan — until the egg thickens. Some sherry is poured over the jammy sponges, and then the custard, when it's cold. The final layer of cream is piled on top and there is a twirl with the fork. No decoration. Nothing to detract from the intensity of the three contrasting layers. We sit eating bowls of it with tea and shortbread in the middle of the afternoon. And there are no leftovers.

AUNT AILEEN'S TRIFLE

INGREDIENTS

For 4-6 servings:

Sponge / jam:
250g (8oz) sponge cake
375g (12oz) pot strawberry jam
4-5 tablespoons medium sherry

Custard:
500ml (16fl oz) milk
6 large eggs
1 tablespoon caster sugar

Cream:
600ml (1 pint) whipping cream

METHOD

First layer:
Cut up sponges into one inch cubes and put in the base of a glass dish. Melt the jam till it is just warm and runny. Pour over the sponges. Pour over the sherry. Leave for a few hours or overnight to soak up the jam.

Custard:

Heat the milk in a pan. Break the eggs into a bowl, add the sugar and beat up. When the milk is hot pour over the eggs and return to the pan. Cook over a low heat, stirring all the time till it thickens, coating the back of the wooden spoon. Leave to cool a little before pouring over the sponge.

Cream:

When the custard is set, beat up the cream and pour over. Serve chilled.

SHETLAND YULE BREAKFAST

MID NINETEENTH CENTURY

The Rev Biot Edmonston's dining-room table was groaning with good things. First for breakfast: a huge round of cold corned beef, savoury sausages (sassermaet), fried fish, eggs, rolls steaming from the oven, flour scones kneaded with milk and butter, a species of oatcake called 'fat brunnies', so rich and free they will scarcely hold together, jam, marmalade and tea with plenty of sugar and rich cream.

'But before we rise from the table,' he says, 'we have yet to partake of the crowning glory of a Yule breakfast. From the sideboard are now brought and set before our host a large old china punch bowl, kept expressly for the purpose; a salver with many ancient, curiously shaped large glasses — also kept sacred to the occasion — and a cake-basket heaped with rich crisp shortbread. The bowl contains whipcol, the venerable and famous Yule breakfast beverage …

'I not know if it was a Yule drink of our Viking ancestors … But I know there was never, in the old house, a Yule breakfast without it.

'The yolks of a dozen eggs are vigorously whisked for half an hour with about a pound of sifted loaf-sugar; nearly half a pint of old rum is added, and then about a quart of rich sweet cream. A bumper of this, tossed off to many happy returns of Yule Day, together with a large square of shortbread, always rounded off our Yule Day breakfast.'

WHIPCOL

INGREDIENTS

For 8-12 servings:
4 egg yolks
175g (6oz) caster sugar
½ cup (125ml/4fl oz) rum
2 cups (500ml/16fl oz) whipping cream

METHOD

Beat the egg yolks and the sugar till thick and foamy, add the rum. Beat the cream till stiff and add to the mixture. Serve with shortbread.

TWENTIETH CENTURY

SASSERMAET

(SAUCERMEAT, SAVOURY SAUSAGE)

Shetland butchers make up this spiced sausage mix which is moulded into 'Lorne sausage' tins producing a slicing sausage. Or it may be sold unshaped for making into *bronies* (hamburgers) at home or a meat loaf. It's a modern development of an old cure for preserving meat (the word appears to come from the French *saucise*). Early recipes have a high proportion of salt and spices used to flavour the meat. Made in its original form in the croft house, it was usually made up in large quantities in the autumn to last the winter. The heavily spiced and salted sassermaet was kept in an earthenware crock and used as required, mixed with fresh meat and/or breadcrumbs along with chopped onions and egg or milk to bind. Though some traditionalists continue to make up their own mix, most sassermaet is now made by butchers in the ready-to-use milder form.

Beef and fat are minced together and mixed with the binder (rusk), water, salt and a spicing mixture which includes, cloves, ginger, white pepper, black pepper, allspice (Jamaica pepper), mace and cinnamon. Every butcher uses his own spicing mix and regards it as a trade secret. All ten butchers in the Shetlands make weekly supplies, Peter Anderson in Commercial Road, Lerwick, making approximately 200kg (400lbs) a week.

LATE TWENTIETH CENTURY

If a supply of the spice mix is handy in a jar it can be quickly mixed into minced beef.

Spice mix to store in a jar
with a tight-fitting lid:
1 teaspoon black peppercorns
1 teaspoon white peppercorns
1 teaspoon whole allspice
1 teaspoon whole mace
3 sticks cinnamon
pinch of whole cloves

Meat mix:

250g (8oz) minced beef

1 teaspoon spice mix

1 teaspoon salt

1 tablespoon oil

METHOD

Grind spices until fine and store. Mix the beef, spice and salt thoroughly. Roll into small round balls about the size of a small egg.

Heat the oil in a frying pan and fry, tossing them around in the pan to cook on all sides. Serve with mashed potatoes, clapshot or stovies.

D E C E M B.

Trench and prepare grounds. Gather together composts. plant Trees in nuseries. and sow their seeds that can Endure it.

Gather Firr feed, holly berries, &c. Take up liquorish. Continue your care in preserving choice Carnations, Anemonies, and Ranunculuses from Raines and frosts. And keep the green-house close against the piercing colds. Turne and refresh your fruit in a clear and serene day. Sharpen and mend tools. Gather oziers and haffell Rods and make baskets in stormy weather. Cover your water pipes with leitter left the frosts do crak them, feed weak bees.

Garden Dishes and Drinks in season.

Colworts, Leeks, &c. Housed Cabbage, Onions, shallot. Several dryed sweet herbes. Housed Parsneeps, Turneeps, Skirrets, Carrots, Potatoes, Beat-rave, Scorzonera, parsly. Fennel Roots. Pickled Cucumbers, Barberries, Artichocks, Asparagus, Purslain, &c.

Housed Aples, Pears. Conserved Cherries, Plumes, Peaches, Apricocks, &c.

Wine of Aples, Pears, Cherries, Liquorish, Hony, &c.

John Reid, *The Scots Gard'ner*, (1683)

Immortalizing Robert Burns Making Marmalade

Haggis, Orange Marmalade, Caledonian Cream

HAGGIS DINNERS

Around the world

Blasts of January chill find Scots deeply involved in steaming haggis puddings, warming toasts of whisky and many spirited addresses to the haggis. But for Burns Suppers, the ugly old pudding might never made it into the 19th century, let alone survived the 20th century's fast-food revolution.

It's now 200 years since Burns's death, yet thanks to him this ancient method of stuffing an animal's innards into its stomach bag remains more or less intact. Developments with plastic casings notwithstanding, we still eat the same old pudding which inspired him to write his 'Address to a Haggis' in the winter of 1786.

It appears to have found its way to Scotland via Ancient Greece, Rome, France and England, but until Burns there was nothing particularly Scottish about it. Recipes appear in English cookery books at the same time the 'Address' was written. But Burns strikes the celebratory note, dear to Scottish hearts, while at the same time honouring something which has little, if any, visual appeal. It was appropriate that he should celebrate a haggis. Do not judge by appearances, he says. Honour the honest virtues of sense and worth, not in French ragouts and fricassés, but in a more democratic dish which makes the least attractive parts of an animal into something worth celebrating.

It was a challenge, firstly to Scots, but as it has turned out, also to the rest of the world, with Burns supper celebrations taking on a universal meaning. Yet at the same time the influence of the haggis on the national food image has been extremely powerful. 'An assertion,' says James Kinsley in Volume 3 of his edition of Burns *Poems and Songs* (1968), 'of peasant virtue and strength, expressed in harsh, violent diction and images of slaughter.'

Just as there is no escape from reality in life, there is no escape in Burns's poem. The image is of a nation celebrating in hospitable and open-hearted ways a hearty, wholesome, unsophisticated yet highly distinctive food at a unique occasion.

Around 1801, five years after his death, the first Burns Club was formed in Greenock. In 1805 Paisley had formed a club, and two years later Kilmarnock.

The Edinburgh literati, including Sir Walter Scott and Alexander Boswell, son of the biographer James Boswell, had their first Burns celebration in 1815 and resolved to have one every three years. In London, Scots along with some English poets had a Burns anniversary supper in 1819. But it was not until 1885 that The Burns Federation was formed with 51 Burns Club members.

In the two centuries since his death a worldwide cult has developed with deep roots founded on the poet's appeal, not just to the literati, but to everyone. Though there may be greater poets, none have surpassed Burns in touching the spirit which bonds people of all nations, creeds and colours. For Scots, he is among a handful of makars who have written from the heart in their own tongue, adding an emotional nostalgia to Burns suppers with the colour and character of the rarely heard native Scots language.

The proceedings for the night may be formal or informal. A formal supper organized by a Burns club begins when all the guests are seated with a piper entering the room, followed by the cook or chef carrying the chieftain haggis — from 5-10kg (10-20lbs) — on a large ashet. Behind him comes the waiter with a bottle of whisky. The procession then walks sunwise round the company, ending up at the chairman of the club, who takes the whisky from the waiter and pours out two glasses. The piper stops playing, the haggis is placed on the table and the piper and the chef are given whiskies.

A guest then recites 'The Address', plunging a dirk into it and cutting a St Andrews Cross on the top, turning back the flaps and inserting the serving spoon. Before the meal begins someone will recite Burns' Selkirk Grace:

> *Some hae meat, and canna eat,*
> *And some wad eat, that want it,*
> *But we hae meat and we can eat,*
> *And sae the Lord be thankit.*

The meat for the meal, besides the haggis, should be in keeping with the festive fare of hamely folk, the traditional menu can be written in Scots and might include: *Het Kail* (a broth); *Caller Fish* (fresh fish); The Haggis; *Het Joints* (meat or poultry, usually roasted); *Ither orra Eattocks* (sweets and puddings); and *Gusty Kickshaws* (hot savouries).

The meal over, there are the toasts, accompanied by glasses of whisky. Firstly The Queen, proposed by the Chairman, followed by The Immortal Memory, proposed by the guest of honour. There may be other informal toasts, but there is usually a formal proposal and reply to both The Guests and The Lassies. The evening's entertainment continues, usually dominated by Burns songs. The ending is a communal singing of Auld Lang Syne when everyone joins hands in a circle and when the fifth verse is reached — And there's a hand, my trusty fiere — everyone crosses their arms in front and grasps their neighbour's hands again, thus contracting the circle. As people come closer together, they move their arms rhythmically up and down, and at the end give a rousing three cheers for auld aquaintances, the world o'er.

Wherever there is a haggis, there can be a supper. Caledonian and Scottish societies around the world have original ways of producing a haggis. US import laws prevent fresh haggis being taken into the country so it might be made by a local butcher or a haggis-making enthusiast. On a trip to Texas in the late 1980s for a Scottish celebration, I found the expatriate Scots community employing the services of one of their members who had taken up haggis-making as a hobby which eventually became a business. It began in the family kitchen, but had soon moved into a purpose-built haggis-making shed at the bottom of his garden.

Not all countries have such enthusiastic haggis-makers and the haggis for Burns suppers is often carried in the luggage of the Scots visitors, though at one customs checkpoint in Africa, the airport was cleared when the official thought he had uncovered a bomb. On a trip to the Baltic republic of Lithuania in 1994, I carried 20lb of haggis, successfully, through the customs for a Burns supper in a restaurant in Vilnius.

In the grim economic climate of post-communist Lithuania (its national culture and language had been suppressed by the Soviets for over 50 years), a new businessman, Dalmantas Todeas, and Lithuanian poet, Violeta Palchinskaite, had decided to host a celebration of Burns in his restaurant. Would I like to come? Would I bring the haggis?

And so one snowy January night we gathered round a long communal table: Lithuanian artists, actors, writers, journalists and haggis-carrying Scot. There was no piper but we made the procession nevertheless. The Address was recited in Scots, the Selkirk Grace in Russian, the Immortal Memory in Lithuanian. And the night went on with toasting, recitations, stories, singing and dancing. Lithuaninans, Russians, Scots and English communicating together quite successfully until Auld Lang Syne which, as I remember, was an emotional occasion about three o'clock in the morning.

HAGGIS

Though the method has remained more or less constant over the years, the ingredients have varied. Fifteenth-century recipes use the liver and blood of the sheep, while later in the 17th century a meatless *Haggas Pudding in a Sheep's Paunch* uses parsley, savoury, thyme, onions, beef suet, oatmeal, cloves, mace, pepper and salt, sewn up and boiled; served with a hole cut in the top and filled with butter melted with two eggs.

Another recipe uses a calf's paunch, and the entrails, minced together with grated bread, yolks of eggs, cream, spices, dried fruits and herbs, served as a sweet with sugar and almonds. Meg Dods has what she calls a 'finer haggis', made by parboiling and skinning sheep's tongues and kidneys, and substituting these minced, for most of the lights (lungs), and soaked bread or crisped crumbs for the toasted meal (oatmeal).

While the recipes vary, few dare to speculate on the issue of — Who makes the best haggis? It's true there are annual haggis competitions, held by the Meat Traders Association, where the range of flavours and textures arouse much controversy. There are also enterprising individuals who run haggis tastings like Bill Costley's attempt to find the best haggis in his native Ayrshire. As the proprietor of Lochgreenan Hotel in Troon, he had invited a leading Glasgow chef, a local haggis connoisseur, and myself, to judge seven local haggis including his favourite.

Only a few mouthfuls into the blind tasting it became clear that severe differences of opinion existed about the definition of a correct haggis flavour. As it turned out, we did not even rate Costley's favourite, and the award was given, very reluctantly by one of the judges, to a compromise two joint winners. One of which was Lawrence Hood who runs his own butcher's shop at Prestwick Cross. His haggis recipe had been given to him by an old butcher who was just about to retire, and who had guarded the secret of his haggis all his life. It was only when Hood suggested that it would be a great pity if such a good haggis were to go with him to the grave that he relented, and gave Hood the recipe.

Such is the competition among haggis-makers that Hood maintains the secrecy and is unwilling to divulge the details of the handed-down recipe. The only thing he will admit is that his haggis is made with proper 'pluck' meats from a sheep, which he says makes the best flavour, and coarse pinhead oatmeal, which he claims makes the best texture.

The other winner was a moist, perfectly seasoned, not too rough and not too smooth controversial haggis, made by the pig processors Hall's of Broxburn. The High Street butchers, and one of the judges, were not happy with this haggis. While there is no quarrel with a large-scale manufactured haggis, they cannot agree with the idea that haggis is made with pig's rather than sheep's pluck.

'It has far too much liver,' says one.

'It tastes more like a French pâté than a haggis,' says another.

'It's far too smooth for a haggis.'

Will anyone ever agree about anything?

METHOD

To make a modern haggis, the pluck (liver, heart, lights or lungs) is washed and put to boil until tender. When cool, the meat is chopped or minced finely and mixed with the oatmeal, onions, salt, pepper and spices. It's then put again through a coarser mincer. The mixture is moistened, usually with meat gravy, put into a filler and pumped into the prepared natural, or artificial casings which are then sealed. The haggis is then cooked in boiling water for about an hour, depending on size, the mixture swells up to fill the skins, then it's left to cool. An independent butcher specializing in haggis might make an annual 200 tons, while a large meat-processing company may make the same amount in a month. It is also sold tinned. The weight can vary from 75-100g/3-4oz (individual size) to 4-5kg/8-10lb 'Chieftain' haggis which would feed 20. An average over-the-counter haggis to feed a family of four is around 250g-500g/½-1lb.

COOKING AND SERVING

The safest way of reheating a whole cooked haggis is in the OVEN. Wrap it in foil, in its skin, and heat it through in the oven gas mark 4/180C/375F for 30 minutes per 250g/8oz haggis.

For reheating in a MICROWAVE, the outer casing should be removed. Allow approximately 8-10 minutes on high for 500g/1lb haggis.

Re-boiling in hot water is risky since the haggis may burst and does not make good soup.

ALTERNATIVE WAYS OF SERVING

Traditional:
It can be served in its skin with mashed potatoes and mashed turnip (tatties and neeps), or with clapshot (mashed potatoes and turnip mixed together [see p.18]).

As a shepherd's pie:
It can also be served in a pie dish with a layer of clapshot on top, finished with pats of butter and browned under the grill. 'Haggis meat,' says Meg Dods (1826), 'for those who do not admire the natural shape, may be poured out of the bag, and served in a deep dish.'

As a haggis-bap:
This is best made with a slicing-sausage haggis, though it can also be made with the traditional round pudding-shape. Remove the skin and grill or fry 1cm (½in) thick slices until browned on both sides (some haggis holds together better than others during frying or grilling), then put them, with a spoonful of chutney, between large buttered baps.

With bacon and eggs for breakfast:
Grill or fry 1cm (½in) slice.

Deep-fried haggis:
Fish and chip shops do a deep-fried haggis in a sausage-shaped haggis which is coated first in batter.

To make: use 500g (1lb) haggis plus a Tempura Batter mix (see p181). Divide the haggis into 14-16 pieces and roll into small balls about the size of a small egg. Make the batter. Toss the haggis balls in the batter and deep fry until they rise to the surface, crisp and browned.

Haggis without meat

A 'sweet' meatless haggis recipe has been handed down through my family for four generations. It is something akin to the Hebridean *Marag*, a steamed pudding made with flour, oatmeal, beef suet, dried fruit, and a little sugar. Though the ingredients are the same, the sweet haggis is less solid, more crumbly in texture. Another mention of a similar meatless Scottish haggis is in Dorothy Hartley's *Food in England* (1954) under the description of 'Gold Belly' which she describes as a version of an 'English oatmeal pudding; Scotch mountain recipe'.

In 1984 an Edinburgh butcher, John Macsween, was challenged by Scottish poet Tessa Ransford to make a vegetarian haggis for the Burns Supper opening of the Scottish Poetry Library. After a number of experiments, he developed a recipe with kidney beans and nuts. The enthusiastic response from guests and press encouraged him to start making the meatless haggis commercially. The volume of production has increased steadily every year.

The Macsween meatless haggis is made with oatmeal, water, vegetable margarine, kidney beans, lentils, mixed nuts, carrots, turnip, onions, mushrooms, salt, pepper, spices, and is suitable for vegans. To make it, the lentils, black beans, onions and oatmeal are soaked in water overnight; the next day the mushrooms are washed, the turnips and carrots peeled and chopped and put through a fine mincer along with the black beans and mushrooms. The mixture then goes through a coarser mincer with the lentils, oatmeal and onions. It is seasoned, and melted margarine is added and mixed in. The mixture is then fed into a 'filler' which pumps it into the skins which are sealed and boiled in water.

MARMALADE

In the years since hot toast and marmalade took a grip on the breakfast habits of the British, nearly all the bitter Spanish Seville oranges harvested in January and February are made into marmalade. Spaniards are not greatly excited by marmalade, but earthenware pots of it have followed Brits around the world for decades. In the early 1900s, the Empress of Russia and the Queen of Greece, both grand-daughters of Queen Victoria, had supplies sent regularly from Wilkins of Tiptree. Frank Cooper of Oxford still have a tin which was taken on Scott's expedition to the North Pole in 1911, which was discovered there in perfect condition in 1980. Marmalade has also been taken with UK expeditions up Everest, although it may not have been eaten on hot buttered toast.

In the course of its tangled life history, the marmalade story has generated at least a couple of myths which have livened-up the letters pages of our national newspapers over the years and for which the Scots must accept some responsibility. One involves the belief that it was an invention of Janet Keiller whose Dundee family built the first marmalade factory in 1797. Another, that it gets its name from Mary Queen of Scots.

Its first appearance — in both Scotland and England — was in wooden boxes. A solid, sugary mass of marmelos (quinces), exported from Portugal, and first mentioned as 'marmelada' in port records at the end of the 15th century. This is what travelled with Mary Queen of Scots when she became seasick on the crossing from Calais to Scotland in 1561 and which may, or may not, have helped to restore her equilibrium since quinces were regarded at the time as healing fruits.

Her request: 'Marmelade pour Marie malade' was no more than an amusing medicinal pun. 'Marmelade' had become a useful name for a thick purée of fruit in the days before the more vulgar *jam* (jammed into pots) appeared. At this time, the medicinal properties of oranges were highly regarded. Candied orange peel was eaten during a fast, so it was a natural thing to pulp and sweeten oranges into a 'marmelade'. According to C A Wilson in *The Book of Marmalade* (1985) it makes its first appearance as a recipe in 17th-century English cookery books, when it was eaten as a sweetmeat to aid digestion.

Now enter the Scots. Their dram of whisky and bowl of ale with floating toast had, until about 1700, been regarded as a warming way to start the day. But now there was tea. And what was to go with it? One solution came in a bargain-load of bitter oranges from Spain, bought by Janet Keiller's husband from a boat in Dundee harbour.

According to English recipe instructions, pounding with much patience, in a pestle and mortar to make a 'thick paste' was the thing to do. But being a resourceful and inventive character, and with an awful lot of oranges, she decided to forego this time-consuming procedure. She would use another method, based on a different (French) recipe in which the peel was chopped into shreds, taking less time and effort. With a shrewd eye on economy, she also worked out that since this 'marmelade' was not concentrated to a thick paste, it would produce many more pots and the cooking time would be shorter. It would produce a better marmalade, which it did, the first Dundee Keiller marmalade.

MAKING MARMALADE

EIGHTEENTH CENTURY

TO MAKE ORANGE MARMALADE

'To the largest best Seville oranges, take the same weight of single refined sugar; grate your oranges [this means, rub the sugar, which would have been in the form of a hard sugar loaf, on the skin of the oranges to absorb the zest]; then cut them in two, and squeeze out the juice; throw away the pulp; cut down the skins as thin as possible, about half an inch long; put a pint of water to a pound of sugar; make it into a syrup; beat the whites of three or four eggs, and clarify it; put in your rinds and gratings, and boil it till it is clear and tender; then put it in your juice, and boil it till it is of a proper thickness; when it is cold, put it in your pots, and paper it up; this is much the easiest and best way of making marmalade.'

H Robertson, *The Young Ladies School of Arts*, 1766.

LATE TWENTIETH CENTURY

The best flavour and colour is achieved with small quantities of oranges (maximum 1.5kg/3lbs). Then the marmalade reaches setting point faster, avoiding prolonged boiling which spoils the finished flavour.

INGREDIENTS

1kg (2lb) Seville oranges
1.7 litres (3 pints) water
2 lemons
500g (1lb) preserving sugar for every 500ml (l pint) fruit pulp

METHOD

Cooking the oranges:
Wash the oranges and put into the preserving pan. Pour over boiling water and simmer until soft (about an hour) or pressure-cook for about 15 minutes. Leave to cool. Cut the fruit in half. Take out the pith and pips, put this back into the cooking liquor and boil steadily for about 15 minutes to extract all the pectin. Sieve. Depending on your taste, press more or less pith through the sieve. More will make it more bitter. For a sweeter, clearer result press very little through, but make sure that all the liquid goes through since it contains the pectin for setting.

Shredding / boiling / potting:
Shred the skins finely. Add to the strained pulp and measure the volume. Add sugar

accordingly. Put into the preserving pan with the juice and grated zest of the lemons, dissolve the sugar and boil up for a set. Test on a chilled plate when the surface should wrinkle when pushed with the finger. Reduce heat while testing or the setting point will be missed and the marmalade will be overcooked. Leave 10 minutes before potting. Put a tablespoonful of rum, brandy or whisky on top. Seal tops.

Food processor method:
Wash and halve the fruit. Squeeze out juice. Set aside pips and put into muslin bag.

Shred everything on the slicer and put into a large bowl with juice, pips and water. Leave overnight.

Measure pulp and put into pan. Boil 1-2 hours till soft, then add sugar and continue as above, boiling for a set.

Cooking with marmalade

While most marmalade will inevitably find itself as a spread on hot-buttered toast, creative cooks have always investigated its potential as an intense flavouring for cakes, puddings and sauces. Mrs Dalgairns in her cookbook (*c.* 1829) put a tablespoon of minced marmalade, mixed with a glass of brandy and the juice of a lemon, through a couple of pints of cream to make a sumptuous pudding which she called Caledonian Cream. Just a simple mix of marmalade, brandy and lemon juice on its own, with additional sweetening was also used as a sauce.

Rich fruit cakes and gingerbreads were regularly laced with spoonfuls of marmalade. A steamed marmalade pudding was another old fashioned favourite. Usually spoonfuls of the marmalade were placed in the base of the pudding bowl — trickling down the sides when it was turned out.

To achieve any distinction in marmalade flavour it's necessary to use a Seville orange marmalade. The Seville orange tree, *Citrus aurantium*, which still decorates the pavements of the Spanish city which takes its name, has a strong distinctive perfume, not just in its fruit but also in its flowers and leaves.

LATE TWENTIETH CENTURY

CALEDONIAN CREAM

INGREDIENTS

For 4 servings:
2 large sweet Spanish navel oranges
300ml (10fl oz) whipping cream
2 heaped tablespoons Seville marmalade

2-3 tablespoons brandy
lemon juice to taste
sugar to taste

METHOD

Strip the zest from the oranges with a zester into the bowl of a food processor. Cut off all the white pith and remove each segment of the orange with a sharp knife avoiding the white pith. Squeeze out any remaining juice from the leftover pith. Put in the base of a glass serving dish. Put the marmalade and brandy into processor with the orange zest and blend until smooth (this can also be used as a sauce). Add all but two teaspoonfuls to cream. Mix and add sugar and lemon juice. Pour on top of oranges. Sprinkle the remaining teaspoonfuls on top and swirl with a knife. Serve chilled.

JANUARY.

PRepare the ground, foils and manures. Fell trees for mechanical ufes. Prune Firrs, plant Hawthorn Hedges, and all Trees and Shrubs that lofe the leaf weather open. Alfo prune the more hardy and old planted. Dung the Roots of Trees that need, draining exceffive moifture, gather Graffs e're they fprout, and near the end Graff; begin with the Stone Fruits. Gather Holly-berries, Firr hufks, &c. Secure choice plants as yet from cold and wet, and earth up fuch as the frofts uncovered.

Feed weak bees, alfo you may remove them.

Garden Difhes and Drinks in feafon.

Coleworts, Leeks, &c. Dry fweet Herbes. Houfed Cabbage, Onions, Shallot, Parfneeps, Skirrets, Potatoes, Carrots, Turneeps, Beat-rave, Scorzonera, Parfly and Fennel Roots in broth.

Pickled Artichocks, Beet-raves, &c. Houfed Aples, Pears, and other conferved Fruits.

With Cyder and other Wines as before.

John Reid, *The Scots Gard'ner*, (1683)

Fasting

Pancakes

After a final fling

As riotous feasting gives way to everyday routine, the mood is anti-climax. It's time to sober up, hibernate, slow down, conserve energy — and fast: a natural period of denial during the bleakest period of empty, late-winter larders which was adopted by Christians as a period of religious atonement. Never mind self-denial being good for the soul, fasting was as expedient as war-imposed rationing and the church simply fashioned it with its own doctrines. Depending on the historical timewarp, religious abstinence from food might have meant no meat, fish, eggs, milk, butter, cream and cheese. Had the medieval church been in control, the full-blown denial would have been 40 symbolic days of bread and water, only after sundown. Sounds grim.

But before it began there was a final fling of pre-Lenten merriment, starting at the festival of Candlemas, on 2 February, involving dressing-up and street processions. Until the Scottish Court moved to London in 1603, it led the fun and frolics which ended on the Tuesday in February after the first spring moon, known as *Fastern's E'en*, *Fester E'en*, *Shreftis E'en*, or Shrove Tuesday which marked the beginning of a period of *shriving*, or *shrivelling* when pre-Lenten pancakes were made with the remaining eggs and milk in the larder.

The Scots version of Lenten pancakes were known as *bannocks*, made with oatmeal, eggs, milk or beef stock and cooked on a girdle. There was also the custom of making a special milk-brose or gruel to eat with the bannocks, so that the festive night was known in different parts of the country as Bannock Night, Brose Day (Brosie for short), or Milk-Gruel Night. While there was communal merriment, the night's ritual also involved gatherings of young people round the family hearth for superstitious rites and customs pre-dating the Christian church.

It would start with fortune-telling. Then the ritual pouring of batter onto the hot girdle would be undertaken by one person, while another turned the pancake and a third removed them when they were ready, handing them round the assembled company. When the bowl of batter was almost empty, a small quantity of soot was added to the mixture to make the large *sooty* bannock, also known as the dreaming-bannock. The magic soot was a relic of the ancient sun worshippers symbolic fires, and their belief in the magical properties of the fire's ashes which they had symbolically added to food and scattered over fields.

A sooty bannock filled the whole girdle. Symbolic charms were dropped into it: button (bachelor); a ring (married); thimble (old maid); farthing (widow); scrap of material (tailor); straw (farmer). Once the bannock was turned and cooked through, it was cut into bits and put into the baker's apron for people to take their lucky dip. At the end of the evening, a piece of the sooty bannock was put inside a sock and placed under pillows where the dreamer hoped to dream of their future partner.

In today's pre-Lenten pancake culture Scots no longer believe in the power of a sooty bannock, hidden under their pillows, but they still make thick spongy pancakes on a girdle for Shrove Tuesday, rather than thin tossable French crepes in a frying pan. Like the soot, the large bannock with charms also appears to have been abandoned and the pre-fasting pancakes have shrunk to small rounds about four to six inches (15cm) across.

I was barely five years old when I was allowed to stand on a stool to reach the girdle on the cooker where my mother let me make pancake-people. Great fat, sprawling figures which covered the whole girdle and into which — before they were turned — we put decorative currants for eyes, nose and mouth on their faces. Today, my teenage daughters hold a *continuous girdle-baking*, of the kind organized in WRI tents at rural shows or Highland games, when the enthusiasts gather in a corner of the tent and turn pancakes and soda scones on a hot girdle for the day's entertainment.

Any *continuous girdle-baking* is a social event as people stand round waiting for each batch to come off the girdle, buttering, sugaring and squeezing with lemon. While we revelled in the childish fun of eating our pancake people — limb by limb — my daughters make big pancakes and pile them into a stack, hot off the girdle, with lashings of butter melting between each layer. It's a style adopted from the Americans. Long or short pancake stacks, once the mainstay of the early American settlers, have been converted into a vehicle for original experimenting with tastes and flavours on adventurous pancake menus stretching to many pages, making lemon, butter and sugar appear timid.

Girdles

Large heavy-duty, or non-stick frying pans also make good girdles. Some electric hot plates are also suitable.

Seasoning:
A new girdle should be covered with a thin layer of oil, heated up slowly until very hot, then left to cool before removing the oil.

Using:
Dust with a dry cloth after use. Heat up gently to get an even temperature. Lightly grease the surface between each batch. A piece of suet or fat wrapped in a muslin can be used, or

some kitchen paper soaked in oil. To test the temperature: Judge the heat with the palm of your hand held about an inch from the surface of the girdle. It should feel hot, but not too fiercely hot.

Turning the pancakes:

For old-fashioned bannocks, which were made the size of the girdle, bannock 'spades' were used. A modern palate knife is not a good shape for turning large pancakes and crumpets but a paint stripper with about a 10cm (4-inch) blade works well. Check that it has a good bend in the blade.

Buttermilk and raising agents:

Buttermilk gives a moister, more springy, more pliable pancake.

Commercial baking powder was invented in the 1880s, a mixture of neutral starchy filler with an acid (cream of tarter) and alkali (bicarbonate of soda) in the proportions 2 parts acid to 1 part alkali. When it's moistened it produces the leavening gas (carbon dioxide).

Of course it's always quicker and easier to use commercial baking powder or self-raising flour than soda and cream of tarter. But there is a difference in texture when an acid ingredient like buttermilk is used along with altered proportions of acid and alkali.

When using this method, however, the gas is released immediately moisture is added. Commercial baking powder and self-raising flour, on the other hand, are double acting. They begin to leaven the mixture when it's moistened, but produce most gas when the mixture is heated. This means that a mixture with either self-raising flour or baking powder can be mixed and left before baking with no adverse effects while one using buttermilk, acid and alkali must be used immediately.

TWENTIETH CENTURY

BUTTERMILK PANCAKES

This method combines the two ways of aerating to get the best of both worlds: you have a springy texture from using buttermilk, plus the safety of a double-acting raising agent in a specially 'light' cake flour, ensuring a very light pancake.

INGREDIENTS

Makes 6-8 large or 12 small pancakes:
125g (4oz) fine plain flour
125g (4oz) self-raising 'cake' flour
1 level teaspoon bicarbonate of soda
pinch of salt

1 tablespoon golden syrup

2 medium eggs

2 tablespoons oil

1½ cups (375ml/12fl oz) approximately buttermilk or
sweet milk soured with the juice of a lemon

Filling ingredients:

Lemon, sugar, butter, syrup, jam, marmalade, fresh
or stewed fruits, chopped nuts, chocolate chips,
whipped double cream, sour cream, yogurt,
fromage frais, etc

METHOD

Heat the girdle and grease. Sift all the dry ingredients into a bowl. Put the syrup, eggs and oil into a small bowl, add some buttermilk and beat until the syrup has dissolved and the eggs are beaten. Make a well in the centre of the flour and add this along with most of the buttermilk. Mix lightly until smooth but do not beat. The consistency should be about that of thick pouring cream.

Pour in ladlefuls onto the prepared girdle; they should spread to about 13-15mm (5-6in) and be about 5mm (¼in) thick. Do not turn until the top is covered with bubbles and the pancake well cooked through. Remove from the girdle, and eat immediately, or wrap in a cloth to keep warm.

To eat:

Sprinkle with lemon juice and sugar; or spread with softened butter and syrup or jam. Use fresh fruits in season with cream, the permutations are endless. Pile in stacks of three or four with filling in between or roll up with filling in the centre.

FAST PANCAKES WITH SWEET MILK

This method uses the special cake flour, milled very finely and sifted very thoroughly to make it flow freely and mix easily. It makes very light spongy pancakes, but less moist and springy than the buttermilk version.

INGREDIENTS

Makes 6-8 large-12 small pancakes

250g (8oz) self-raising 'cake' flour

2 tablespoons vegetable oil
1 egg
1 tablespoon honey or syrup
sweet milk to mix

METHOD

Sift the flour into a bowl and make a well in the centre. Pour in the oil, egg, honey or syrup and milk. Mix with a fork, until smooth then beat briefly with a whisk to remove any lumps. Cook on the girdle as above.

POURING BATTER PANCAKES FOR TOSSING

Plain:

INGREDIENTS

For approximately 15 pancakes:
125g (4oz) plain flour
pinch of salt
1 large egg
300ml (10fl oz) milk
oil/lard or butter melted for brushing pan

METHOD

Stir flour and egg together and gradually add the other ingredients using enough liquid to make it the consistency of thick pouring cream. Or blend all the ingredients in a blender for a minute. Leave in a cool place for about an hour.

Heat a 15cm (6in) crêpe pan over a high heat and grease. Pour in enough batter to just cover the base and cook for a minute. Toss, and cook on the other side for half a minute. Continue with the rest of the batter. Pile up on a plate. They may be cooked in advance and wrapped in cling film. Serve dusted with sugar and with lemon wedges.

Rich:

INGREDIENTS

For approximately 15 pancakes:
150g (5oz) plain flour
3 eggs
250ml (8fl oz) milk

4 tablespoons water

half a teaspoon salt

40g (1½oz) butter, melted and cooled

oil and pastry brush for greasing the pan

METHOD

As above.

FEBRUARY.

PLant any Trees or Shrubs that lose the leaf, also lay and cir-
cumpose such for increass, see *June*. Likewayes sow all your
Seeds, Kyes, Kirnells, Nuts, Stones; also the seeds of several
Greens, as Holly, Yew, Philyrea, Laurells, &c. Prune
Firrs, &c.

Continue to destroy Vermine.

Graffing is now in season, see the last moneth.

Prune all Trees and Shrubs except tender Greens. Nail and dress
them at the wall. Cover the Roots of Trees layed bair the fore-end
of Winter, if any be. Plant Hawthorn Hedges, Willows, &c.

Plant Liquorish, Potatoes, Peas, Beans, Cabbage. Sow
Parsly, Beets, Spinage, Marygold, and other hardy Pot-herbes.

Let carnations and such sheltered Flowers get Air in mild weather. But keep close the Green-house.

Now you may remove bees and feed weak stocks.

Garden Dishes and drinks in season.

Cole, Leiks, sweet Herbes. Onions, Shallot, housed Cabbage, Skirrets, Turneeps, Parsneeps, Potatoes, Beat-rave,
Scorzonera, Carrots, besides Parsly and Fennell Roots.

Pickled Beat-rave, Artichock. Cucum: Housed Aples, Pears,
and other conserved Fruits with Cyder and other Wines and drinks,
as above.

John Reid, *The Scots Gard'ner*, (1683)

Farming Fish

Atlantic Salmon

ONE FISH, TWO LIFESTYLES

Wild Atlantic salmon returns to the river of its birth in the spring. Full of flavour at this time from feeding on the rich plankton around Greenland, its purpose in returning is to breed. But this is the time to eat wild salmon. Records in the 18th century show the salmon fisheries on the rivers, Tay, Spey, Tweed, Don and Dee, producing colossal catches which were eaten both fresh in season and *kippered* (dried and smoked) in winter. The quantity caught each year was such that salmon was as cheap and common as fish and chips a couple of centuries later.

The subsequent fortunes of Scotland's Atlantic salmon have risen and fallen over the years, from cheap-everyday-filler, to expensive-rare-gastronomic delicacy. Now it's back to relative cheapness and availability. The reason, of course, has been the development of the salmon-farming industry, which began in Scotland in 1969. Before this time, legitimately-caught wild Scottish salmon was an expensive and rare luxury; within hours of catching, much of the fish was boxed in ice and loaded onto the London train, an operation which my family witnessed first hand while on holiday in the North-West Highlands when an entire netful of about a hundred salmon — except for one fish — disappeared before our eyes.

We had been standing on the beach at Glenelg on the North-West coast when a salmon-net fisherman got into difficulties. His colleague had been called to row out for some passengers from the steamer which had just come into the loch, so we helped him pull in his net of heaving silver fish. Nothing unusual for him in the size of the haul, but for us it was an amazing spectacle as the net came in closer and we saw the size of it. Without our help, he might have lost the lot. Once the fish were safely up on the beach we were told to leave a jacket lying on a rock nearby, and come back later when the eyes of the village had returned to their houses. Except for the one we found under my father's jacket — and which we relished for the rest of our holiday — no local person, nor even the local hotel, had more than a passing glimpse of one of the richest flavours of the sea.

More recently, as I hung over the rail of a cage which is home to thousands of Atlantic salmon of a different generation, I thought of the salmon we had enjoyed at Glenelg, and the illegitimate taste which had been my only childhood memory of this long-travelled, stunningly-beautiful, amazingly-flavoured fish. Salmon farming in cages may have become an issue of environment and ethics — and not all of it may be the best-quality fish — but it has brought availability. Scots can now afford to taste their own Atlantic salmon. It has also provided work in fragile rural communities, now that fishing the high seas no longer provides enough employment for everyone. Fish farming is the logical solution. Its success depends, of course, on avoiding pollution and death in the marine environment, and also on preventing the less genetically robust farmed fish from escaping into the native stocks of wild salmon with unknown, and possibly disastrous, consequences.

In the past few years some consortiums of farms have developed, the largest in Shetland, where 63 farms have joined together. Native fishermen of Norse ancestry in both Orkney and Shetland have a strong sense of protecting their marine environment. In Shetland, where the main source of their livelihood is the sea, they have many natural advantages which produce exceptionally fine salmon. Voes (sheltered inlets) not only have good currents flowing through them, but also very few freshwater rivers running into them so the salinity remains high. The water temperature is also cooler. All of which helps to produce a high-quality farmed fish which can hold its own in the markets of the world. There are now 6,000 jobs involved in the fish-farming industry in Scotland.

For the salmon, however, which have made the journey across the Atlantic to the winter feeding grounds in the rich waters around Greenland, and back again, there is another story. While supplies of wild salmon remained plentiful for the best part of the 19th century, there has been a gradual but steady decline throughout the 20th century. Over-fishing, and netting have been just two of the problems, and research is being undertaken to discover the reasons for the decline.

Wild salmon fishing in Scotland begins in February and carries through to September, with variations for rod-caught fish on certain rivers. The best quality are caught in early spring and summer, when still fat and flavoursome from the rich sea feeding grounds. They are likely to weigh around 4kg (8lb) upwards; a large fish is 15kg (30lb) while exceptionally large fish may reach 25-30kg (50-60lb). When, and if, they reach their original birthplace and the female spawns and the male ejects his milt on top of the spawn, they become either *spent kelts* and die from exhaustion and lack of food, or *mended kelts* who make it back to the sea. Around five per cent return to spawn again. They will usually spend two to three winters in the sea, maximum five.

Salmon farming depends on breeding stocks which are 'milked' for their eggs in November. The eggs are checked to ensure they are free from disease and then they are kept in controlled conditions until they hatch in March. The young fish are very tiny, and are carefully monitored. They are reared in special tanks, and as they grow in size, are transferred to larger tanks in fresh-water lochs, where they grow until they are large enough to be transferred to the sea farms in lochs fed by sea water.

They will be silver along the belly turning to blue/black along the back, with an internal colour a variety of shades of reddish-pink according to feeding and condition. Currently, around 50,000 tonnes of salmon are farmed, while only about 600 tonnes are legitimately caught wild — possibly another 200 tonnes are illegally caught or poached.

SEARED SALMON STEAKS WITH WARM ROCKET SALAD

This was the choice of English chef, Alastair Little, at the 1993 Scottish Food Proms Chefs' dinner in Perth when he took over the kitchens, with Shaun Hill, to show what could be done with Scottish produce.

Alistair's salmon was Shetland farmed, and the rocket came from Robert Wilson in the Carse of Gowrie (Scotherbs see p.). He tossed the rocket in a warm hollandaise-type dressing just before serving with new potatoes and butter. The skinned, boned fillets were cut at an angle of 30 degrees, making an inch-thick (2.5cm) slice which he then threw onto an oil-free smoking hot-plate. The fish stuck at first. Then after about 30 seconds, the natural oil in the flesh released it, and it was turned to the other side for another 30 seconds. While Alistair's salmon was judged a huge success, there was one thing missing — the skin. Use the skin, says David Wilson of the Peat Inn, in *The Flavour of Scotland* (1995). It has natural oils which are a very good flavour, and should not be thrown away. He's right of course. Pan-fry and grill it, he says, to make a crisp crunchiness which contrasts with the moist succulence of the fish.

Serve rich salmon with a hot, sharply pungent orange vinaigrette, says Sonia Stevenson, previously chef at the Horn of Plenty in Devon, but now travelling the length of the country teaching her sauce and fish courses. She has just made this splendid sauce for us in Mo Scott's demonstration kitchen at Earlshill Farm, at Lochwinnoch, just outside Glasgow. The recipe is in her book *The Magic of Saucery* (1995).

DAVID WILSON'S SALMON WITH CRISP SKIN, SERVED WITH SONIA STEVENSON'S HOT ORANGE VINAIGRETTE

INGREDIENTS

4 x 100/125g (4oz) salmon fillets, boned, descaled with skin left on

sea salt

mixed green salad leaves

For the hot orange vinaigrette:
150ml (5fl oz) water
200g (7oz) sugar
300ml (10fl oz) white wine vinegar
zest of 1 large orange
2 teaspoons Dijon mustard
300ml (10fl oz) groundnut oil

METHOD

To prepare the salmon, slash the skin 5-6 times with a sharp knife. Sprinkle over some sea-salt.

Heat a frying pan until it is very hot but not burning. Place in the salmon, skin-side down. The skin will stick at first but as the fat is released in the skin it will loosen. Cook for 2-3 minutes or until the fish is about half cooked through. The time will depend on the thickness of the fish.

Remove from the pan and transfer to a foil-lined baking sheet. Place skin-side up. Cook the skin until crisp under a very hot grill, for 3-4 minutes. Serve, skin side up.

To make the orange vinaigrette:
Dissolve the sugar and water in a pan and bring to the boil, simmer until it reduces and turns golden and lightly caramelized. Averting your face, but stirring well, add the vinegar and then the orange. Boil to reduce until about 300ml (½ pint). All the caramel should have dissolved but if some still remains, add some more water and boil down again to 300ml. Add mustard and mix in by boiling the mixture and shaking the pan. Pour into a heated wide-necked jar, add oil, put on lid and shake hard to emulsify.

Serving:
Place salmon on heated plates and pour vinaigrette round the fish. Serve with boiled potatoes and salad leaves in season. Store leftover vinaigrette in the fridge.

MARCH.

Redelve, mix, and Rake your ground for Immediat ufe. Delve about the Roots of all your Trees. Yet plant Trees and rather greens. Alfo prun fuch except the Rofinious. Propagate by laying circumpofition, and efpecially by cuttings. Sow the feeds of moft Trees and hardy greens. Cover thefe Trees whofe Roots lay bair, and delve doun the dungs that lay about your young Trees all winter, covering on leitter again topt with Earth to prevent drought in fummer: this is a material obfervation and more efpecially for fuch as are late planted. Slit the bark of ill thriving Trees. Fell fuch as grow croked in the nurferie. Graffing is yet in feafon, (but too late for ftone fruit) cut off the heads of them Inoculated.

Set peas, beans, Cabbage, Afparagus, Liquorifh. Sow parfly, beets, Endive, Succory, Buglofs, Burrage, Sellery, Fennell, Marigold. Plant fhollot, garleeks, Potatoes, Skirrets. Sow Onions, Lettice, Creffes, Parfneep, Beet-rave, Radifh, &c, And on the hotbed coleflour, and if you pleafe cucumber, &c.

Slip and fet phyfick herbes, *July*-flowers, and other fibrous Rooted flowers. Be carefull of the tender, the peircing colds are now on foot. Turne your fruit in theRoom but open not yet the windows.

Catch Moles, Mice, Snails, Worms, deftroy frogs fpawn, &c.

Half open paffages for bees, they begin to fit, keep them clofe night and moring: yet you may remove them.

Garden Difhes and Drinks in feafon.

Both green and houfed herbes and Roots: alfo Pickled, Houfed, and conferved fruits: with their wines as in the former months.

John Reid, *The Scots Gard'ner,* (1683)

APRIL

Feasting

Easter Bread, Paskha,
Easter Tree Cake, Decorated Eggs

THE EGG-SYMBOL OF NEW LIFE

Though the April festival of rebirth at the end of Lent is now established in Scotland as Easter, for nature-worshipping Celts it came a month later at the beginning of May with Beltane. *Ne'er cast a cloot till May is oot*, say canny Scots, meaning that cold winter can still come hurtling back when farther south it is already well into warm summer. A longer spring, shorter summer, and therefore later growing cycle made the festive times different in nature-worshipping Scotland. But Christianity, when it became established, took the southerners springtime as the festival of rebirth and not the Scots Beltane.

Easter was formerly known in Scotland as Pace, Pasch or Pesche, from the Latin *pascha*, itself from the Hebrew *pesach* passover (Gaelic *Càisg* from the same root), its name later conformed with English to become Easter after a Saxon goddess of spring *Eastre* or *Ostara*. The egg-symbol of new life had been the nature-worshippers' analogy with the miracle of the earth: apparently lifeless, then dramatically alive. In the mystical and magical religion of the Druids, eggs were sacred and their priests wore symbolic egg-shapes round their necks to denote rank.

Their *Feast of the Eggs*, had involved rolling eggs downhill to symbolize the movement of the sun. So the Christian church took the custom and related it to an imitation of the stones rolling away from Christ's tomb. Today, children continue to egg-roll at Easter, the lucky ones are those whose eggs roll the farthest without breaking.

While all kinds of natural eggs were coloured and painted from the time of the early Egyptians, the development of painted wooden, ceramic and exotic bejewelled gold and silver eggs developed in the 19th century reaching its height of extravagance with the legendary eggs made for the Russian royal family by Peter Carl Fabergé. Decorative eggs were, first and foremost, lucky talisman presents. Eggs simply covered in gold leaf were carried by travellers for good luck.

The first chocolate Easter eggs were made by Fry and Cadbury in the mid-1870s and were sometimes filled with sweets. By the 1890s the style was developing and eggs were being covered individually by decorative wickerwork. Later, moulded cards were used with a decorative print before they were finally sold in square boxes. Cadbury had introduced their 'creme' eggs in the 1920s and by the 30s Easter novelties were an important part of the celebrations. But it was not until the 50s that the packaging extravaganza really took off with the idea of using a card case, with holes on either side (an invention of a designer experimenting with packaging for light bulbs), which made the egg visible. Since then, the art of Easter egg origami has never looked back.

Hot-cross buns, the other symbolic food at Easter, can be traced back to ancient, nature-worshipping Greeks and Romans. Their crossed buns were a signal of the four seasons, dividing the bun into the four quarters of the year. Superstition had it that marking with a cross also released the evil spirits lurking in the rising dough, making them lucky buns. The crossed buns suited the Christians very well since they could be linked to Christ's death on a cross. Though Christians made them an Easter-only bun, the old pagan magic carried on and a leftover crossed bun continued to be regarded as a powerful healer, threaded and hung from the rafters, along with the cured hams and salt fish, it was used when illness struck, its crumbs moistened with some liquid and given as a cure.

Apart from the symbolic egg, the Scots have no rich tradition of native Easter foods. So Scotland has borrowed hot-cross buns first, and now English simnel cakes have appeared. While all Scottish High Street bakers make their own version of a decorated Easter sponge cake, simnels are not universal. They were sold first in branches of English-based multiple retailers and some Scottish bakers have taken up the idea successfully while others report a lack of interest in the heavily marzipaned fruit cake.

For festive Easter celebrations my borrowed traditions have come from Finland, from the happy accident of meeting J, who came to live next door and who turned up on Good Friday with a present of her eggy-rich, yeasted Easter bread and soft spreading cheesy *paskha*. For more than twenty years J had lived in a small town in northern Finland, bordering on Lapland, where the long, very severe winters make the coming of spring a tremendous cause for celebration. This was her first Easter in Scotland. Later, when we became close friends, we spent many Easters together, making her rich eggy bread and sweet cheesy paskha (the word coming from the same Hebrew root as pasch, the old Scots name for Easter).

Her festivities focused on an Easter 'tree' made with new-budding twigs which she decorated with eggs and Easter symbols. It was a pagan superstition that bringing new-budding branches of certain trees into the home brought good luck. Her favourite twigs were silver-birch. Secured in a plant pot, the delicate little tree was decorated with eggs, ribbons and feathers which she had dyed yellow, turquoise and orange. It was put in the centre of the table, the family presents piled beneath to be opened at a special breakfast on Easter Sunday. The hassle-free cold-table menu was a simple assortment of pickled, salted and smoked fish and meats, along with boiled eggs, and rye breads, followed by the eggy bread and creamy paskha.

To make the 'tree':

Secure a small glass which will hold the twigs in a flower-pot full of earth or sand. Any branch which is just beginning to sprout green leaves can be used, catkins, forsythia or flowering cherry. Fill the glass with water and secure the twigs. To decorate the branches, tie yellow, orange and turquoise ribbons or small bunches of coloured feathers onto the branches (white chicken feathers can be dyed yellow, orange and turquoise with fabric dyes). Decorate with blown, decorated eggs tied on with ribbon or wool. Sit fluffy yellow chickens on the branches. Make your own style with original creations.

To blow and decorate eggs:

Soak the eggs overnight in a weak solution of vinegar and water which makes them easier to paint. Make a tiny hole at either end of the egg. Blow slowly and steadily until the yolk emerges. Rinse, dry and decorate. They may be simply painted with felt-tipped pens, acrylic or water colours, or they may have tiny beads, dried flowers, shells, sequins, lace etc glued on. They may be varnished, or they may have one side removed (with a razor blade) and used as tiny hanging windows with a chicken inside or a flower or a sweet. To hang the eggs, tie a short matchstick to a piece of cotton and insert the matchstick in one end of the egg.

To decorate hard-boiled eggs:

Eggs may be boiled in plain colours with initials, names or designs drawn on beforehand with melted candle wax. Either soak in vinegar beforehand or add a spoonful of vinegar to the boiling water which makes the shell more receptive to colour. Onions skins produce a deep yellow colour.

RICH EASTER BREAD

INGREDIENTS

625g (1lb 4oz) strong white flour

25g (1oz) sugar

25g (1oz) fresh yeast

6 (size 2) eggs

milk to mix (about ½cup/125ml/4fl oz)

250g (8oz) butter, softened

egg for brushing

METHOD

Preheat the oven to gas mark 8/230C/450F. Line the base and sides of an 18cm (7in) round cake tin with double thickness foil, extending the sides to 15cm (6in).

Put the flour and sugar into the bowl of a mixer. Add the eggs and yeast dissolved in milk. Mix into the flour lightly by hand, add the butter and then mix with the dough hook until it comes together. Stop the machine to test the consistency. If it is too stiff, add more milk. Beat for about 7-8 minutes to stretch the gluten and until the dough is springy and elastic.

Remove the dough, press out on a floured board. Fold in three and put into a floured bowl, cover with cling film and put in a warm place to rise.

When almost doubled in size, remove dough, knock back and knead until smooth. Cover and place in the fridge for two hours. Turn out onto a lightly floured work surface and shape into a large ball. Place in tin. Cover with greased cling film and leave to rise till almost double in size.

Brush with egg and bake for about one hour till risen and browned. Knock on the base of the bread and it should sound hollow. Serve with paskha.

PASKHA

Originally an end of Lent expedient when stock-piles of Lent-forbidden eggs, butter, cheese and milk had been accumulating. The solution was to make a rich spreading cheese, flavoured with vanilla essence, candied peel and nuts. There are a number of different methods of making paskha. The simplest is just cream cheese, sweetened and flavoured with vanilla, glace fruits and nuts.

INGREDIENTS

250g (8oz) cottage cheese
250g (8oz) cream cheese
2 eggs
2 tablespoons double cream
50g (2oz) unsalted butter
75g (3oz) caster sugar
2 teaspoons vanilla extract
glacé fruit and nuts to decorate

METHOD

Sieve the cottage cheese, mix with the cream cheese and put in a muslin cloth. Tie and hang up to drain for about 12 hours. Put into a pan with the eggs, cream, butter and sugar. Mix well over a low heat, stirring all the time until the mixture thickens. Add the vanilla. Put into the muslin again and leave to drip for a day. Press into a mould to make a shape.

Turn out and decorate with fruit and nuts. Alternatively, omit draining for a thinner, spreading-consistency paskha.

EASTER TREE CAKE

A ring-mould shape is used to make this dense, richly-flavoured sponge cake which can become a base for the Easter Tree, or it can be simply decorated with spring flowers. It's made using a quick-and-easy sponge method which dispenses with lengthy creaming and produces as good, if not a better, result.

INGREDIENTS

115g packet of white chocolate drops
1 teaspoon vanilla extract
75g (3oz) self raising 'cake' flour
75g (3oz) plain flour
125g (4oz) caster sugar
50g (2oz) ground almonds
1 level teaspoon bicarbonate of soda
150ml (5fl oz) soured cream
2 eggs
75g (3oz) butter

For decoration:
2 tablespoons apricot jam for brushing the cake
500g (1lb) yellow marzipan
125g (4oz) small chocolate eggs
Easter Tree (see p.67)

METHOD

Preheat the oven to gas mark 4/180C/350F. Grease and flour a 1.5 litre (2½ pint) fluted 9cm (3½in) deep ring mould.

Coat the chocolate chips with vanilla and toss in a teaspoon of flour so that they are all coated. Sift the flours into a bowl and add the sugar, ground almonds and bicarbonate of soda. Beat with an electric beater for 30 seconds.

Add the soured cream, eggs and butter. Beat for 60 seconds or until the mixture has lightened and become fluffy and creamy. Mix in the chocolate chips.

Pour into the prepared tin and bake for 50-60 minutes until a skewer comes out clean. Leave in cake tin for ten minutes to cool. Turn out and leave to cool completely.

Decoration:

Roll out three quarters of the marzipan on a board or work surface dusted with icing sugar to a round shape about 5mm (¼in) thick. Place cake in the middle, with the rounded bottom of the mould shape on the marzipan and the baked crust uppermost.

Paint the outsides very lightly with jam and bring up the marzipan to coat the sides. Bring about 2.5cm (1in) over the top and press well. Cut off excess.

Turn the cake over and cut off the base piece of marzipan which is not sticking to the cake in the middle. Turn the cake back onto the base again. Cut away some of the centre sponge and place small glass in the centre.

Finish off the top edge of the basket by plaiting the remaining marzipan into a length which will go round the top edge. Wet the edge and stick on plait.

Use any remaining marzipan to make round egg shapes and put on top or use ready-made small chocolate eggs. Fill the glass with water and fill with twigs to make an Easter Tree (see p.67). Alternatively the glass can be filled with a bunch of spring flowers.

A P R I L E.

Plant Holly Hedges and Hawthorn too if not too foreward. Ply and fheer Hedges. Nail and prun Wall-trees, &c. Sow and plant firrs, and other greens. Slip and fet fage, Rofemary, thym, Rue, Savory, and all fibrous Rooted herbes and Flowers. uncover and drefs ftrawberries. Plant Artichocks, flip them and delve their plottes. Set Cabbage, Beans, Peas, Kidnees. fow Afparagus, Parfly, Beets, and Beet-card. Set Garleeks, Shallot, Potatoes, Skirrets, Sorral. fow Onions, Leeks, Lettice, Crefles, Radifh, Orach, Scorzonera, Carvy, Fennel, &c. And on the hotbed Cucumbers, Coleflowers, Purflain, fweet Marjorum, Bafill, Summer Savory, Tobaco, &c.

Set Strawberries, Violets, July-flowers, &c. Alfo fow the feeds of july flowers. &c. Sow all your Annuall flowers and Rare plants fome requiring the hotbed. Deftroy Moles, Mice Worms, Snails. Lay, Beat, and Roll gravel and grafs. Fall to your mowing and weeding.

Open the Doors off your bee-hives now they hatch.

Garden Difhes and Drinks in feafon.

Onions, Leeks, Colworts, Beets, Parfly, and other herbes: Spinage, Sorral. Scorzonera, green Afparagus, Lettice and other Sallads. Pickled Artichocks, Beet-rave, Barberries, Cucumbers.

Houfed Aples and Pears, Conferved Cherries, Plumes, Peaches, Apricocks, Goosberries, Currans. Alfo the wines of Aples, Pears, Cherries, Liquorifh, Hony, &c.

John Reid, *The Scots Gard'ner*, (1683)

PART TWO

Summer and Autumn

Worshipping Summer's Beginning

Beltane (The Celtic Spring), The Festive Bannock, Curds and Whey

FIRE FESTIVALS AT DAWN

The feast of summer-come-again in the Celtic calendar was the springtime fire festival held in honour of the sun at Beltane. It divided the Celtic year equally into two: Samhuinn (Halloween) on 31 October when fires were lit at sundown in graveyards and sacred places, Beltane on 1 May when fires were lit on hilltops at sunrise. Though the Christian church established Christmas and Easter as their most important feasts, in the nature-worshipping Celtic calendar the most important feasts have always been at these emotional times when the earth's rhythm changed.

Samhuinn was the more powerful of the two, and has been the most vigorous survivor, but Beltane has also lasted into the 20th century, almost dying out, then taking on a new lease of life, with Beltane fires re-lit recently on Calton Hill in Edinburgh, a symbolic reminder that rebirth is always possible.

As with the end of October, the beginning of May marked a time when the earth was in turmoil and change, but this time with new growth. Once again the spirits of the netherworld were disturbed from their sleep and came alive, some just to visit their loved ones, but others to do mischief. While in October there was thanksgiving for the earth's harvest, in May there was supplication for protection from the ill luck of bad weather, crops failing and animals dying. Many rites and customs relating to nature's birth were practised round the daybreak bonfires which were surrounded by a wide circular trench, within which the people gathered. Focus of the festivities was the Beltane Wedding, when the bride was the earth and the bridegroom the sun.

Because the earth's rebirth required moisture as well as heat and light, Beltane celebrated water as well as fire. The water from sacred wells took on magical powers, and pilgrimages were made to certain wells. There are about 600 sites of wishing wells in Scotland; one of the best known is the Cloutie Well just outside Inverness. But the most sacred water for nature worshippers was the early-morning dew collected on 1 May which the Druids used in secret rites. The superstitious custom of washing faces in the May dew has survived into the 20th century. In 1934, the *Daily Record* reported the 1 May ritual when, 'About two hundred young women climbed to the top of Arthur's Seat in the King's Park, Edinburgh, early yesterday morning to bathe their faces in the May dew.' The practice still continues.

The customs and festivities on 1 May were not only influenced by the Celtic fire and water rites, but also by the Roman floral festival known as *Florilia*. A springtime flower festival which was predominant in Europe, even in areas which had never been occupied by a Roman legion. When parts of southern Scotland ceased to be Celtic, Florilia was grafted onto Beltane. In some of the burghs, the maypole became the focal point of the festivities with games and dancing and the election of a May Queen and King. The maypole was decorated with flowers, houses were filled with flowers, and newly green branches of protective trees, such as the rowan, juniper and elder were taken into the house. In many burghs the habit of Common Ridings developed, which involved a ride or walk round the commonlands attached to the burgh with subsidiary practices, originally derived from the Beltane celebrations. Meantime, people in the more strongly Celtic areas of the north continued to light the Beltane bonfires on the tops of hills, visit sacred wells, gather the May dew and wash faces in it. On the special Beltane hills around the country, where huge bonfires had been burnt year after year for many centuries, geologists have identified a thick stratum of charcoal underneath a covering of fine loam.

Among the eating traditions recorded at Beltane there was a custard-type mixture of eggs, milk and oatmeal, known as the Beltane Caudle which was cooked on the Beltane bonfire. Some of it was poured symbolically onto the ground so that the hens would lay plentifully in the coming year, the cows give abundant milk and the fields a rich harvest. The remainder was either eaten or poured over the Beltane Bannock.

'These cakes or bannocks, as we call them in Scotland,' says Sir James Frazer in *The Golden Bough* (1906), 'were oatcakes baked in the usual way, but washed over with a thin batter of whipped egg, milk, and cream.' The nature of the festive bannock appears to have varied throughout the country with some bannocks remaining in the form of large round inch-thick cakes of barley or oatmeal while others took on a triangular shape.

A Beltane Bannock on the Isle of Mull is recorded in *British Calendar Customs* by M M Banks, as being a large round cake with a hole in the middle, through which the cows were milked on 1 May for luck. In Ross-shire they were called hand-cakes (Gaelic, *dearnagan*) because they were entirely worked by hand, not rolled out on a board or table. After baking, they were put immediately into the hands of the children to eat.

The Beltane Bannock survived on the Isle of Lewis, at least to the beginning of the 20th century, where it is recorded as being made with barley meal, spread over with a mixture of switched egg, oatmeal and milk and toasted before the fire. The ritual bannock, in its most sophisticated form, appears to have been made with a batter coating of flour, cream, eggs and sugar which was cooked onto the already baked bannock. A layer of about a quarter of an inch was spread on one side and this was put to toast at the fire. When that had browned, another layer was added and the procedure repeated. Several layers were built up on each side of the bannock, each toasted separately before the fire in the same way that Germans make their *Baumkuchen* (tree-cake), the cake revolving on a spit before the fire while the layers of thick batter are cooked onto it.

In many parts of Scotland a newly made sheep's-milk cheese was specially prepared for Beltane. It was cut and laid on the Beltane bannock and eaten before sunset. According to the 16th-century poet Alexander Scott, other festive foods included:

> Butter, new cheise, and beir in May,
> Connan [rabbits], cokkelis, curds and quhey [whey].

THE FESTIVE BANNOCK

Of Selkirk fame

The word 'bannock' referred originally to a round unleavened piece of dough, usually about the size of a meat plate, which was baked on the girdle and used by the oven-less Scots in place of yeast-raised oven-baked bread. It is now generally applied to any baking item which is large and round.

Inch-thick (2.5cm), unleavened bannocks in the style of the original Beltane bannocks are no longer made; the thickest oatcake is unlikely to be more than ¼in (5mm) thick and they are usually divided up into four farls (quarters) rather than left whole. The only remaining large round bannocks made of barley are Orkney beremeal bannocks (see page 141) though they are soft and aerated with modern raising agents. Another traditional round bannock with a more recent history is the Selkirk bannock — a yeast-raised, buttery flavoured bun which is made with sultanas. The first Selkirk bannocks were made by a baker, Robbie Douglas, who opened a shop in the Market Place in 1859 and started making a rich yeasted bannock which eventually took on the name of the town.

He used the best butter from cows grazing on local pastures and the best Turkish sultanas, establishing a quality product with a distinctive flavour. It made its reputation when Queen Victoria, on a visit to Sir Walter Scott's granddaughter at Abbotsford in 1867, is said to have refused all else from the tea-table spread, save a slice of the Douglas bannock.

While a number of bakers now make the bannock, the original recipe has been handed down via Alex Dalgetty, one of the bakers who baked for Robbie Douglas. Dalgetty's descendants continue to make the original recipe at their bakery in

Galashiels, though Houstons in Hawick now own the bakery where Robbie Douglas made his first bannocks. Hossacks in Kelso have recently developed a Tweed Bannock made with 100 per cent wholemeal stoneground flour from Heatherslaw Corn Mill at Cornhill-on-Tweed.

Though the original bannock was made with a portion of everyday bread dough, bakers now make up a special bannock dough. Some, but not all, continue to follow the original method of making a 'sponge' dough first which is left to prove and ferment, developing flavour overnight. Those who follow the faster-rising method produce a less well-flavoured bannock.

At Dalgetty's, a yeast dough is made up with approximately 4 parts flour to 1 part butter and lard. It is left to rise overnight and then knocked back when the remaining ingredients, 1 part sugar and 2 parts sultanas, are added. The dough is shaped into small or large rounds and set to prove. When they have doubled in size they are glazed and baked in a hot oven. Time depends on the size from 25-30 minutes for the smallest to about an hour for the largest.

They make around 2-3,000 in a week varying in size from: 450g/1lb (small) to 800g/1½lb (large). The Selkirk Bannock is now made by all independent bakers in the Borders.

CURDS AND WHEY

At Aikwood Tower

The 1993 midsummer junketing of the Scottish writer's group of Pen International was held at Aikwood Tower in the Ettrick valley, an old tower house restored by Sir David and Lady Steel, which has become not only their home but also a public place for gatherings, literary, artistic and social.

Judy Steel had made lunch, which ended, appropriately, with junket. The delicate, flower-scented curd had been set with rennet in large crystal bowls, on top of which (following an old recipe) she had poured an inch-thick layer of whipped cream. Her original summer symbol was a scattering of shocking pink rose petals from old-fashioned rose bushes in the garden, which had been thrown over the cream just before serving.

JUNKET

INGREDIENTS

1 teaspoon of rennet

1 litre (2 pints) milk

300ml (10fl oz) whipping cream

2 teaspoons rosewater

3 handfuls of (insecticide-free) rose-petals

METHOD

Stir the rennet into the milk, pour into the serving dish and leave to set. Beat up the cream and flavour with sugar and rosewater. Spread on top of curd. Just before serving, scatter over rose petals.

M A Y.

PUll up fuckers and haw about the Trees. Rub-off unneceffary buds. Sheer or clip Hedges. Prun tender Greens, (Not the Rofinious) bring furth the houfed ones refrefhing & trimming them. Plant all forts of medicinal Herbes. Sow all fweet ones which are tender.

Gather Snails, Wormes, catch Moles.

Sow Letice, Creffes, Purflain, Turneep, Radifh, Peas, &c. Continue weeding and watering.

Near the end watch the Bees ready to fwarm.

Garden Difhes and drinks in feafon.

Coleworts and other Herbes, (being eaten with contentement is better than a fatted Ox without it) fage (with Butter,) Leeks, Parfly, Thyme, Marjorum, forrall, Spinage, &c. Scorzonera, Afparagus, Letice, Purflain, and other Sallades and Pot-herbes.

Pickled Artichocks, Barberries; Beet-rave, Cucumbers, houfed Aples and Pears for many ufes. Early Cherries, Straw-berries, near the end.

Cyder, Metheglin, Liquorifh Ail, &c.

John Reid, *The Scots Gard'ner*, (1683)

Bed and Breakfasting
Breakfast Bakery

Oatcakes, Rowies, Quick-mix
Breakfast Loaves and Muffins

Private hospitality

Scotland's bed-and-breakfast industry operates from about March through to the end of October and is based on the idea of opening your home to visitors for a night's rest and breakfast. It's a tradition throughout the country, but particularly strong in remote areas like the Highlands and Islands where hotels are few and far between, and where people who make a living from a number of other freelance activities, such as crofting and fishing, vacate their houses in summer, often living in sheds at the bottom of the garden, to do B&Bs.

It has developed from an old custom of private hospitality, when a welcome was always given to travellers in outlying areas. A knock on any door guaranteed a bed and food for the night. A gift, rather than money, was given in lieu of payment and it's still traditional to carry gifts when visiting. In the old clan system, hospitality was a matter of honour. No one, not even a deadly enemy, who turned up looking for shelter and food was ever turned away. The legendary 'Highland Welcome', which Burns enjoyed on a visit to the area, prompted him to claim that he would be happy to arrive in Heaven, if only he could be sure of a Highland welcome.

Universal private hospitality meant that there was much less need for public inns. When the outrageously rude English doctor Samuel Johnson and his polite Scottish travelling companion, James Boswell, took their tour of the Highlands and Islands in the late 18th century, they did not stay at inns, but enjoyed the hospitality of the lairds who operated a system of passing-on with a letter of introduction. It was a custom which, inadvertently, created a much lower standard of public inns in Scotland. From accounts in the early days it seems that they were rough and ready affairs, used mainly as stables for horses and bothies for servants. Compared with a comfortable English inn, they were not a pleasant experience. As Englishman Edward Burt who lived in Inverness during the 18th century, discovered as he travelled around the Highlands: 'Some of the inns in these remote parts are not very inviting. Your chamber, which you sometimes enter from without doors by stairs as dirty as the streets, is so far from having been washed that it would be no wonder you stumbled over clods of dried dirt in going from fire-side to bed.'

Burt was equally unimpressed with the food. The Highland table at the inn might have been a risky experience but there was nothing wrong with food presented at homely tables such as the Highland breakfast which was described by Tobias Smollett in Humphrey Clinker (1771): 'One kit boiled eggs; a second full of butter; a third full of cream; an entire cheese made of goat's milk; a large earthen pot full of honey; the best part of a ham; a cold venison pasty; a bushel of oatmeal made into thin cakes and bannocks, with a small wheaten loaf in the middle for the strangers; a large stone bottle full of whisky, another of brandy, and a kilderkin of ale.'

To a roast-beef-eating English traveller, these were novel tastes: wild game, goat's and sheep's milk cheeses, peat-smoked fish, heather honey, mellow oatcakes, earthy barley breads, and potent distilled whisky. It was a vast choice of food, by modern standards, eaten first thing. But in Smollet's time, before disrupting-lunch took over, everyone ate heartily at breakfast. Breakfast and dinner were the two main meals of the day. People rose early, between five and six, and worked for a few hours before breakfast around nine, when there was always something substantial like a pie or cold beef, or a sheep's heid. And they never ate again till dinner, which was in the mid to late afternoon.

The two young Germans who were sitting at Mrs McPhail's breakfast table, in a remote corner of North-West Sutherland, had just finished their modern version of Smollet's 18th-century breakfast feast. No sheep's heid or potent whisky, but bacon and eggs, sausages, black pudding, haggis, tomatoes and mushrooms. Their bed-and-breakfast deal had also included plates of porridge and cream, while Mrs McPhail's home-made oatcakes, baps and marmalade came with a pot of tea or a cafétière of freshly ground coffee. 'This is wonderful,' said one. 'Now all we need is a biscuit in the middle of the day to keep us going till dinner. Your breakfasts are fantastic.'

Those who provide such a breakfast feast which makes lunch redundant, preserve a distinguished tradition of Scottish hospitality. They are often to be found baking their own breads and oatcakes, making their own marmalades and preserves, ensuring that the bacon is water-free, the eggs free-range and the kippers and smoked fish free from unwanted colourings. They have sensibly banished characterless plant-baked bread, along with packaged portion-controlled butter and jam, in their early-morning effort to make an unforgettable start to the day.

BREAKFAST BAKERY

Oatcakes

An oatcake may take a number of different forms. It can be an oven-baked, manufactured biscuit containing a proportion of wheat flour. Or it can be a girdle-baked version, containing no flour, which takes on a life of its own as a thin curling triangle as it dries out. A hybrid of this is the toasted oatcake, which has not only been dried-out on a girdle, but also gently toasted before a live fire, or other source of heat, to sharpen up the oatmeal flavour and increase crispness. They are rarely found for sale commercially, though farmer's wives who bake for rural shows and Highland games sometimes produce a batch for sale. Wafer-thin, girdle-curled, dusky-coloured, crunchy-textured, nutty-flavoured — they are a distinctive product of the home-baker's art. A method which requires both skill and care, which accounts for their rarity.

'Toast very slowly at a distance from the fire,' says an old recipe, 'first on one side and then the other, on a toaster of open bars that lets the moisture escape.'

Lacking both the open fire and the old-fashioned oatcake toaster with the open bars, a compromise is to cook them first on the girdle, and finish them with a toasting under a very low grill. To get a curl on the oatcake it's necessary to cut them into triangular farls.

MID TWENTIETH CENTURY

OATCAKES — TOASTED

INGREDIENTS

125g (4oz) medium or fine oatmeal
1 tablespoon melted fat, preferably bacon fat
1-2 tablespoons boiling water
pinch of salt

METHOD

To mix and shape:
Add the fat to the meal and mix through. Sprinkle over the boiling water and bring together into a soft, firm ball. The rolling out must be done quickly before the mixture cools, when it will be much more difficult to roll. Dust the work surface with oatmeal and roll out with a rolling pin, pinching the edges to stop them cracking, to a circle about ⅛in (½cm) thick. Leave whole or cut into four, six or eight triangles. They can be left to dry out for an hour or longer if wished. This helps them to curl.

Heating the girdle:
Heat up slowly to a moderate heat. Test by holding your hand just above the surface when it should feel pleasantly, but not fiercely, hot. Firing the oatcakes: Put on the girdle and leave until they have dried out and started to curl. If they are too thick they will not curl. Remove and toast in the oven (gas mark 4/180C/350F) for 10-15 minutes, or toast under

a cool grill, or in front of the fire, or in a toaster. Cool on a rack and store in an airtight tin between layers of greaseproof paper. Toast again before use.

LATE TWENTIETH CENTURY

OATCAKES — BAKED IN THE OVEN

INGREDIENTS

250g (8oz) medium oatmeal

125g (4oz) pinhead oatmeal

125g (4oz) wheaten flour

pinch of salt

1 teaspoon sugar

50g (4oz) butter, dripping or lard, or a mixture

4 tablespoons boiling water

METHOD

You will need two 19 x 28cm (7½ x 11in) baking tins or two 20cm (8in) round sandwich tins — greased and floured. Preheat oven to gas mark 4/180C/350F.

Put the oatmeal, flour, salt and sugar into a bowl. Melt the fat in the water and add. Mix to a fairly stiff dough. Divide between tins. Level with a spatula. Dust with oatmeal. Cut into squares or triangles. Bake for 40 minutes.

Aberdeen Rowies

Legend has it that the Aberdeen rowie, roll or butterie came into being when a local fisherman, scunnered with living off hard ship's biscuit on long forays into the North Sea fish, met up with his friendly local baker.

'Fit wey can ye no mak a better rowie for takkin on the boatie?' asks the fisherman.

'Nae bother ava,' says the baker. 'Jist gie me a few days, an I'll hae something for ye.'

So the baker starts off with a lump from his daily bread dough. To make a keeping-rowie, he knows he must add fat. The most readily available is meat dripping from the butcher, it's also the least likely to toughen the rowie. He mixes the dripping with some dough to make it more pliable, rolls out some plain bread dough and covers it with the fatty-dripping dough. Folds it, rolls it, kneads it and then cuts it up into misshapen mounds which he flattens into the same large thin round shape as his normal softies.

His fisherman friend is delighted. And so, too, are the people of the town, who have sampled the new fisherman's rowie. The news of this crisp, crunchy rowie, with its faintly burnt saltiness, spreads. It's soon being made by every baker on the East coast from Caithness to Edinburgh. Its endearing homely shape and good taste, ensures its success. It may have none of the stylish pretensions of a French croissant, but for the people of Aberdeen it has become the favoured roll.

The first recorded literary mention of a butterie (in the *Scottish National Dictionary*) is of a street-seller in Arbroath in 1899: 'Between butteries, Rob Roy's [a kind of Bath Bun], an' turnovers, her basket was weel filled.' But the name of the baker who first took up the fisherman's challenge remains a mystery. No written evidence has yet been found and my search among the elders of Aberdeen's baking fraternity to find the first butterie baker has drawn a complete blank.

The important thing, however, is that they survive, despite attacks by healthy-eating propagandists on foods with a fatty overload. Aberdonians, and all those who face a chilling blast, need sustaining inner fuel. Butteries fulfil that practical purpose.

Though they are known in Aberdeen as rowies, or just rolls, outside the city the term *butterie* has become attached to them. On a *rowie crawl* around the town one arctic wintry day (total sampling: 16) the textures varied enormously from very crisp to very 'bready', while the taste also varied from quite bland to very salty and well-fired. Chalmers of Brocksburn, just outside Aberdeen, made a *wee rowie*, about two thirds the normal size, and in some of their branches they sell a *double rowie* for serious rowie eaters, which is two stuck together with butter.

In rowie technology, the differences between its finished characteristics can vary from one batch to the next coming from the same baker's oven. Some rowie experts claim that baker George Robertson, ten miles south in Stonehaven makes the best-flavoured and textured rowie. Food writers, myself included, have attempted to explain the rowie technology with recipes, but none, myself included, have got it right.

The only way to unravel the correct baker's procedure is to visit in the middle of the night.

At Aitken's bakery in Glenbervie Street the night's production is counted by the thousand — all shaped by hand. David Aitken is the fourth generation on this site among the grey granite tenements in the Torry district of the town. When I arrive at 4.30am it is cold and dark. There are lights shining from an open doorway and a police car is drawing up outside. Not to investigate a crime, but to collect their daily supply of hot-out-the-oven rowies. I make my way through the lighted doorway and into the source of warm, yeasty smells where the bakers are about to begin the last batch of rowies for the night. The dough is lying in a giant mound on the table, waiting to be made into 4,000 rowies. It is Friday night and by morning a total of 27,000 will be shaped by hand for the weekend consumption (through the week the production drops to 18,000).

At their stations round the white mountain of dough on the table are a team of flour-dusted bakers, ready to start carving it up. It has been made from two separate doughs, already mixed: the fatty-dough and the bread-dough. The men start to cut it up.

'Want to have a go?' says one of the young bakers and he pushes a tray towards me. Flouring his hands and lifting one of the soft, sticky lumps of dough, he shows me the knack of using masses of flour which prevents the sticky dough sticking to your hands.

He picks up the piece of dough and throws it onto the floured board. As the soft dough hits the board it spreads out into a misshapen mound. He now spreads it out more thinly. I copy him, pressing the sticky mass out with four outspread floury fingers. Next, he flours the backs of his fingers on his right hand and the fronts of those on his left.

'Yes, I've got that.'

Now he clenches his right hand into a fist and presses the rowie simultaneously with his left outstretched fingers till it is roughly a quarter of an inch thick. It takes a bit of practice, but after the fourth tray I'm beginning to get the hang of it. Now they go off to a hot steamy cupboard beside the ovens where they will prove for about 20 minutes, before going into the oven for another 18 minutes or so.

Some come out darker than others and they are put in a separate pile for customers who like a 'cremated' rowie. Some are so brittle that they break up, so the broken bits are put into paper bags for those who like a 'baggie of bities'.

Over breakfast tea and freshly-out-the-oven rowies, David Aitken tells me that he was waiting for a plane last summer in Majorca when he spied a family with a bag of Aitken's rowies. They had, he discovered, taken a fortnight's supply on holiday. Aberdonians love their rowies.

AITKEN'S ROWIES

INGREDIENTS

Bread-dough:

3 teaspoons sugar

25g (1oz) fresh yeast

375-450ml (12-15fl oz) warm water

500g (1lb) very strong bread flour, slightly warmed

METHOD

Dissolve the yeast and sugar in a little of the water and leave for ten minutes. Add to the warmed flour along with most of the remaining water and knead in. Add enough water to make a very soft sticky dough.

INGREDIENTS

Fatty-dough:
325g (11oz) solid vegetable fat
12-25g (½-1oz) salt
3 teaspoons sugar
150g (5oz) very strong bread flour

METHOD

Mix all the ingredients together till thoroughly blended. Preheat the oven to gas mark 7/220C/425F.

Mixing the two doughs:

Put a very thick layer of flour on the board and place on the first dough. Flour it on top and spread it out with well-floured hands, or a rolling pin, till it is about 1cm (½in) thick and roughly rectangular. Spread half of the second dough all over. Fold down one third to the centre and fold the other third up. Roll out to about 1cm (½in) thick and repeat with the remaining second dough. Roll out and fold up the dough one more using plenty of flour to prevent sticking.

Shaping the rowies:

Divide up the dough into 50g (2oz) pieces — approximately 20-24. Flour your hands well, take up a piece, toss to coat it evenly with flour, place it on the baking tray and press down in it with four outstretched fingers so that it spreads out. Fill the baking tray, leaving a small space between them. To finish shaping, flour the fronts of the four fingers on your right hand. Make the final pressing-out of the mis-shapen rowies by pressing down and then spreading out with the right and left floured fingers together. The rowies should by this time be roughly 5mm-1cm (¼-½in) thick.

Proving:

Oil a sheet of clingfilm and cover the tray to enclose the rowies and prevent air getting in. Leave for about 20 minutes to double in size. It is important to keep the surface from drying out.

Baking/cooling:

Bake for 18-20 minutes in a fairly hot oven till they are crisp and golden. Leave on the tray till they have cooled a little. Then stack them together, end on, in a tray. If they are stacked too soon they will have too much moisture and be soggy, on the other hand, if they are left till they go cold they will become very crisp and brittle and may break more easily.

QUICK-MIX BREAKFAST LOAVES AND MUFFINS

Half-way between a yeasted bread and a sweet cake, quick-mix loaves and muffins have many uses but their value at breakfast is speed. Make the loaves in two small loaf tins and they will take less than ten minutes preparation and no longer than 40 minutes to bake. The muffins are faster, from start to finish less than 30 minutes.

SEED AND WALNUT LOAF

An easy-mix loaf with walnuts and sesame seeds as the flavouring combined with soured cream to make a dense moist, springy texture. May also be used as a savoury loaf with soups, salads and cheese.

INGREDIENTS

2 tablespoons sesame seeds

250g (8oz) self-raising 'cake' flour

½ teaspoon bicarbonate of soda

60ml (2fl oz) olive oil

50g (2oz) soft brown sugar

2 eggs

150g (6oz) finely chopped walnuts

300ml (10fl oz) soured cream

METHOD

Preheat the oven to gas mark 5/190C/375F. Grease and coat with sesame seeds: two 1 litre (1¾ pint) loaf tins. Sift the flour and bicarbonate of soda into one bowl and mix well. Put the oil, sugar, eggs into another large bowl and beat to mix thoroughly for about 30 seconds. Add the flour, nuts and soured cream and stir in, mixing until smooth. Pour immediately into prepared tin. Bake for 40 minutes in the middle of the oven.

Test for readiness when a skewer inserted into the middle comes out clean. Cool in the tin for ten minutes, finish cooling on a rack. Serve while warm, or wrap tightly in cling film.

OATMEAL AND HAZELNUT LOAF

Another easy-mix savoury loaf with a dense crumb and lively character.

INGREDIENTS

125g (4oz) fine oatmeal

250g (8oz) self-raising 'cake' flour

½ teaspoon bicarbonate of soda

125g (4oz) ground hazel nuts

60ml (2fl oz) olive oil

1 tablespoon blossom or heather honey

2 eggs

300ml (10fl oz) soured cream

METHOD:

Preheat the oven to gas mark 5/190C/375F. Grease and flour two 1 litre (1¾ pint) loaf tins. Take one tablespoon of the oatmeal and put into the tins. Shake round the sides so that they are thoroughly coated. Reserve about two teaspoons of the oatmeal for sprinkling on top.

Sift the flour and bicarbonate of soda into one bowl. Add the oatmeal and nuts and mix well.

Put the oil, honey and eggs into another large bowl and beat to mix thoroughly for about 30 seconds.

Add the flour mixture and stir in, mixing until it is smooth. Add the soured cream and mix in.

Pour into the tin immediately, leave for ten minutes before baking. Bake for 40-45 minutes. Test with a skewer inserted into the cake, which should come out clean. Cool in the tin for ten minutes then remove to a rack. When completely cold, wrap in cling film and store.

TOASTED OAT AND RAISIN MUFFINS

Using a ready-mixed crunchy cereal and a food processor method speeds up the preparation of these muffins which can be served with bacon and eggs for breakfast.

INGREDIENTS

For 8-12 muffins:

50g (2oz) raisins

250g (8oz) crunchy toasted oat cereal

150g (5oz) self-raising superfine cake flour
½ teaspoon bicarbonate of soda
75g (3oz) butter
1 egg
250ml (8fl oz) buttermilk or fresh milk soured
with 2 tablespoons lemon juice

METHOD

Preheat the oven to gas mark 5/190C/375F. You will need a tray of 12 individual muffin tins. Grease and flour the tins. Sprinkle a few raisins in the base of each tin.

Put the crunchy cereal into the food processor and add the flour. Pulse for ten seconds, remove 2 tablespoons for the topping. Add the butter and bicarbonate of soda and pulse until the mixture is like fine breadcrumbs. Add the egg and buttermilk and pulse for a few seconds. It should form a soft batter. Spoon into the muffin tins. Sprinkle over the crunchy topping. Bake for 15-20 minutes. Cool for 5 minutes in the tin and serve warm.

J U N E.

Cleanfe about the Roots of Trees. Suckers and weeds, water their Covered Bulks: efpecially the new planted.
Fell the long fmall ill-train'd Forreft-trees in the nurferie within half foot of the ground. Unbind graffs. Prun all Wall and Standard. Trees. Towards the end you may Inoculat. And Increafe by circumpofition.
Gather Elm feed and fow Immediatly.
Tranfplant Coleflowers, Coleworts. Beets, Leeks, Purflain, &c. In moift weather; at leaft water firft the ground if dry.
Sow Peas, Radifh, Turneep, Letice, Chervil, Creffes, &c. Deftroy Snails, Worms, &c.
Begin to lay carnations or July-flowers: fhade, fupport and Prun fuch as will blow. Water pots and thrifty plants. Weeding and mowing is in feafon; and fo is diftillation.
Bees now Swarm, look diligently to them.

Garden Difhes and Drinks in feafon.

Cole, Beets, Parfly, Sorrall and other Pot-herbes. Purflain, Letice, and other Sallads; Radifh, Scorzonera; Afparagus. Green Peas and Artichocks. Green Goosberries. Ripe cherries, Rafps, Currans, Straw-berries.
Houfed Aples and Pears.
Cyder, Metheglin, &c.

John Reid, *The Scots Gard'ner*, (1683)

Growing
Fishing
Eating Out

Berries and Herbs, Crabs and Lobster,
Tea and Scones, Ice Cream

BERRY GROWING IN COOL SUMMERS

While delicate berries shrivel under the blistering heat of a tropical sun, in cool northern summers, where the light still shines at midnight, raspberries, strawberries, tayberries, blackcurrants, blaeberries, brambles, redcurrants and gooseberries thrive. In Scotland, commercial berry-growing is concentrated in Tayside and Fife, with lesser amounts in the Borders, the Clyde Valley, Arran, Ayrshire, Caithness, Morayshire and Aberdeenshire. But provided the soil is suitable, berries will thrive in any part of the country, even the far north.

I cultivate berries, for my own use, in a remote corner of the North-West Highlands on land once used by crofters for growing potatoes. Because of the warming effects of the Gulf Stream the ground seldom freezes and one year the temperature on Christmas Day was the same as 1 July. Which is the reason Osgood Mackenzie was able to cultivate tropical plants in his now much-visited Inverewe garden, on a similar lochside site two lochs further north.

The blackcurrants, raspberries, gooseberries (as well as apples, pears, plums and cherries) in my lochside garden were planted by my father in the early 1970s, and have provided generous crops annually for the last couple of decades. About 15 years ago, on a trip back home to his native Angus, he discovered a fruit farmer throwing out some experimental American highbush blueberries and rescued a dozen to add to his collection. These have also flourished, providing supplies of the large, blue-black, tangy berries which Americans use for Blueberry Pie.

Highbush blueberries were first developed in Scotland at the Scottish Crop Research Institute at Invergowrie, just outside Dundee, as an alternative to the native wild blaeberries. The blueberry was originally created in 1920 for use on the acid, boggy soils of New Jersey which had previously been thought worthless. The cultivated varieties of blueberry are mostly hybrids of three native American species, of which Berkley and Blue

Crop are grown in Scotland. Trials are in progress in Caithness and in Angus with a number of fruit farmers (one farmer has five acres, and another five farmers are experimenting with around 400 trial bushes).

Though wild berries are no longer collected for commercial markets, as they are in other northern European countries, wild berry-picking enthusiasts in Scotland continue to harvest brambles, rowans, sloes, elderberries and blaeberries for domestic use. Wild berries were once an important part of the summer diet, and sold commercially, as my father recalls the wild blaeberries sold commercially by tinkers and travelling packmen in the early 1920s and 30s when he worked on a farm in an Angus glen.

When the blaeberries were ripe on the hills, a berry-picking packman, known as Sandy 'Pints' (bootlaces) would appear with his travelling companion 'Sweet' Marie, carrying baskets of ripe blaeberries. Sandy had invented a wide-toothed wooden comb on a stout handle, which he put underneath the bushes, 'combing' off the ripe berries in one easy move. He called it his 'picker for the purpose' and the kenspeckle pair were given a warm welcome when they arrived at the back door of the farmhouse, with their baskets of sharp-tasting, blue-black mountain berries. The farmer's wife served up bowls of the berries with sweet thick cream, making the surplus into pots of jam. During the winter months, a spoonful of the dark purple preserve would be heated up with rum as a cough or cold cure.

Raspberries

But of course the berries which have made their name as the country's premier commercial crop are raspberries. Grown in Europe for centuries, it was not until the 17th century that British horticulturalists began to take the fruit seriously and by the 18th century most cookery books included recipes for raspberry wine and vinegar.

It was a group of Scottish market gardeners in Angus, at the beginning of the 20th century, who decided to move out of the traditional strawberry production and into raspberries. They joined together as a cooperative, and in subsequent decades established the Scottish crop as the dominant British supply. In 1946 the Scottish Raspberry Investigation was set up at University College, Dundee, transferring to Mylnefield Farm at Invergowrie in 1951, when the Scottish Crop Research Institute was established as a horticultural research station in the heart of berry-growing country. Over the years it has supported the industry, and been largely instrumental in its success, by developing varieties with a view to increasing yields, producing disease-resistant plants and improving flavour while retaining quality.

The quest for perfection in raspberry variety is, however, never-ending. Currently in production is Glen Clova, one of the oldest (1969) which is still used commercially; also

Glen Moy and Glen Prosen (both released in 1981). Along with Clova these three make up the bulk of the crop. Other minor varieties are Glen Garry (1990), Glen Lyon (1991) and Glencoe (1989), a purple raspberry. There is also the autumn-fruiting variety Autumn Bliss, which serves a niche consumer market, while varieties Magna, Ample and Rosa are currently under trial.

Visual and taste differences between the three main varieties are minimal, but Clova is a medium-sized, light to medium coloured fruit with a sweetish-sharp flavour; Prosen is a slightly larger fruit, medium red coloured and has a sourer flavour but a firmer, more easily transportable fruit, while Moy is a large berry of a medium red colour generally regarded as the best flavoured of the three but also the most difficult to grow.

In 1992 the Scottish Soft Fruit Growers Ltd was set up and members now commit 100 per cent of all their raspberries destined for processing to the group. Of the total raspberry crop around 7 per cent is sold fresh; 8 per cent in frozen punnets; 26 per cent quick frozen in bulk; 25 per cent canned and 34 per cent puréed. Since 1992 both canned and pureed have declined while there has been an increase in fresh, and frozen. Average production in a year is around 5,000 tonnes fluctuating according to the weather conditions. There are 311 growers, of which 183 have holding areas of less than 50 hectares.

'Ra berries'

On the fertile Tayside soils — at one time favoured by farming monks in the Middle Ages — the raspberry produces a high-quality berry around the beginning of July. Though local schoolchildren and the unemployed are the main berry pickers, in the early days of the development of the crop, the pickers were tinkers and travelling people (like Sandy and Marie) plus a contingent of Glaswegian unemployed. They arrived each year to live for 'the season' in wooden shacks which the owners had provided. In its heyday, from the 1930s through to about the 60s, *ra berries* was the highlight of the year for many city children, cooped-up in a Glasgow tenement, whose parents could not afford a holiday. In the fields of Angus the weans ran wild, swimming in rivers, sitting round camp-fires and occasionally picking *ra berries*, in city slang still used as a term for any good thing.

Today, there are new varieties grown for mechanical picking and no doubt people-pickers will one day become totally redundant. Where they will survive, though, is on the Pick-Your-Own fruit farms (see p.189) where a telephone call to the farm in advance will provide up-to-date information about the state of the fruit. The weekends are peak picking time when entire families often take to the fields to pick the fruit in its prime.

John Laird runs the PYO fields at Cairnie Fruit Farm just outside Cupar in Fife, providing one of the largest areas of a PYO farm. Over the years the field-plan of varieties has changed according to new variety developments, but for the 1995 season there were the dessert berry varieties of Elsanta, Pegasus as well as the much larger, juicier Hapil (EM227) which is only suitable for PYO since it must be picked and eaten as quickly as possible, having a minimum shelf-life.

For jam-making there was Tamella and Cambridge Favourite. Among the rasp varieties was the comparatively new variety, Glen Lyon. A dark red, round-shaped berry with a deeply citric tang which is the perfect foil for mellow cream and sweet meringue in a pavlova. There are strawberry-teas at the farm and preserves for sale which are made by Mrs Booth, who has been boiling the jelly-pans in the Cairnie farm kitchen for the last ten years and has recently published a book of recipes, *Mrs Booth's Preserves*.

BERRY-FEASTING

BERRIES WITH MERINGUES AND CREAM

Berries demand simple foils and easy combinations. The crusty crunch of meringue with a squidgy marshmallow centre, plus sweet mellow cream, is the richest feast of flavours and textures.

INGREDIENTS

For 6 servings:
6 large egg whites
pinch of salt
350g (12oz) caster sugar
2 teaspoons cornflour
1 teaspoon vinegar
300ml (10fl oz) whipping cream
500g (1lb) mixed berries
125ml (4fl oz) rum-pot liqueur (see p.96)
or crème de cassis

METHOD

Pre-heat the oven to gas mark 4/180C/350F. Line a baking sheet with baking parchment or rice paper.

Making the meringue:
Beat the egg whites with the salt till stiff. Then start adding the sugar, a tablespoon at a time, beating well as you add and carry on beating until they are very stiff and glossy. Finally beat in the cornflour and vinegar.

Pour onto lined baking sheet in a large circle about 25cm (10in) across. Or make into six separate mounds for individual pavlovas.

Baking:
Bake for five minutes at the high heat and then turn down to gas mark 1/140C/275F and cook for about an hour until very pale cream on top.

Leave to cool, remove from tin and cover the top with whipped cream and berries and liqueur.

BERRIES WITH BREAD

In the restaurant at the Gallery of Modern Art in Edinburgh they serve bread and summer berries, not in the usual summer pudding style, but in a large rectangular tray. A thick juicy crimson mixture of stewed berries and soaking bread. It is invitingly colourful — and for the cook a quick and easy method which was created by Helen Ruthven.

For economy in the restaurant, the berry juices are sweetened with concentrated blackcurrant syrup. At home she flavours with red wine and crème de cassis.

INGREDIENTS

For 6-8 servings:
350g (12oz) strawberries
250g (8oz) raspberries
250g (8oz) other available soft fruit — black or
redcurrants, brambles (blackberries), blaeberries,
blueberries, cherries
1 tablespoon sugar
1 cup (250ml/8fl oz) liquid — rum-pot liqueur (see p.96) or
fresh fruit purée or commercial juice, red wine,
crème de cassis, grenadine, other fruit liqueur to taste
125g (4oz) white bread, crusts removed

METHOD

You will need a 1½ litre (3 pint) square, round or rectangular dish or pudding bowl/basin.

Wash and shaw the strawberries and put them with the other fruit in a bowl. Sprinkle with sugar and leave for a few hours or overnight. Turn once. Put into a pan, bring slowly up to almost simmering point and remove from the heat. Add the liquid and taste. Add more sugar if necessary. Cool slightly.

Cut the bread into squares and put into the still hot liquid two or three pieces at a time. Make sure each piece of bread is thoroughly soaked before adding more.

When the bread has soaked up all the liquid and the mixture is quite solid looking, turn into the pudding bowl. Add more bread if necessary. Cover with a plate and put in a cool place, preferably overnight or longer, before turning out. Serve with cream.

Alternatively, the mixture can be poured into a shallow serving dish, as it is served in the Gallery, and cut into square portions or just spooned out.

BERRIES WITH EATING-JAM

Before solid-spreading jam was jammed into pots in factories, fruity-tasting preserves were part of the dessert ending to a meal. Pots of preserved summer fruits, became useful winter puddings. Thickly made concentrations of damson, gooseberries and apples, known as *cheeses*, were made from thickly puréed fruit, set in straight-sided earthenware pots and slid out onto a dish where they were stuck with almonds, dredged with port and eaten with thickly whipped cream. Sometimes they were cut in slices and served with ripe apples and mature cheddar cheese.

We were sitting down to tea with hot-out-the-oven scones, when my mother went for a pot of her newly-made raspberry jam. 'The jam's gone,' she announced. And sure enough the pot had been cleaned out. Her jam is a type of freezer-jam, which she makes by stirring liquid pectin into ripe raspberries and sugar. It's left to set like a jelly so that it retains the sharp, fresh tang of the uncooked berries, normally lost in the boiled variety.

The jam-thief, it turned out, was my teenage daughter who had found the pot and finished it off.

'What! All of it?'

'Yes. It was very good.'

In food cultures where jams are not jammed-into-pots but known as conserves or preserves my daughter's behaviour would have been quite normal. Thin-set, tasting of fruit, and good enough to eat on their own, they often have a runny consistency and are served as a pudding with thick cream or as a sauce with hot pancakes.

Elizabeth Grant of Rothiemurchus describes in her memoirs a jam-eating session when she was a young girl, visiting a relative on the Rothiemurchus estate in the summer of 1812. Inside her hostess's deep-shelved pantry there were oatcakes, barley scones, flour scones, butter, honey, sweetmeats, cheese, wine, and spiced whisky. Also the key to the dairy, which she recalls taking to the cook, who went to skim and whip some cream which was then poured over the contents of 'a whole pot of jam'. They called the dish, which was a great favourite, *bainne briste*, meaning broken milk.

MY MOTHER'S RASPBERRY EATING-JAM

INGREDIENTS

To make approximately 3 x 450g (1lb) pots:
450g (15oz) fresh raspberries
575g (19oz) caster sugar
juice of 1 lemon
125ml (4fl oz) liquid pectin (Certo)

METHOD

Put the rasps into a large bowl sprinkle over the lemon juice and add the sugar. Stir to mix the sugar through. Leave to stand for an hour or overnight, stir again before mixing in the liquid pectin. Make sure the sugar is thoroughly dissolved and ladle the mixture into pots which have a lid. Cover and leave for about 24 hours till the jam sets.

Keep in the fridge for 2-3 weeks or place in the freezing compartment.

STRAWBERRY EATING-JAM

This a quick-and-easy recipe (15 minutes) which produces a runny strawberry-flavoured syrup with whole berries in it. Choose small, perfectly ripened strawberries (Cambridge Favourite or Tamella) for this intensely flavoured, but not sickly-sweet, preserve.

INGREDIENTS

To make approximately 3 x 450g (1lb) pots:
500g (1lb) strawberries
juice of ½ lemon
500g (1lb) sugar

METHOD

Wash and drain the strawberries. Put them into a wide, shallow pan with the lemon juice. A deep frying pan would do. Put the sugar on a plate in a warm oven to dry out. Cook the berries on the lowest heat until soft and the juice running.

Add sugar, bring to the boil and simmer for ten minutes. Stirring gently from time to time. Pot and cover. It does not matter whether it sets or not.

BERRIES SOAKED IN RUM

Fruits which are preserved in alcohol usually means cherries in brandy, prunes in Armagnac, sloes in gin … But a rum-pot is more versatile. Almost any fruit can be used and added to throughout the fruit season.

To start the rum-pot in early summer:

INGREDIENTS

250g (8oz) strawberries washed and hulled
250g (8oz) granulated sugar
1 bottle of dark rum

METHOD

Use a large, lidded stoneware pot around 4-5 litre (8-10 pint); smaller will do but gives less scope for adding. Store in a cool room, cellar or garage away from central heating.

Put the strawberries into the pot, cover with sugar, stir well and leave for half an hour. Add enough rum to cover. Stir the fruit gently every two or three days.

To continue adding throughout the summer:

Add about 250g (8oz) at a time of prepared gooseberries, cherries, redcurrants, blackcurrants, raspberries, plums and apricots as they become available and cheap. Before adding to the pot, mix each 250g of fruit with 125g (4oz) sugar. And each time the fruit is added, add more rum to cover.

While the fruit is being added stir the pot every two or three days. After this it is only necessary to stir it every two or three weeks.

At the end of October:

Add another 300ml (½pint) of rum to the pot, by which time the fruit and its liqueur will be ready for use. Serve with ice cream or whipped cream. Use with sponge cakes or meringues, as a sauce to accompany rich game, or serve it simply on its own in a tall chilled glass as an effortless ending to a meal.

GROWING HERBS AND FLOWERS

A salad a day

John Evelyn's claim in *Acetaria, A Discourse of Sallets* (1699) that he could make a green salad for every day of the year from the 35 salad herbs growing in his garden, makes the modern use of salad herbs seem timid. Some of the plants which he used are now totally obscure, while others like sorrel, lovage and rocket are experiencing a modern revival. Like others, his knowledge and understanding of plants was linked not just to culinary uses but also to medicinal herbal cures. In the days before the modern drug industry, folk medicine's use of natural cures meant that people were much more acutely aware of the power of plants. Without being told by their doctor, they knew to take mint for digestion, garlic for infections, camomile to calm nerves ... Neglected herbal remedies are now experiencing a revival: in healing, as in cooking there is more understanding of the plant's potential.

'Try mushroom soup flavoured with astringent lovage,' says herb-gardener Robert Wilson of Scotherbs in the fertile Carse of Gowrie, 'or lightly cooked cauliflower tossed with a handful of marjoram ... what about aniseed-flavoured sweet cicely chopped into rhubarb jam ... a bed of apple ringy leaves on the base of the tin before you bake a victoria sponge ... here's some Moroccan mint which makes the best mint tea ... and rocket flowers — what could you do with them?'

Robert was a dairy farmer who converted to herb-growing in the 1980s when the 'set-aside' EC directive was first brought in. To visit his garden in the late afternoon of a hot summer's day, is to enjoy not just the heady herbal aromas, but also his enthusiasm for herbs.

Classic combinations, of course, will always remain powerful — sage with pork, horseradish with beef and rosemary with lamb — but adventurous herb-thinkers can transform ordinary foods. Some grow their own herbs and are constantly experimenting, original cooks like Joyce Molineux at the Carved Angel in Dartmouth.

She had just finished cooking lunch for the restaurant, her face flushed from the cooking heat. Tied tightly round her head was a blue and white spotted head-scarf which hid her hairline, emphasizing the directness of her gaze, and the laughter in her smile. Did she remember, we had met in London some years ago? Yes, of course. How good of you to visit.

The detour, a matter of a couple of hundred miles to Dartmouth, had been viewed by my North Cornish hosts as a ridiculously long way to go for lunch. Joyce is neither young nor trendy, and her unfussy appearance is not the stuff television cooks are made of. What she has created, however, is a remarkable open-plan cooking and eating space in a shop-front restaurant which overlooks the sailing ships in the harbour. In English restaurant culture it is unique, her cooking philosophy totally at one with local produce and eating food in season: the freshest growing things, the best fed and most cared for animals and the fish and shellfish in best condition. She is a natural 'seasons' cook, as she describes in her book *The Carved Angel Cookbook*:

'The seasons set natural parameters. In summer months the charcoal grill comes into play, giving its smoky outdoors flavour to marinated chicken or guinea fowl. Autumn introduces the first of the game, gradually bringing stronger, earthier tastes and heartier dishes to the menu. Rich stews and casseroles replace the lighter dishes of summer and the weather chills to winter. The last days of February see the end of the shooting season and, with luck, the first intimations of spring. Domestic fowl replace the game and fresh flavours start to oust the mellow winter comforters. And, so, full circle, back to summer.'

FEASTING ON HERBS

TARRAGON CHICKEN

Joyce's first experience of tarragon and chicken was at the Hole in the Wall, in Bath when she cooked with the legendary George Perry-Smith. He would roast a chicken and scent it with lots of tarragon, then finish it with a butter and cream sauce, in the Elizabeth David style.

It was served in the restaurant in its full glory and carved at the table. What might sound like a recipe for financial disaster, was in fact the opposite. An elderly lady chose a thin slice of breast, a man a whole leg. Everyone got what they wanted.

The carcass was returned to the kitchen where it was picked clean of all the meat which was made into a gratin with the leftover sauce, while the bones went into the stock pot.

INGREDIENTS

For 4-6 servings:

For the roast chicken and roast potatoes:
1 x 2kg (4lb) free range chicken
50g (2oz) butter
2 tablespoons chopped tarragon
salt
1kg (2lb) Kerr's Pinks, Golden Wonder, King Edward,
or Maris Piper potatoes, peeled
1 tablespoon olive oil
2 tablespoons brandy

For the sauce:
1 tablespoon plain flour
2 cups (500ml/16fl oz) chicken juices plus water
1 cup (250ml/8fl oz) dry white wine
½ cup (125ml/4fl oz) double cream

2 tablespoon chopped tarragon

salt

freshly ground white pepper

METHOD

To roast the chicken and potatoes:

Pre-heat oven to gas mark 8/230C/450F. Remove the wishbone with a sharp knife and release the breast skin by sliding your hand under it. Mix the butter and tarragon and push under the skin, spreading out over the breast. Keep back a little tarragon butter and rub the outside of the bird. Season all over with salt.

Put potatoes into roasting tin and coat in oil. Place chicken on its side and roast for 20 minutes. Turn onto other side. Turn the potatoes and roast for another 20 minutes. Turn chicken onto its back and roast for a final 20 minutes. Remove from the oven. Pour over the brandy and set alight. Leave to rest in a warm place for ten minutes before making the sauce.

To make the sauce:

Remove the juices from the roast and make up to two cups with water. Take off some of the surface fat and mix with the flour. Put into a wide, deep, frying pan and cook for few minutes. Add the rest of the juices and the wine and bring to the boil. Simmer to reduce and concentrate the flavour. Taste. Add the cream and tarragon and continue to reduce until the correct consistency. Season. Serve with the chicken and potatoes.

CHICKEN GRATIN: Pick over the remains of the chicken, chop up roughly and heat through in leftover sauce. Put in a gratin dish and cover with breadcrumbs. Brown under the grill.

Nettles

It appears that the Scots had some knowledge of culinary and medicinal herbs. Highlanders used the fresh young shoots of nettles in springtime soups. Three platefuls was the prescribed dose as an iron and vitamin tonic after a winter of vitamin-deprived salt fish and meat.

The young nettle shoots were made into a thick green broth, often with a chicken stock. Today, medical herbalists use an infusion of nettles for curing anaemia.

A Northern herb garden

Margaret Mackenzie taught cookery in schools, before moving to live in the old Brin school house at Flichity, seven miles off the A9 west of Daviot on the B851 to Fort Augustus. The schoolhouse had a large garden which was a jungle 14 years ago but she cleared it and started growing and selling vegetables and herbs. Some of her customers said that they were picking out the raw bits from her pre-packed stir-fry packs to put into salads which is when she had the original idea (in 1986) of ready-to-serve salad bags.

In the tearoom adjoining the herb garden there are bowls of herb salads. No cutlery is provided and no dressing. Neither are needed. Picking out each tiny leaf and flower there is a feast of flavours: licoricy sweet cicely, aniseedy dill, pungent sweet marjoram, spicy nasturtium. There are also refreshingly succulent leaves from the first shoots of garden peas which taste, surprisingly, of peas (a new experiment); fleshy miner's lettuce with its tiny white flowers and round cup-shaped leaves and small scraps of bitter red oak leaf. These are background lettuces which act as a foil to the pungent herbs. For colour highlights there are tiny petals of bright yellow violets streaked with purple and primroses provide a springtime note.

Because it's early in the season, there are smaller snippets of a wider variety of plants. But later on, once the plants are larger, she will make up the salads with a smaller selection: between 9 and 12 different plants, using around three to four each of herbs, flowers and lettuces. But whatever the size of the salad, she says, the intensely flavoured herbs, should always be used in small quantities.

Casual main course salads with herb bowl

Protein and starchy ingredients are the most dominant elements, which provide a unifying effect while the herbs, flowers, oils and vinegars provide the seasoning. Serve with an undressed herbal salad.

As a general rule:
Meat and fish should not be mixed.
Everything should be in bite-sized pieces.
Hard cheeses should be grated or chopped; soft cheeses mixed into the dressing.
Use cooked potatoes, rice, bulgar wheat, couscous or pasta. One starchy element is usually enough.

Seasonings:
Edible flowers: chive, thyme, borage, nasturtium flowers, marigolds, primroses, violets, roses, pinks, scented-leaved geraniums and herb flowers. Do not use any from gardens which have been sprayed with insecticide.
Oil: experiment with difference flavours.
Vinegar: experiment with different flavours, or use lemon juice.
Herbs: experiment with different combinations.
Juices from roast meats can be used in the dressing to give flavour.

Hard-boiled eggs balance bitterness, especially the yolk, and should be considered as part of the seasoning.

Garlic: crush the clove, add it to the dressing without chopping, and leave it to soak when it will release its pungency. Remove before serving. Alternatively, rub the bowl with a crushed clove.

Mustard, salt and pepper: according to taste.

To make the salad:

Put some oil in the serving dish and beat in vinegar/lemon juice, gradually, tasting as you go, till it is beginning to sharpen a little. The proportions are entirely a matter of taste and can vary from three to five or six of oil to one of vinegar/lemon juice. Add meat juices, salt, pepper, mustard and any herbs and flowers which are to be used in the dressing as seasoning. Add chopped hard-boiled eggs and any other seasoning. Taste and adjust.

Mix in all the protein/starch ingredients along with sweet peppers, courgettes, mushrooms, cucumber or tomatoes.

Pile delicate herbs, lettuces and flowers in a separate bowl and serve separately without a dressing with the main-course salad.

ICED SUMMER SOUP

INGREDIENTS

For 4 servings:

4 cloves garlic, crushed with a little salt

125g (4oz) ground almonds

50g (2oz) white bread

125g (4fl oz) extra virgin olive oil

1-2 tablespoons lemon juice

1-2 tablespoons dry sherry

water to dilute

4-8 nasturtium flowers for garnish

METHOD

Put the garlic, salt, ground almonds and bread into a food processor and blend until fine crumbs.

Add the oil gradually, then the lemon juice and sherry. Dilute with water to a thin creamy consistency. Taste and season. Add more lemon juice or sherry to taste.

Serve chilled with ice cubes, garnished with nasturtium flowers.

FISHING CRABS AND LOBSTERS

Streamlined lobster or dumpy crab

Before commercial creel-fishing in the mid-18th century, crabs and lobsters from cool, unpolluted Scottish waters were caught under seaweed-covered rocks, howked from their hiding places with a bent stick. But then English fish merchants cottoned on to the value of live lobsters and the system of catching them in lobster pots fitted with bait was invented. Such was the attraction of intensely flavoured lobsters that they were put into floating chests or 'keep boxes' and collected each week by large fishing boats which sailed off to the London market. Crabs were not rated, but in the 1790s around 60 boats were creel-fishing for lobsters in the Orkneys, and the landings in the early years are reputed to have been huge.

Creel-fishing for edible crabs (partans) has been concentrated more on the East Coast of Scotland and on Orkney. Landings have been greatest from Montrose south to the Berwickshire coast, also around Peterhead, Fraserburgh and Wick while West Coast fishermen have only recently taken crabs more seriously. As recently as the 1960s they were still throwing them back into the sea. But now a niche has been created for this more affordable quality shellfish, with processing plants set up to boil crabs in large tanks where the meat is removed (mostly by hand) before packing and freezing.

Streamlined, elegant lobster may have claimed the gastronomic high ground over dumpy sideways-walking crab, but to my mind crab is in many ways the more attractive shellfish. Besides its cheaper price, it's also more plentiful. Currently, the price of Scottish lobster makes it an extremely expensive luxury (even chefs in top London restaurants complain it's beyond their budget). Dumpy crab, on the other hand, has an equally interesting range of flavours, from strong-flavoured dark meat (liver) to the more delicately flavoured white meat from the claws. Though it has no 'meaty' tail muscle like lobster, it has enough flavour and character to become a meal without a rich accompanying sauce.

As children, we 'fished' for crabs each summer with sticks under the seaweed-covered rocks on the beach in front of my grandmother's house on the Firth of Tay. Learning to grasp the live crab behind its back, to avoid getting nipped, was a daring challenge which we mastered very quickly. Boiling them when we got home, our idea of heaven was to laze about picking the tasty meat from the shells with long-hooked shellfish picks. Crabs need nothing added and nothing taken away. Crabs are easy.

The lobsters, on the other hand, which we bought from a local fisherman one summer during a holiday in a croft house on the Isle of Harris, created more debate and work in the kitchen than had been seen in the entire holiday. What to do with them?

Something rich? Something original? Definitely a sauce … they must have some cream … a little white wine perhaps …

There was a suggestion that Drambuie was the thing for lobsters, S had tasted them flavoured with this in a hotel once. So off he went to the nearby Rodel Hotel for a bottle of the rich liqueur. The cooked lobsters were halved, the edible parts sorted out, and the meaty tail chopped into bite-sized pieces. Some butter was put into the frying pan, then the tail meat, and while it heated gently in the pan a generous slurp of Drambuie was poured over, and the contents of the pan set alight. As the flames died down, the lobster meat was removed and returned to the shells. White wine was added to the pan along with the lobster debris and some cream. Much scraping, tasting and reducing went on before the sauce was finally declared perfection and sieved over the waiting tail meat in the shells. Lobsters are difficult.

Partan

Brown Crab, Common or Edible Crab (*Cancer Pagurus*). The width across the shell may be up to 30cm (12in) though the minimum legal size is 12.5cm (4½in). The colour is reddish, pinky-brown tinted with purple, the legs reddish and the claws black.

They are now commercially caught in deep-water lobster pots (creels) with fresh fish bait and may be sold live, frozen or processed. Average annual production by approximately 1,607 registered creel fishing vessels is 5,202 tonnes. They are caught mainly in the coastal waters on the West and North Coasts and around the islands, as well as on the East Coast.

Season/buying:
From April to September. Though their quality is generally regarded as best throughout the summer months, they have an improved flavour just after they have grown larger and cast their shells, which usually occurs in August. Avoid while spawning in the early spring months.

If buying cooked, a good fishmonger will release the central undercarriage and let you check that its fresh and free from excess water. Otherwise you can only judge by the weight. Live crabs should be lively when picked up, and thrash about. If they don't they have been lying around too long.

Lobster

The body shell (carapace) length may reach 45cm (18in), its weight varying from 375g to 1.25kg (12oz-2½lb). It is illegal to land lobsters with a shell of under 8.5cm (3in). Its colour varies according to habitat, usually dark blue or greenish but after cooking, the red pigment in its shell is 'released' and it turns bright red.

There are around 1,607 registered creel-fishing vessels catching live lobsters in baited pots (creels) in rocky areas and the average annual production is around 463 tonnes. The areas where they are fished are all unpolluted coastal areas around Scotland.

Season / buying:
From April to November. Though their quality is generally regarded as good throughout the summer months, they have an improved flavour just after they have grown and cast their shells usually in August. Avoid while spawning in the early spring months.

Pick up to check liveliness. Avoid those which do not thrash their tails; they have been lying around too long.

COOKING CRAB

Both crabs and lobsters should be eaten as soon after cooking as possible, since their flavour deteriorates by the hour, and freezing destroys much of it. A 750g-1kg (1½-2lb) crab will serve two. Immerse in fresh water for 24 hours to flush out intestinal tract and improve flavour.

Fill a large pan with water, the larger the volume of water the less likely the temperature is to drop below the boil when the crab is put in. Add 2-3 teaspoons salt to every 2 litres (4 pints) water and bring to the boil. Add the crab and hold down for the first few seconds. Turn down the heat and simmer gently 15 minutes for the first 500g (1lb), then another 5 minutes for each pound after that. When cooked take it out of the water, lay it on its back and leave to cool.

Twist off the claws and legs. Using your thumbs together, push hard on the base part of the underside of the body to release this central undercarriage from the top shell. Pull it all out, discard the small mouth with the bitter grey stomach sac behind. Discard the dull beige feathery 'dead man's fingers' which lie along the internal part.

Separate the sweet white fibrous meat from the brown body meat. Pick out the central undercarriage meat with a skewer, or shellfish pick. Use crab (or nut) crackers for the claws. Keep the meat separate or mix them together. Season with salt and pepper.

To prepare the shell: Press along the curved line on the underside of the shell which is near the edge. It will break cleanly, remove the broken shell and give it a good scrub. It can be oiled lightly to give it a gloss. Replace the seasoned crab meat, white separated from brown or mixed and serve with brown bread and butter.

NINETEENTH CENTURY

PARTAN BREE

'Pick all the meat from 2 crabs, except that in the large claws; boil 5½oz of whole rice in milk till soft, but not to a pulp, and pass it with the crab meat through a tammy into a basin; stir with a wooden spoon till perfectly smooth. Add to it in the basin, very gradually, sufficient white unseasoned stock for a party of 12 or 14; season with salt, white pepper, and anchovy; put all into a pan, and stir over the fire till quite hot, but do not let it boil; add pieces of meat from the claws, and just before serving stir ½ pint of cream into the tureen. This must not be as thick as a purée, or it will be too rich.'

Lady Clark of Tillypronie (1841-1897)

LATE TWENTIETH CENTURY

There is an intense crab aroma wafting from Kenny Wilson's partan bree at The Cabin restaurant in Whiteinch, Glasgow. Less cream, more crab flavour plus a fishy stock is his formula.

INGREDIENTS

2 large live crabs

2 litres (4 pints) cold water

Fish stock:

1kg (2lb) monkfish heads

½ onion, chopped

½ leek, chopped

2 sticks celery, chopped

4 peppercorns

1 star anise

bay leaf

parsley stalks

For the bree:

2 tablespoons olive oil

1 large tablespoon tomato puree

1 large carrot, finely chopped

1 medium onion, finely chopped

2 sticks celery, finely chopped

1 white of leek, finely chopped
75g (3oz) long grain rice
125ml (4fl oz) double cream (optional)
salt
freshly ground white pepper

METHOD

To make the stock:
Boil the crabs in the water, see method (p.104). Place all the fish stock ingredients into a pan and strain crab water on top. Simmer for 30 minutes, removing any scum that rises.

To make the bree:
Remove all the meat from the crabs (see p.104), liquidize and reserve. Crush the shells finely in pestle and mortar. Heat the oil in a pan and add the tomato purée and the shells. Sweat for about 5-10 minutes, stirring all the time. Add the strained stock and simmer gently for about an hour to extract all the crab flavour. Strain.

To finish:
Add the vegetables and rice to the strained bree, simmer to cook. Add the crab meat and cream (according to taste). Season.

COOKING LOBSTER

A 750g-1kg (1½lb-2lb) lobster will serve two. Boil as for crab. Cut in half lengthwise. Remove and discard the dark often greeny sac from behind the eyes. Also the dead men's fingers and any thin, dark or greenish intestinal tract from the length of the body. Do not confuse this with the flavourful, olive green mass of liver from the centre of the body. Preserve the coral mass of roe, if it is there. Crack the claws and remove the white meat. Pick over with a skewer or shellfish pick. Serve meat in shells with mayonnaise and brown bread and butter.

EATING OUT

Cranston and Mackintosh tearooms

While Stuart Cranston created the original, it was his sister Kate who made her name as the first lady of the tearoom. With the help of her architect business partner, Charles Rennie Mackintosh, who provided the avant-garde interiors, she created a tearoom legend in Glasgow which developed 'sight of the city' status on a par with the coffee houses of Vienna. Stylish Bohemians, and art lovers from all over the world came to view the Glasgow tearoom interiors, some fashioning their private houses in the Cranston-Mackintosh style right through to their crockery and cutlery. In the visual art world, it was an early 20th-century phenomenon, though neither Cranston nor Mackintosh became fabulously rich, Mackintosh dying in London, prematurely, and without resources in 1928.

The initiator of the tearoom cult, Stuart Cranston, was a well-established tea merchant (Glasgow had been trading in tea directly with China since 1833, later with India and Ceylon) with premises at 44 St Enoch Square. For some time the habit of 'perpendicular' lunchtime eating had been common among city businessmen and Stuart Cranston saw the opportunity of turning his tea merchant's shop into an eating place. He was, in any case, already providing his clients with a sample tasting-cup of tea, so it was only a short step to introduce food, provide seats, and charge customers for their tea.

The idea of the tearoom also appealed to him on moral grounds, since the consequences of poverty and urban deprivation had taken its toll in industrial cities like Glasgow. Alcoholism and ill health were serious problems and the Cranstons were members of an active temperance movement. They regarded their non-alcohol-serving tearooms as a service to the community at a time when there were no alternatives to the pub.

The first Cranston's Tearoom was opened by Stuart Cranston in 1875 at the corner of Queen Street and Argyle Street (it was demolished in 1954). Three years later Kate Cranston opened Miss Cranston's Crown Tearooms in 114 Argyle Street. With a distinctiveness, described as 'Cranston from the chairs to the china', she opened another in the same mode in Buchanan Street, and then in 1903 created the sophisticated Miss Cranston's Willow Tearooms in fashionable Sauchiehall Street.

By the turn of the century, tearooms had caught on. Though many of the old male order found the idea of the tearoom extremely distasteful, there were others who felt differently. The Bohemian élite of the city, whose paintings often decorated the tearoom walls, felt very much at home in them. Progressive women who needed a place to meet outside the home, pubs and cafés being forbidden territory, found them extremely attractive. Then there was the vast army of young city clerks, often with artistic temperaments, who also felt at home. There was tea, a place to smoke, talk, play cards and dominoes and meet extremely well-dressed and attractive waitresses, with whom they could become friendly — even date. For the social class, however, who most needed to escape from the pub-alcohol culture, the sophisticated Cranston's tearooms were an expensive luxury, rarely affordable.

In its first era the tearoom menus showed a versatile style of eating. First and foremost they satisfied the need for a simple cup of tea, but they also provided a more substantial meal. From the 'Snack Teas' menu there was a choice of: ham and egg; sausage and bacon; a boiled country egg; a hot mutton pie; potted meat; kippered herring; or a fried split haddock.

'High Tea' was a fixed price affair. For 1s/3d there was a choice of ham and egg or filleted fish, three breads (varied) and a pot of tea. For 1s/6d you got an extra egg and chips with your fish. Going the whole hog with an 'A la Carte' high tea gave a choice of cold Tay salmon and salad, fried cod steak, Aberdeen haddock, baked fish custard, Wiltshire bacon and poached eggs, fried turkey egg, cold roast beef, lamb and tongue. Bread and butter or toast, scones and cakes, known as 'fancies' were accompanied by a pot of tea.

Though the Cranston tearoom era ended shortly after World War I when Kate Cranston retired, many other tearooms, run by similar female characters, such as Miss Buick and Miss Rombach, carried on in similar style but without the Mackintosh genius. The next era of the tearoom involved a number of well-established family bakeries who began to open tearooms. Craigs, Hubbards and Fullars were among the leading bakers in the city who brought an exceptionally high standard of baking to the tearoom tradition. Craigs imported continental bakers and the 'French cake' was introduced. Fullers were known for their eclairs and marzipan walnuts with toffee topping. Hubbards made 'paving stones' which were square-shaped chewy gingerbreads with a hard icing on top. Craigs, the most successful and popular of the bakery chains, were renowned for their chocolate liqueur cakes.

Because the 'spend' in the old tearooms was not high, their economic success depended on cheap female labour, which after World War II became less available. By the 1950s social habits were changing. Starched tablecloths and good furniture may have satisfied the previous generation, but young people in the post-war years were looking for something more modern. Old bakery firms were taken over by conglomerates and only a few survived.

The Greek Cypriot, Reo Stakis, who arrived in Glasgow selling lace from a motorbike, sensed the mood for change and grasped at the chance to make a new style out of the old. He began with the old Ceylon Tearoom at the top of St Vincent Street, which he turned into the Prince's Restaurant in 1949. And then began the systematic takeover of the old-fashioned Cranston-inspired tearooms, turning them into modern restaurants by providing a congenial atmosphere and affordable food. A typical Stakis menu would begin with a prawn cocktail, followed by steak-and-chips, accompanied by a bottle of cheap and cheerful 'plonk'.

Though Glasgow lost its reputation as tearoom capital of the world, the tearoom concept survives. It lives on in a number of forms in both city-centre tearooms and country stopping places for travellers. Recently a journalist from the New York Times arrived to do a 'good-tea-and-scone' gastronomic tour of Scotland as a tourist feature. Once set in the right direction, she put together a creditable trail of good tearoom venues ranging from five-star hotels to off-the-beaten-track rural retreats.

Visits were made to old-established venues which have made their reputation on reliable Scottish baking and tea freshly made in pots, like Kind Kyttock's Kitchen in Falkland, the Laigh Kitchen and the Gallery of Modern Art in Edinburgh, Fisher and Donaldson's tearoom in Dundee, Bradford's tearoom in Glasgow, The Granary in Comrie, The Abbey Cottage Tearoom in New Abbey, the Old School Tearoom near Castle Douglas. The tearoom lives.

CREAM SCONES

To get the best of both worlds these scones are made with a very fine self-raising cake flour for lightness, plus plain flour with sour cream and bicarbonate of soda for a moist springy texture.

INGREDIENTS

To make 6 large scones:
125g (4oz) 'supreme' self-raising cake flour
125g (4oz) extra-fine plain flour
1 level teaspoon bicarbonate of soda
1 egg
2 tablespoons oil
200ml (7fl oz) sour cream

METHOD

Preheat the oven to gas mark 9/240C/475F. Grease and flour an 18 x 28cm (7 x 11in) baking sheet.

Sift the flours, bicarbonate of soda into a bowl. Make a well in the centre. Add the egg, oil and sour cream.

Mix with a fork to a soft, light dough. Dust on top liberally with flour. Divide into six while still in the bowl. Flour hands. Lift out each scone, handling gently, then put onto tray shaping into a round. Dust with flour. Bake for 15 minutes, till risen and browned. Cool in a cloth and serve warm with raspberry or strawberry jam (see p.95).

ITALIAN ICE-CREAM

A roaring trade

Brought to Britain as cheap labour in the late 19th century, recruited by agents working for a 'padrone' (master), the original ice-cream makers were grossly exploited, lodged in poor conditions, and very badly paid. They worked during the winter as hurdy-gurdy men, but in summer cranked and froze the ice-cream mix they had made the previous night, before setting off with their barrows around the city streets.

They laid the foundations for what was to become a flourishing industry, particularly in Scotland, which in the space of about 70 years (1850-1920), transformed them from itinerant ice-cream salesmen to rudimentary shop owners in slum areas, and finally to owners of luxurious ice-cream parlours in Sauchiehall Street with mirrors on walls, wooden partitions and leather-covered seats.

Chinese and 'Indo-Pak' restaurants may have had a major influence on the national palate, but it was the Italians who arrived first with their new foods and new eating styles. Ice-cream parlours, fish-and-chip shops, restaurants and sophisticated Italian delis have all made their mark, but none more so than the Tally's ice-cream.

According to police statistics, in 1903 there were 89 Italian cafés selling ice-cream in Glasgow, a year later, 184, and by 1905 there were 336. As the numbers increased, problems developed. At the turn of the century, Glasgow was a thriving industrial centre of the British Empire full of appalling slums and serious social problems, including drunkenness. But it was also a fun city with cinemas, dance halls and music halls for the prospering classes seeking new entertainments. The 'tallys', in the early days, however, did not fit naturally into the middle class eating out scene. Though the owners had ambitions to appeal to this more prosperous class, the tallys were largely frequented by the lower social classes and widely regarded by the middle classes as filthy dens run by Catholic foreigners.

Writers like A J Cronin did a great deal to change the tallys' image in the city with books like *Hatter's Castle* (1931) where the young middle class heroine Mary is taken into the forbidden territory:

'He took her arm firmly and led her a few doors down the street, then, before she realised it and could think even to resist, he had drawn her inside the cream-coloured doors of Bertorelli's cafe. She paled with apprehension, feeling that she had finally passed the limits of respectability, that the depth of her dissipation had now been reached, and looking reproachfully into Denis' smiling face, in a shocked tone she gasped:

"Oh, Denis, how could you?"

Yet as she looked round the clean, empty shop, with its rows of marble-topped tables, its small scintillating mirrors and brightly papered walls, while she allowed herself to be guided to one of the plush stalls that appeared exactly like her pew in church, she felt curiously surprised, as if she had expected to find a sordid den suited appropriately to the debauched revels that must, if tradition were to be believed, inevitably be connected with a place like this.'

Scandalmongering, conservative, Presbyterian xenophobes in Glasgow (including many jealous shopkeepers) did their best to wreck the reputation of the Glasgow tallys who were doing such a roaring trade in ice-cream. In an article in the *Glasgow Herald* (2 October, 1907 — Ice-cream 'Hells') there is a report of a United Free Church conference on ice-cream shops in which one of the church's representatives describes the ice-cream cafés as, 'perfect iniquities of hell itself and ten times worse than any of the evils of the public-house'. According to them, this sensuous ice-cream made by Catholic foreigners was sapping the morals of Scotland's youth.

In fact the hard-working Italians who made it have been entirely responsible for at least three generations of Scots who can tell a real ice-cream from a fake with their eyes shut. For my generation, brought up without a fridge, pocket-money was religiously saved for the addictive, refreshing, light, cold, clean-tasting, milky-flavoured tally's cones dripping with raspberry juice — the tally's blood. For a family treat, the largest jug would be taken to the tallys for a fill-up of ice-cream. We were certainly addicts, hooked on its sensuous charms. The rest of Europe might have considered Italian *gelati* an expensive luxury, but for us it was as common as mince and tatties. By the time we had a fridge, there was an Italian café within walking distance of practically every street in Glasgow, ice-cream vans touring the outlying estates, as they still do today.

Besides its inner city attractions there was also the opportunity of a seaside ice-cream *doon the water* on the Clyde Coast where every seaside town also had its tallys. One of the most sophisticated ice-cream parlours was at Largs on the Firth of Clyde. Among other attractions at Nardinis was the art deco style, the low wicker chairs for lounging, and the delectable sundaes.

Today, not much has changed — the same chairs, the same decor, the same buzz — just a new generation of teenagers and a more challenging choice of sundaes. The waitress is sent away three times before our party of old-generation nostalgics and new-generation enthusiasts, can come to the difficult decision: Which Nardini 'special' to have today?

Out of a choice of 17 sundaes, orders are eventually placed for a *Garden Festival* (vanilla ice with chocolate sauce, whipped cream and roasted nuts soaked with Frangelico hazelnut liqueur), an *Amaretto Special* (vanilla ice with amaretto macaroons, fresh whipped cream and amaretto liqueur), and a *Mista Coppa* which contains five different-flavoured luxury dairy cream ices. One of the new generation chooses from the selection of real fruit luxury ices (in season) from a total range of 20. More difficult decisions.

Then we sit back waiting and watching as trays of tall glasses, with their glitter sticks jauntily stuck into swirls of whipped cream, float past us on their way to other tables.

MAKING ITALIAN ICE-CREAM

There are two distinguishing features of Italian ices which sets them apart. The fact that full-cream milk, and not cream is used, and the low percentage of air which is beaten in during freezing. It's the milk, rather than cream, which gives them their distinctive 'icy' tag, compared with the creamier French or American-style ice. Italian ices, because they have less cream, take longer to freeze which produces their clear, clean light taste. Compared with the not-so-natural tasting, fluffy-textured 'soft scoop whippy' there can be no doubt about their refreshing quality.

'There are three ways to make cheap ice-cream,' says Stephano Boni, of Mr Boni's Ice-cream parlours in Edinburgh. 'Firstly by using cheap ingredients, such as artificial flavourings and whey powder instead of milk, secondly by making it in a large-scale industrial plant which reduces labour costs, and thirdly, by beating huge amounts of air into it.'

Though small-scale traditional ice-cream makers would like a change in the law, at the moment there is no legislation to limit the amount of air which is beaten into ice- cream.

'People don't understand why a quality ice-cream can be so much more expensive,' says Stephano, 'but if you think of blowing up a balloon, that's what happens to ice-cream when you start pumping air into it.'

To make ice-cream commercially, the ingredients are first pasteurized, then homogenized under pressure — the degree of pressure depends on the percentage of solids in the mix. The mixture is cooled quickly by passing through chilled coils, it is then put into an 'aging' vat, where the mixture is left to mature. Then it goes into the freezer, which may be a batch-type taking about 25 litres at a time, or a continuous freezer. In the batch-type, which is the most common method for small scale traditional producers, around 30-40 per cent of air is beaten into the ice-cream. In a continuous freezer any amount can be pumped in under pressure.

Traditional Italian ice-cream makers are reluctant to declare the exact percentage of air added, but maintain it is much less than 100 per cent but not lower than 30 per cent. Stephano claims their level is around 30 per cent.

ICE-CREAM SUNDAE

Pile in a very tall sundae glass:
vanilla ice (3 scoops)

To taste:
chopped roasted hazelnuts
whipped cream
fresh raspberries
Frangelico (hazelnut liqueur)

Decorate with glitter sticks or decorative cocktail sticks. For special occasions use lighted sparklers.

J U L Y.

FAllow ground as foon as the crop comes off. Prune and purge all Standard-trees. Ply, Nail, Prune, and drefs your Wal-trees. Pull up fuckers and weeds. Haw and Water where need-ful. Inoculat Fruit-trees, Shrubs, rare Greens, Flower-trees; Increafe the fame by laying. Clip your Hedges after Rain. Suffer fuch Herbes and Flowers to run to feed as you would fave: Cut-ting the reft a handful from the ground.

Sow Turneep, Radifh, Lettice, Onjon, Cole-flower, Cab-bage, and Coleworts in the full Moon. Near the end fow Beets, Spinage. &c. You may plant Strawberries, Violets, Camomile. Lay July flowers. Plant their feedlings. Slip and fet Hypaticas, Bears-ears, Couflips, Helibors, &c. Take up Bulbo and Tube-rous ones that are dry in their ftalks (if you mind to change their places) and keep till *September*, but fome would be fet imme-diatly.

Supply voids with potted Annualls. Lay Grafs and Gravell. Make Cherrie and Rasberrie Wine, &c.

Prevent the Bees latter fwarmes, Kill Drons, Wafps, &c.

Garden Difhes and drinks in feafon.

Beets and many Pot-herbes and Sweet-herbes.
Beet-card, Purflain, Lettice, Endive, &c.
Cabbage, Cole-flower, Scorzonera, Beetrave, Carrot, Ra-difh, Turneep, Peas, Beens, and Kidnees, Artichocks, Straw-berries, Rafps, Currans, Goosbeeries, Cherries, Plumes, fummer Pears and Aples, Cyder, Metheglin and other Wines.

John Reid, *The Scots Gard'ner*, (1683)

AUGUST

Hunting Game
Cheesemaking

Roast Grouse, Skirlie Toasts, Venison Haunch,
Farmhouse Cheeses, Factory Cheddar,
The Cheesemakers

HUNTING GAME IN 1892

It's more than a hundred years since the ritual shooting of the first grouse, on 12 August, signalled the start of the hunting season. Given the royal seal of approval by Queen Victoria, when she moved her court to Deeside, the hunters also moved north. Lured, not by the sunny climate, but by the sense of solitude and freedom among dramatic Scottish mountains, it was a huge contrast from crowded city to spectacularly beautiful wild open spaces.

To escape the midsummer city heat, the politician had packed his rods, guns and cartridge cases and was waiting with his two setters when the cab came to take him from his home in Bloomsbury to King's Cross Station for the overnight 'Scotch Mail'. By late evening on 11 August 1892, he had settled into his sleeping compartment on the train — the hectic business of the House of Commons already fading.

About half an hour from his destination, the steward wakened him and he opened the window to sniff the morning air. Dawn sunlight was slanting across purple, heather-clad hillsides while puffs of curling mist lay in the hollows. When he got off the train, there was a short journey in the dog-cart with a fast-trotting pony to the shooting lodge, a quick breakfast and a change of clothes. By 11am he was off to the moors. Sixteen hours from Bloomsbury and he had shot his first grouse. It had been a glorious day.

It was in 1892 that the British Government passed Game Laws with special conditions for Scottish game, prohibiting hunting during the breeding seasons and attempting to restrict those who were exploiting Scotland's natural wild game. It was a vital move, ensuring the survival of Scotland as a destination for hunters. In the decades following it has continued to attract those who shoot for sport, providing a natural food resource which is largely unknown to most native Scots. Though game dealers have tried to make it more generally available, the Scots with the best knowledge of game continue to be those who live or work on shooting estates.

In the 18th century — before shooting parties and royalty invaded the Highlands — native game had been an essential part of the diet, hunted and shared out among the clanspeople. It was more common on Highland tables than beef, mutton, veal or lamb as the English author of *Letters from the North of Scotland* (1754) Edward Burt discovered, while living for several years in Inverness: 'Our principal diet, consists of such things as you in London esteem to be the greatest rarities — salmon and trout just taken out of the river; partridge, grouse, hare, duck and mallard, woodcock, snipes etc each in its proper season.'

Despite the loss of game as a common food, there are still those who continue to enjoy native game. When I arrived in a remote area of Wester Ross, to cook in the local hotel which had a large shooting and fishing estate attached, I had never tasted game birds, or even venison, let alone cooked with them. But for M, it would have been trial and error with a recipe book.

Behind her kitchen door, scenting the kitchen, was a pheasant which had been hanging by its head for the best part of a fortnight. We plucked, cleaned, trussed and made it ready for the oven, wrapping it up like a parcel in thin streaky bacon. Into the roasting-hot oven it went, turned from breast to back a couple of times, to prevent the juices running out and drying up the breast meat. We had a few slices hot, but most of the roasted bird was left to go cold. Sliced thinly, and eaten the next day, the powerful flavours had mellowed. Hot-from-the-oven, the flavours were intense. Like strong-flavoured terrines or pâtés, the flavour of well-hung game is best when it has cooled and the complex flavours mingled. So the tradition of eating it cold rather than hot was the Highland preference. We ate it with sharp tangy jellies, and floury Golden Wonders. That was my first lesson.

Two of M's sons were gamekeepers, and she had lived with her husband on a large shooting estate on Lewis as well as on the north side of Loch Maree, before moving to another shooting estate at Kinlochewe. Now widowed, and living in a stable cottage in the yard behind the hotel where I cooked, her years of coping in remote areas had made her an unusually resourceful cook. Though her kitchen was tiny, the tastes and smells which passed through it were big, bold and amazingly varied.

In an entirely erratic fashion, since there was no knowing what would be shot or caught the next day, her menu would change from hare broth thickened with blood, to venison tripe stewed with onions and served up on triangles of toast which she called Poca Buidh (yellow bag). This was one of her specialities, in great demand by those who had had the privilege of sampling the creamy unbleached tripes, which she camouflaged so successfully that tripe-haters were oblivious of their real origins.

Of course there was a certain amount of poaching for the pot, but since her eldest son was also the estate gamekeeper, some of the tastes were entirely legitimate. Wild goose and ptarmigan were unforgettable flavours, while the melting quality of a tender venison liver, cut thinly and fried quickly with crisp bacon, made memorable breakfasts. Encouraged by her, I had a go at venison haggis, also broth using a stag's head for flavour.

While others might suggest throwing the tripes and heads to the dogs, M would never tolerate such waste. It was not just her instinctive thrift which made her economize in this way, she also enjoyed the cooking challenge. For those of us who sat at her table, these were rare tastes from animals which roamed freely among the high crags. Had history been different, they might have continued as part of the Highland diet which in other parts of the country were considered 'the greatest rarities'.

Game birds

Grouse:

Red Grouse (*Lagopus Scoticus*) is a medium-sized game bird with a reddish-brown plumage speckled with white and black. It's weight is approximately 500g (1lb). It has a distinctive red comb over the eye which is more prominent in the cock. Both sexes have feathered legs and feet which some people have made into kilt pins. Since their principal food is the flowers, seeds and young green shoots of ling heathers they have a distinctive flavour which is thought to be the reason why grouse meat is darker and stronger flavoured than other game birds. They also eat blaeberries and the seeds of sorrel which, depending on their local availability, add further distinctive flavours to the meat. The flavour of grouse varies from region to region. It also varies according to its 'hanging' time usually from two to seven days, depending on weather conditions, temperature and humidity.

Other members of the grouse family include Black Grouse (Blackcock); Wood or Great Grouse (Capercaillie) and White Grouse (Ptarmigan).

Red grouse are native to Scottish, Northern English and Welsh heather moors. They have also been introduced to Dartmoor and Exmoor. The season is 12 August-10 December. Production is variable from year to year depending on weather conditions in late spring, which can destroy the young chicks if it is very cold and wet. They are wild birds and cannot, like pheasant, be reared by hand. Their survival, however, is managed on the shooting estates by burning small patches of the heather on the moors so that there are areas at different stages of regeneration. Grouse need areas of young shoots, plus mature heather for nesting. Grouse shooting is a highly organized affair with groups of beaters driving the birds towards the guns which are usually concealed in small, dry-stone shelters or 'butts'.

While red grouse inhabit the heather moors, black grouse are to be found in mixed woodland, capercaillie in pine woods and ptarmigan on the very high tops. These birds are much less common than red grouse and very rarely reach the domestic market.

Hanging / cooking / eating:

All game needs to hang. Yet theatrical events continue to be organized with freshly shot grouse, helicoptered-and-parachuted from hill to dining room in the space of a few hours. Attempting to bring the bird from hill to table in the same day, without a period of at least two to three days hanging, is a gimmick which game aficionados regard as totally misguided. It means missing out on the real flavour. Just as trying to serve them off the bone means missing out on the different flavours to be found in different parts of the bird.

While the whole bird may not be acceptable on sophisticated hotel menus, small game birds demand a proper chew on a bone; a finger bowl; and an acceptance that part of the fun is in picking over all the carcass.

Cooking on a spit was the old way with young birds, and is still the best method, since the turning birds baste themselves as they go, cooking quickly without drying out. Failing this, they should be roasted quickly in a hot oven or split up the back bone, spread out flat, brushed with fat or oil and put under a very hot grill for 10 to 15 minutes.

ROAST GROUSE (OR OTHER SMALL GAME BIRDS)

INGREDIENTS

4 plump young grouse
125g (4oz) softened butter
herbs/berries for the cavity: strong flavours like thyme,
tarragon, bay leaf, juniper berries, brambles, blueberries or blaeberries
600ml (1 pint) robust red wine and/or water
salt and freshly ground white pepper

METHOD

Pre-heat the oven to gas mark 8/230C/450F. Mix the butter with the herb/berry flavouring. Divide into four and stuff into the cavities. Keep a little back to rub over the birds. Leave in a cool place for a couple of hours or overnight for the flavours to mingle.

Heat up a large sauté pan or frying pan which will take the four birds and can also be put into the oven. When hot, sear the birds on all sides, turning after two minutes. Place all the birds on their backs and place the pan in the oven. Roast for about ten minutes and leave in a warm place for the meat to relax.

Meanwhile make the gravy, add red wine/water to the pan scraping up the debris and boiling it up, reducing to a concentrated flavour. Taste and season. Strain. If brambles, blaeberries or blueberries are available add a handful to the sauce. Keep warm. Serve on skirlie toast with rowan jelly and floury chappit potatoes.

SKIRLIE TOASTS

INGREDIENTS

4 tablespoons bacon fat, or other fat or oil
1 large onion, finely chopped
125g (4oz) medium oatmeal
salt and pepper
25g (1oz) butter
4 slices of crusty bread, toasted and buttered

METHOD

Heat the fat and cook the onion until soft and lightly browned. Add the oatmeal and cook for another five minutes stirring occasionally. Season.

Alternatively cook everything in the microwave for 3-4 minutes, stirring half way through.

Mix the skirlie with the butter so that it can be spread more easily. Spread on buttered toast.

Venison

Red deer venison comes from either a mature stag weighing approximately 105kg, or a hind weighing 70kg (cleaned weight). The meat is close-grained, dark crimson red with a firm white fat. The flavour depends on the age and condition of the animal, as well as the hanging time. Deer are culled in the wild and gralloched (innards removed) immediately. They are then transported on hill ponies to a collection point where they are trucked in refrigerated vehicles to a production unit; skinned; inspected by a vet; hung for approximately two to three days and then butchered into prime cuts and other products such as sausages and mince. There are approximately 40,000 wild red deer culled each year, also a few herds of farmed red deer.

Wild red deer can be found on all remote areas of high land throughout the country from the Cheviots northwards. The season for hinds is 21 October-15 February and for stags it is 1 July-20 October.

Roe deer inhabit forests and are around a quarter the size of red deer. The season for bucks is 1 May-20 October and for does it is 21 October-end of February. The best time for eating is the same as red deer.

Availability / hanging:

Now that Eastern European venison is more available, both the price and the demand for

Scottish venison by Germany has dropped. Since the end of World War II, West Germany has imported the largest amount but there is now an opportunity for more to be sold in Scotland. It can be found on a few supermarket shelves, but fishmongers or butchers with a game licence are still the most reliable sources. Continental demand has encouraged a Continental system of 'filleting out' individual muscles so that a sinew-free piece of meat is produced which does not require a long slow wet cooking method to tenderize.

Most of the meat sold commercially has been lightly hung and has none of the pungency of estate hung game with a 'high' flavour. In the current craze for youth and tenderness, the flavour of well-hung game may be in danger of being lost. Hanging not only develops a unique flavour, it also allows enzymes to develop which tenderize the meat.

Robust game flavours have, in the past, been matched up with equally strong partners. Spices such as mace, allspice, cayenne and nutmeg were favourites in old cookery recipes for venison. They also combined robust game flavours with claret and port, redcurrant, rowan and sloe-flavoured jellies. In continental venison cookery, gin and juniper are widely used; also sharp, tangy fruits. In summer ripe soft fruits are used, in winter stewed prunes and apricots.

Venison cuts:

The HAUNCH is a prime cut and can either be roasted or cut into slices (collops) and pan-fried (the classic method finishes the pan juices by making a sauce with red wine and a sharp jelly such as rowan or sloe).

The SADDLE includes the loin cut and fillet, it may be roasted whole, on the bone, or the tender meat may be removed and cooked quickly by frying or roasting.

The FLANK may be used for soup or stew or made into sausages.

The SHOULDER may be boned out and used for stewing or in soup or stuffed and braised.

Tender LIVER should be fried: test by holding between finger and thumb and pressing, if it gives easily it will be tender but if it feels hard it should be used for a venison haggis along with the heart, flank and kidney.

The TRIPE in good condition, like the liver, is considered a great delicacy. The whole stomach bag must be cleaned immediately the animal is shot, steeped in salted water for a day, and boiled for six to eight hours till tender, then cut into one-inch squares and cooked for another hour in a white sauce flavoured with onions. Serve with a plate of hot toast.

The HEAD, use for broth.

VENISON HAUNCH

The whole haunch used to be wrapped in a pastry crust but foil is the modern substitute.

The package should be left for a night's rest to allow the flavours to mingle and develop before cooking.

INGREDIENTS

Servings:boneless, allow 125-175g (4-6oz)
meat per person, with bone 250g (8oz):

2-3kg (4lb-6lb) haunch of venison with or without bone

50g (2oz) fresh ginger, sliced

2-4 slices of lemon

2-3 cloves garlic, crushed

4 tablespoons extra virgin olive oil

4 bay leaves

2 sheets extra strong foil

1 teaspoon Maldon sea salt

rowan jelly

roast potatoes

METHOD

Pre-heat the oven gas mark 5/190C/375F. Place the sheets of foil in the roasting tin, on top of one another, crosswise. Place venison on top. Rub all over with oil. Put the flavourings on top, dribble over more oil and sprinkle with flakes of Maldon salt. Wrap up, leaving space above the meat. Keep in a cool place overnight.

Cook the next day allowing 20 minutes per 500g (1lb) plus 20 minutes.

Before serving open up the package and strain off cooking juices. Re-wrap the meat. Pour the cooking juices into a pan, bring to the boil, adust flavouring and pour into a sauceboat.

Serve by opening up the package at the table. Serve with rowan jelly and roast potatoes.

CHEESEMAKING

Farmhouse cheesemaking

Susannah Stone was the trail-blazing cheesemaker in the Highlands who made history by reviving the crofter's *crowdie*. Her first batch, she now admits, was made with ten gallons of surplus cow's milk, hung up to drip in a pillow slip over the family bath. That was in 1962, a practical solution to a farming problem at a time when she had no ambition to make cheesemaking her career. The Milk Marketing Board (MMB) bought everyone's milk and held the cheesemaking monopoly. An enterprising farmer's wife making her own cheese with her own farm milk was virtually unheard-of.

This unusual situation had developed mostly as a result of Government policy during World War II, when it was thought that the most expedient way of conserving food resources was to truck the farmer's milk to large creameries and produce a hard, longer-keeping cheddar. It was all made from pasteurized milk because it was regarded as unsafe to use raw milk coming from different farms. Susannah, and others like her who resurrected other forgotten cheeses, have been responsible for the greater variety of textures, flavours and aromas in cheeses which we now enjoy.

Another trail-blazer was Patrick Rance, author of *The Great British Cheese Book* (1983). An English cheesemonger from Berkshire, Rance visited Scotland on several occasions during the 1970s and 80s, encouraging cheesemakers to persevere despite the difficulties. He was particularly concerned that cheeses should continue to be made in farmhouses with the farm's supply of raw, unpasteurized milk since it is this milk which has the potential to produce the most characterful cheese. Its flavour at the end of the ripening period is richer and more subtle from the bacteria and enzymes which are otherwise destroyed by pasteurizing. Other European cheesemaking countries, though equally stressed during wartime, had allowed raw-milk farmhouse cheesemaking to continue. The French, in particular, had a headstart, and throughout the 1960s and 70s they had the market more or less to themselves in a cheese-bankrupt Britain.

The tradition of cheesemaking in Scotland has its roots in early times, its history is described by John Smith in *Cheesemaking in Scotland* (1995) where he suggests that the earliest cheesemaking skills possibly came with the arrival of Christianity, initially in the South-West, and with the arrival of Celtic tribes from Ireland. A settled community was necessary for cheesemaking to flourish and there is evidence that cheese was made in certain parts throughout the middle ages. There is a record of cheese being given to Robert the Bruce's troops at Bannockburn in 1314.

By the late 19th century cheesemaking had become a growing industry, largely developed in the dairying areas of Ayrshire and the South-West with the growth of large urban markets in Central Scotland. Unlike the soft Highland crofter's crowdie, the traditional cheese in the south of Scotland was a hard cow's milk cheese, known as Dunlop and thought to have been developed in the 17th century by an enterprising and enthusiastic cheesemaker, Barbara Gilmour of the Hill Farm, Dunlop. Its quality was significantly improved after the Ayrshire Agricultural Association brought a Somerset farmer and his wife to teach the Cheddar method to the Ayrshire cheesemakers in 1885. But just over a century later the old Dunlop cheese is almost extinct.

Cheese made by the 'cheddaring' method in Scotland has now taken the English name and accounts for around 80 per cent of cheese made in Scotland. What with the demise of the farmhouse cheesemaker, and the reluctance of the MMB to continue making the old cheese (uncomfortable with the Dunlop tag since it was also attached to the leading make of rubber tyres, not the best marketing image for a cheese, they thought) Dunlop cheese was largely abandoned.

Dunlop is distinguished from cheddar by its creamier, milder flavour and very low acidity. At its prime it should be entirely free of acidity. A well-matured Dunlop, correctly stored, will have a pleasantly sharp aftertaste. It has a thin rind, and when cut across should present a perfectly close unbroken surface. Though it's still made on some island creameries with pasteurized milk, the only farmhouse cheesemaker making traditional Dunlop with unpasteurized milk is Ann Dorward of West Clerkland Farm in Ayrshire (within sight of Barbara Gilmour's Hill Farm).

Encouraged by the growing momentum for clothbound unpasteurized farmhouse cheeses, Ann Dorward has just started (1996) making her Dunlop cheese with unpasteurized milk and clothbinding it, rather than plastic-wrapping. Some are in small clothbound 2-2.5kg (4-5lb) sizes but she has also made larger 15kg (30 lb) sizes, which are more like the size of the original Dunlop's.

The history of Scottish cheeses in the Highlands, post-war, has been equally fraught. Milk, cheese and butter were originally important sources of income, exchanged with Lowlanders for grain, which Highlanders found more difficult to grow in large enough quantities because of the lack of arable land. In the period prior to the Highland Clearances, the native soft cheese, of Viking and Pictish ancestry, had been made by every Highland crofter from surplus milk. Its demise occurred when much of the Highlands was taken over by sheep-farming and shooting estates, ending the crofter's system of sending cattle, sheep and goats to the mountain grazings in summer where the women and children had traditionally made the cheese and butter.

Though the word crowdie is applied sometimes to any food of a porridge or brose nature, it is also used for the soft cheese made from curds which formed when milk curdled.

'The great treat,' said G W Lockhart, in *The Scot and his Oats* (1983) 'was to have crowdie [cheese] mixed with fresh cream and piled on an oatcake with fresh salted butter. Then you had a royal feast of flavours — acid, sweet and salt, and better perhaps, a royal mixture of textures, soft, crisp and crunchy.'

Made on the croft, as part of the daily management of excess milk, the bowl of surplus milk was put at the side of the fire in winter, and at a sunny window in summer and left until it had soured naturally. It was then cooked very lightly, until it 'scrambled' or formed a curd with the whey separating. Finally it was poured into a muslin-lined bowl, the ends of the muslin drawn together and tied with string and hung up, usually outside from the branch of a tree until the whey drained out.

For a more mature flavour, the bag would be left to drip and dry out for several days. Surplus crowdie was mixed with butter (cruddy-butter) and packed into earthenware crocks and covered with melted butter. Kept in a cool barn, it lasted throughout the winter as chunks were cut out and used as a spread on oatcakes and bannocks.

While revivalist cheesemakers often began cheesemaking in an attempt to recreate some of these early memories of old cheeses (some had grandparents who taught them the recipes), those guarding the public health came from an entirely different background. Sanitary inspectors, as they were originally known, had no knowledge or experience of the cheese industry's long history, or any concept of the way cheese had been made for centuries without poisoning people.

Susannah Stone's first encounter with a zealous sanitary inspector occurred when production moved out of the family bath and into a custom-built creamery.

'This cheese won't do,' he told her, after testing a sample in his lab. 'It contains live bacteria. You'll have to sterilise it.'

There followed a long dispute which was resolved when the local councillor for Easter Ross, Marjorie Linklater (Eric Linklater's wife), arranged a meeting of the two parties, during which she read from part of a chapter from a book on cheesemaking which left the sanitary inspector in no doubt that live bugs in cheese were normal, not always harmful.

No sooner had this battle been won, than the North of Scotland MMB decided to make it themselves, using a faster method with rennet which they sold at a cheaper price. Undaunted, Susannah decided to diversify, making a richer version of the crowdie, known as cream-crowdie. The MMB copied that too. Sitting in the dentist's waiting room one day, she came across a magazine which quoted an old Highland ballad telling of the 'cream of the May', flavoured with wild garlic as the cure to all ills. Wild garlic leaves, chopped into the cheese? That's it, she thought. There is no way the MMB will take to the woods and pick wild garlic. So 'Galic' was invented.

The idea of establishing her own distinctive cheeses moved a step further when she made the rich cream cheese which her mother had learned originally from her grandmother on Skye, and had handed on to her. She made up the ancient recipe, rolled the cheese into neat cylinders, and coated them in crunchy toasted oatmeal. Her mother had called it a 'kebbuck' from the generic Scots word for any whole cheese. She would call it a 'Caboc'.

While Susannah, and her late husband Reggie, led the way in a hostile environment, others have followed. The public health disputes, however, have not abated. If anything they have become worse over the years with Brussels bureaucrats adding their restrictions.

The food scares of the late 1980s have not helped either, the 1990 Food Act providing a power-base for public-health protectors.

There have been some ludicrous rules, such as banning of wooden surfaces, making all creameries convert to stainless steel. On the Orkney island of Shapinsay, Jean Wallace and her Orkney farmhouse cheeses became a victim of this regulation, as she gave up cheesemaking in her little shed adjoining Girnigoe farmhouse. Her five milking cows, Nessie, Florrie, Kitty, Agnes and Selina, had been eating the island pastures uncontaminated by modern pesticides for years and Jean had been making remarkable cheese from their milk every day. The cheeses sat on wooden shelves, maturing and intensifying in flavour wafted by the sea breezes which Patrick Rance claimed gave her cheeses their special charm. But no more.

Jean Wallace went quietly out of business, unable to afford the change from wood to stainless steel, closing down without fuss in 1992. Those of us who had been visitors to Girnigoe, and were regular buyers of her cheese, wrote indignantly about the outrageous destruction of an ancient craft. Farmhouse cheesemaker, Humphrey Errington, might also have gone quietly in November 1994 when Clydesdale Environmental Health Inspectors closed him down and sent out a health warning to doctors that a major outbreak of listeria poisoning — with possible deaths — was imminent among people who had eaten his unpasteurized ewes milk Lanark Blue.

Humphrey and his wife spent several sleepless nights, were deprived of their income for three months, and not allowed to make or sell their cheese, during which time they felt very isolated.

'It was an awful struggle to keep going,' he admits, 'and we would certainly not have made it without an aunt's generous gift from her Emergency Fund.'

Then, after the nightmares of the first three months, the momentum of support gathered, and people rallied to the cause. 'Save Lanark Blue' took off, and more than a year later (December 1995) the court ruled that the cheese was safe, and that errors had been made in the EHO's testing procedure. Lanark Blue lives. But it might just as easily have died.

The case for the defence rested largely on the evidence of a microbiologist from Roquefort in France who is the first scientist to attempt to study all the microflora in blue cheese. What he discovered was an equilibrium of microbes in raw-milk cheese — equivalent to acid and alkali balance — which is disturbed when a pathogen (harmful bacteria) enters. He proved that a combination of blue mould, plus acetic acid from using raw-milk, along with free fatty acids in the cheese, all combine to inhibit pathogens in unpasteurized blue cheese. So instead of being a high-risk cheese, it's the opposite. The test case of Lanark Blue has provided a large amount of literature on the issue which has now been circulated, not just in the UK, but also throughout France.

Factory cheddar production

While several revivalist cheesemakers have become well-established in the last couple of decades, their continuing success will always be dependent on the individual cheesemaker. The output of small independent cheesemakers accounts for only about 10 per cent of the cheese made in Scotland. The other 80 per cent is made into cheddar in large-scale industrial creameries on Orkney, Arran and Islay and at Rothesay, Campbeltown, Stranraer and Lockerbie from pasteurized cow's milk. It's made into a natural pale yellow, or artificially coloured orange-yellow cheese produced in varying sizes of rounds, plastic-wrapped, wax-dipped and clothbound, as well as in rindless blocks.

Though it's still Scotland's most popular cheese it's no longer simply a choice of 'red' or 'white' as cheddar has moved out of its mousetrap image and into the speciality cheese cabinet. Now, as never before, it's necessary to study the form. If possible with the help of tasting-samples offered from helpful cheesemongers.

Unfortunately this is not the custom at the supermarket deli counter where some have recently devised a new 'cheese strength' labelling scheme. Make your choice, between 1 to 7, and you will lower the risk of buying a cheese you do not like. Or will you? Not all cheese experts agree with this idea of labelling for strength.

'It can be a strong flavour,' says Robin Gilmore, Director of McLelland's Cheese Market in Glasgow, 'but what we look for in a mature cheddar is not strength of flavour, but a "clean" maturity. Strength is only one aspect, and it can be misleading.'

'Cleanness' — in cheesespeak — is the level of acidity balanced against other flavours. In a well-matured cheddar, acidity should not be too dominant. But at the same time there should be enough to provide a refreshing tingle in the mouth. A badly matured cheese will have a dull, muddy flavour or a sharpness at the first taste, but with no follow-through.

Gilmore manages the maturing of Scottish cheddars in a large temperature- and humidity-controlled cheese store which markets brand-named cheddars with a consistent flavour. He begins by grading cheddar by age: mild (6 months old), medium (8 months) and mature (over 12 months).

Like whisky-blenders who judge the development of flavour throughout the period of its maturing, the cheese-taster's palate must be tuned to changing and developing flavours. He will sell off, as mild or medium, those which he judges will not mature into more interesting cheeses, storing the more characterful cheeses in the hope that they will develop good depth and body.

According to maturity: 12-14 month-old will have a sharp 'bite' to it, while a 4-5 month-old will have a more mellow, rounded flavour. Maturity classification: mild (less than 4 months); medium mature (5-8 months); mature (9-12 months); extra mature or vintage (over 12 months, up to 2 years).

The cheesemakers

As new cheeses are developed, the production of others may cease, so that any attempt to give a run-down of all Scottish cheeses may not always be entirely accurate.

At the time of writing, the following list includes most established cheesemakers, some of them with a longer history than others. They all make unique cheeses.

Ballindalloch, Highland Goats Products, Banffshire. Cheesemaker: Jane Heap.

Hard goats' cheese, natural crust (unpasteurized), vegetarian.

Bonchester and Teviotdale, Easter Weems Farm, Bonchester Bridge, Roxburgh. Cheesemakers: John and Christian Curtis.

Production began in 1980, originally out of a need to use up winter milk from a couple of Jersey cows. There is now a herd of 18, and the full-cream milk (unpasteurized) is made into a soft, lightly pressed, mould-ripened cheese with natural white crust and firm half-ripe Brie texture. Bonchester is made in 100 or 280g rounds. They are creamy yellow with a deep, richly creamy flavour. Teviotdale is a harder pressed, mould-ripened cheese with a natural white mould crust made with four Bonchesters, weighing 1.25kg. Colour is yellow-creamy, the flavour has a deeper more mature tang.

Brodick Blue, Arran Blue, The Island Cheese Company, The Home Farm, Brodick, Arran. Cheesemaker: Ian McClery.

Arran Blue (pasteurized) cows' milk. Brodick Blue (unpasteurized) ewes' milk. Crottin, small goats' milk cheese.

Cairnsmore, Millaines Farm, Sorbie, Newton Stewart, Dumfries and Galloway. Cheesemaker: Alan Brown.

Rich ewes' milk cheese, (unpasteurized) vegetarian.

Crowdie and Caboc Highland Fine Cheese, Tain, Easter Ross. Cheesemakers: Susannah, Jamie and Rhuraidh Stone.

Crowdie is a pasteurized soft, cows' milk cheese which does not use rennet, but a lactic acid 'starter', specially formulated to give a sharp, acidic, refreshing tang to the cheese. Because their cheese has a very low potassium and sodium content, it is used widely in hospitals as part of the diet of kidney patients on dialysis. *Gruth Dhu* (black Crowdie) is crowdie mixed with double cream and rolled in toasted oatmeal and black pepper. *Hramsa* is crowdie mixed with wild garlic and white and red pepper. *Galic* is Hramsa rolled in crumbled flaked hazelnuts and almonds. *Caboc* is a cows' milk (pasteurized) soft, double cream cheese made into a round cylindrical shape, rolled in toasted pinhead oatmeal. It has a rich creamy, buttery flavour with a mild to medium tang depending on age.

Crowdie, Achmore Farm, Plockton, Wester Ross. Cheesemaker: Kathy Biss.

Dunlop, **Bonnet**, **Swinzie**, Dunlop Dairy Products, Ayrshire. Cheesemaker: Ann Dorward.

Dunlop (see p.122), Bonnet, from milk from her herd of goats, and Swinzie from her own ewes' milk.

Galloway Soft California Farm, Wigtownshire. Cheesemakers: Gordon and Dorothy Walling.

Goats' cheese, young, fresh and soft cheeses packed in wooden boxes, plain or with herbs.

Howgate — Brie, Camembert, Pentland, Bishop Kennedy, St Andrews, Strathkinness, Highland Cream Cheese. Cheesemaker: Graham Webster.

Brie and Camembert (pasteurized); Pentland (unpasteurized) brie; Bishop Kennedy (pasteurized) full-fat, soft cheese, rind washed in whisky; Strathkinness (pasteurized) Gruyère-type mature hard cheese; Highland Cream (pasteurized) soft cream cheese rolled in oatmeal; St Andrews, washed rind cheese, cows' milk, (unpasteurized) vegetarian.

Isle of Mull Cheddar, Sgriob-ruadh Farm Dairy, Tobermory, Mull. Cheesemakers: Christine and Jeff Read.

Clothbound, (unpasteurized) cheddar truckles, strong, full-flavoured.

Kelsae and Stichill, Garden Cottage Farm, Stichill, Kelso. Cheesemaker: Brenda Leddy.

Stichill and Kelsae (the old name for Kelso), as well as Stichill Soft are made from a herd of around 30 Jersey cows. Both the recipes were handed on from farmhouse cheesemakers in the Highlands (their origin and history is unknown) but they have been altered and developed to suit the Jersey milk, while retaining the basic characteristics of the original recipes.

Kelsae (unpasteurized) is a hard-pressed cows' milk cheese similar to a Wensleydale but with more flavour. Stichill (unpasteurized) is also a hard-pressed cows' milk cheese more like a crumbly Cheshire, but richer and less tangy. They both have a very rich, creamy flavour.

Lairobell, East Lairo farm, Shapinsay, Orkney. Cheesemaker: Jock Bell.

Semi-soft goats' milk cheese, natural rind (unpasteurized).

Lanark and Dunsyre Blue, Ogscastle, Carnwath, Lanarkshire. Cheesemaker: Humphrey Errington.

Lanark Blue (unpasteurized) is the most successful revival of a blue-veined ewes' milk cheese in Scotland. A sharp creamy cheese with a strong tang and a long aftertaste, it's made from milk from a Friesian-cross dairy flock in an area which was the original stronghold of ewes' milk cheese.

Dunsyre Blue (unpasteurized) is a round blue-veined cows' milk cheese with a creamy, sharp flavour and long aftertaste. It's made from milk from a single herd of Ayrshire cows.

Lochaber-smoked, Macdonalds Smoked Produce, Glenuig, Lochailort, Inverness-shire. Smoker: Simon Macdonald.

A crowdie cream cheese, lightly cold-smoked.

Loch Arthur and Crannog, Loch Arthur Creamery, Camphill Village Trust, Beeswing, Dumfries. Cheesemaker: Barry Graham.

Crannog plain or with herbs (unpasteurized) lightly pressed soft cheese made in small rounds: Loch Arthur (unpasteurized/vegetarian/organic) clothbound cheddar, creamy, full-bodied flavour.

Orkney Farmhouse. A seasonal summer cheese made from cows' milk (unpasteurized) which is available from the farms, or in butchers or fish shops in Kirkwall and Stromness.

Hilda Seater, Grimister, Finstown, distributes her farmhouse Orkney to Neals Yard, Covent Garden, London.

The cheesemongers

A traditional cheesemonger, like Patrick Rance who visited cheesemakers, bought cheese which was not fully matured and had the facilities for ripening the cheese himself, judging when it was ready to sell. McLelland's Cheese Market in Glasgow is the largest and most sophisticated wholesale cheesemonger in Scotland, buying mostly cheddar from large creameries. Iain Mellis, cheesemonger in Glasgow and Edinburgh, is Scotland's Patrick Rance, visiting the cheesemakers, buying direct, maturing and ripening farmhouse cheeses and selling them when he judges they are at their best.

Most farmhouse cheesemakers are delighted to sell from the farm-gate, recognizing that consumer confidence can be greatly improved if a personal contact is made.

SOFT YOGURT CHEESE

A home-made soft cheese can be made with thick live, Greek-style yogurt which has already been strained. It can be flavoured with herbs and garlic or left plain and served with soft fruits in season.

INGREDIENTS

1kg (2lb) Greek yogurt
herb seasonings
1 clove crushed garlic or soft fruits in season

METHOD

Put the yogurt into a square of muslin or a clean J-cloth. Bring the edges together and tie with string. Hang the bag up to drip for a few hours, until the cheese is firm (around 3-4 hours).

Alternatively, remove from the bag while it is still very soft. Put the cheese into a bowl and season with salt. Spoon into moulds (small plastic plant pots will do) which have been perforated (this can be done with a hot skewer) and leave to drip until the cheese has firmed. Turn out and serve.

If you leave the cheese in the cloth until it is firm, remove and season before flavouring with herbs and garlic.

To serve with fresh fruits:
Pile a mound of soft cheese in the centre of a white plate. Surround with ripe berries, in season or mango, peach or pineapple. Garnish with fresh mint leaves.

AUGUST.

Fallow bordures, Beds, Nurferies, and the bulks of Trees. Yet Inoculat. Ply and purge Trees. Pull up fuckers and weeds. Clip Hedges. Gather the Black-cherrie and Morella Stones. Gather Mezerion berries. Gather the feeds of moft Herbes and Flowers. Cut your Phyfick-herbes. In the beginning fow Cabbage (thô I confefs its too late. See the laft moneth) Beets and Beet-card, Spinage, Black-radifh, Chervil, Letice, Corn-fallade, Endive, Scorzonera, Carvy, Marygold, Angelica, Scurvy-grafs, &c. Take up ripe Onions, Garleeks and Shallot, Unbind buds Inoculated. Cut and ftring Strawberries. Lay July-flowers. Sow Columbines, Holyhoks, Larks-heells, Candytuffs, Popies, and fuch as can endure Winter.

Take up your bulbs and plant as in the laft. Sift the ground for Tulips and Gladiolus. Plunge in potted Annualls in Vacants. Keep down weeds by hawing, &c. Lay Grafs and Gravel, Beat, Roll, and mow well. Make Goosberrie and Curran Wines, &c.

Towards the end take Bees, take the lighteft firft; thofe who are near heaths may differ a little. Deftroy Wafps, ftraiten the paffage by putting on the hecks to fecure from Robers.

Garden Dishes and drinks in feafon.

Many Pot-herbes and Sallades, Cabbage, Coleflower, Beet-card, Turneep, Radifh, Carrot, Beet-rave, Scorzonera, Peas, Beans, and Kidnees, Artichocks, Cucumbers, Aples, Pears, Plumes, Apricocks, Geens, Goosberries, Currans, Rafps, Strawberries, &c.

Cyder, Metheglin, Cherrie Wine, Curran Wine, Goosberrie Wine, Rafpberrie Wine, &c.

John Reid, *The Scots Gard'ner,* (1683)

Harvesting
Breeding Beef
Lamb or Mutton?

Fresh from the boats

Every morning, a fleet of small fishing boats steams out of the harbour to hunt the rocky coastline for seafood, returning in the early evening to sell its catch on makeshift stalls at the edge of the pier. The people of the town cluster round, haggling for fish which they will cook that night, while the rest of the catch sizzle on pavement charcoal grills outside bars and restaurants on the waterfront. Neither over-fishing, nor world wars, nor careless pollution, nor factory processing, nor refrigerated transport have changed the centuries-old habits of these fish-loving Europeans.

They are a rare breed now. Few coastal villages like this one in the north-west corner of Spain continue to preserve such an intimate relationship with the sea, and certainly none in Scotland. But to stand on such a pier, surrounded by the freshest fish, the infectious enthusiasm of the local people and the smoky aromas of grilling fish in the background, is an unforgettable experience. It's also a reminder of how it used to be. How coastal communities around the long Scottish coastline must have waited for their supplies of fresh fish straight from the boats.

Scotland's strong tradition of coastal fishing and foraging for seafood, has been largely influenced by its extensive coastline (one of the largest in Europe), its unpolluted waters, and proximity to good fishing grounds in the North Sea and beyond. The 18th and 19th centuries were prosperous times for the fishing industry. There may not have been a tradition of sizzling fish on pavement charcoal grills, but armies of fishwives sold fish and shellfish from market stalls in the towns, as well as door-to-door around the country. In Edinburgh, they made their daily trudge from the fishing boats in Leith and Newhaven up Leith Walk to the Mercat Cross in Edinburgh, to sell fresh fish — straight from the boats.

Supplies are landed now mainly at Aberdeen, Peterhead and Fraserburgh, but there are also landings at smaller ports such as Ayr, Buckie, Eyemouth, Lossiemouth, MacDuff, Lerwick, Pittenweem, Arbroath, Garliestown, Isle of Whithorn, Wick, Oban, Tarbet, Mallaig, Ullapool, Lochinver, Stornoway, Kinlochbervie and Campbeltown.

Though processing plants, and lorry-loads of refrigerated fish for export both account for a large amount of the catch, there are those who still believe in preserving the intimate link with fish, straight from the boats. Some fish merchants have been inspired by visits to other countries, where the link has been better preserved. Some now cooperate with local chefs and sell according to day-to-day quality and availability. This means, of course, that the chef must be able to operate a more flexible menu, his dishes reflecting, not what he wants to cook, but what the fish-merchant has chosen for him as the best of today's catch.

Others see the value of preserving the intimate link with the sea by selling fish and shellfish from seafood bars and fish shops at or near the fishing ports or near the lochs where shellfish is grown and harvested. On the West Coast, the trailblazers of this philosophy have been oyster farmers, John Noble and Andrew Lane who began in 1978, inspired by a rich oyster-eating history in 18th- and 19th-century Scotland. They started by selling their farmed oysters from a makeshift stall at the side of the road and now have three Oyster Bars and a wet fish shop, besides running a seafood fair on Loch Fyne, now into its seventh year.

In the South-West there is the Galloway Smokehouse at Carsluith near Newton Stewart where Alan Watson's wet fish display reflects daily landings at Garliestown and Isle of Whithorn. At Troon, in Ayrshire, there is the MacCallum brothers enterprise selling wet fish to Glasgow and Edinburgh restaurants as well as in two shops in Glasgow plus a seafood bar on the pier at Troon. On the West Coast there is Alba Smokehouse where one of the most welcome sights for seafood lovers touring the West Coast last year was Mike Leng's seafood trailer, parked during the day on the pier at Inveraray selling ready-to-eat seafood snacks, such as hot smoked salmon baguettes, dressed half lobsters and crabs, and langoustine salads. Unfortunately planning permission has been refused this year for Inveraray pier, but the trailer will continue in the less picturesque position of the Lochgilphead Co-op car park with another trailer this year in Oban Co-op's car park.

FARMED AND WILD SHELLFISH

As well as wild-caught crabs, lobsters, squat lobsters, langoustines, whelks and razor fish, there are now reliable, and plentiful, supplies of farmed oysters, mussels and scallops (king, queen and princess) from around 300 registered shellfish farms scattered up and down the coastline. Most are members of the Association of Scottish Shellfish Growers.

Common mussel (*Mytilus edulis*), **Horse mussel** (*Modiolus modiolus*) known as Clabbies or Clabbie Dubhs from the Gaelic *Clab-Dubh* meaning large black mouth. (Common mussel — usually from 5-8cm/2-3in in length; horse mussel — usually from 15-20cm/6-8in in length; blue black shells, bright orange flesh.)

The first recorded evidence of cultivated mussels in Scotland was in the 1890s. Several experiments took place on the East Coast of Scotland growing mussels on ropes, but the idea was abandoned following a series of disasters. In 1966 experiments were resumed, cultivating again on ropes. Commercial ventures were started in the early 1970s using ropes attached to both longlines and rafts. Both methods continue to be used, with each farmer developing a system which suits his particular site. Once harvested they are washed and graded.

Horse mussels are harvested from natural beds lying at extreme low water mark.

Mussels are farmed mainly on the West Coast from Dumfries and Galloway to Shetland, though there are some mussel farms in Lothian. There are 109 shellfish farming sites producing for sale approximately 882 tonnes a year.

Season/buying:

Mussels in Scottish waters will spawn around the end of February, their quality less good for the next three months until they fatten up again in June. In the run-up to spawning, they are at their plumpest.

Clean-shelled, rope-grown, farmed mussels are the best for mussel broths where the shells are part of the dish. These are young mussels, two to three years old, which will have less flavour than wild mussels which are more blue-black in colour and with a deeper orange, richer-flavoured muscle — better for frying with bacon.

Pacific oyster (*Crassostrea gigas*), **European native oyster** (*Ostrea edulis*). Native oysters are fan-shaped, almost circular, one half of the shell is flat, the other cupped. The shell of the Pacific oyster is more deeply cupped, rougher and more elongated than the native. Most of the West Coast oysters are Pacific and are graded by size 70-80g; 80-95g; 95g and upwards. They are a wide variety of colours and textures according to their origin while the sea-tasting flavour is determined by the feeding, and varies from loch to loch. In terms of the quality of flavour, most Scottish oysters are Grade A, meaning they have not been purified by passing through purification tanks or been held in aerated 'holding' tanks before sale.

They were eaten with great relish throughout Scotland during their heyday in the 18th and 19th centuries. So cheap and plentiful was the supply, that contemporary recipes for soups and stews often demanded a mere 60 oysters. These were the large European native oysters which are mentioned by Martin Martin in his *Description of the Western Islands of Scotland* (1703) as growing on rocks and 'so big that they are cut in four pieces before they are ate [sic]'.

The native oyster beds, which were the original source of supply, fell victim to pollution and over-fishing and by the mid-20th century were almost totally wiped out. Their revival, in the last 20 or so years, has depended entirely on farming commercially cultivated oysters. Almost all of this production has been gigas oysters, though some farms are now experimenting with natives in sheltered sea lochs on the West Coast, and also on some of the islands and in Orkney.

The gigas oyster has largely been used for this farming venture since the cold water inhibits breeding, which means they do not retain their eggs and can therefore be sold all year round without tasting unpleasant.

Lochs chosen for oyster farming must have both shelter, total lack of pollution, and a rich supply of natural nutrients in the waters. The most common method is to put the young seed (brought from hatcheries at about 12-15mm/½-⅝in) into mesh bags which are put on metal or wooden trestles at low-water mark, or put into plastic trays which are stacked on the sea bed or suspended from a headline. The first method gives the farmer access to sort and grade during the spring tides and the second, weather permitting, allows the oysters to be worked at any time. Allowing the oysters to be uncovered is considered important since it allows them to close tightly and survive in air, essential when they are eventually transported for sale. They are usually harvested after two to three summers' feeding.

Production: Pacific gigas oysters — 3.4 million; Native — 182,000. Shellfish farming sites producing shellfish for sale — 109. They are mainly farmed on the West Coast from Dumfries and Galloway to Shetland.

Season/buying:
For gigas, all year. For natives the 'R' rule (months with an 'R' in them) when they taste less pleasant because of breeding does not apply in Scotland where spring arrives later. Some would suggest a close season from 1 June to 1 October would be more appropriate.

Norway lobster (*Nephropos norvegicus*); other names: Langoustine — French; Scampo — Italian; Dublin Bay 'prawn'. Maximum length, not counting the claws, 24cm (9½in); minimum legal carapace size 25mm (1in); carapace is pink, rose or orange-red, often quite pale; its claws are banded pink and white.

There is evidence that Norway lobsters were sold in Billingsgate in the 19th century (W B Lord, *Crab, Shrimp and Lobster Lore*, 1867) but it was not until the 1950s that they became an important commercial catch in Scotland, taking a 'gourmet' tag and demanding high prices. The Irish appear to have been the first to appreciate their potential, when fishing boats started landing them in Dublin Bay, though whether they were in fact caught in the bay is debatable. They were certainly sold in the streets, and because of their size and similarity, were initially described as 'prawns'. In fishing lore it is a misnomer which has stuck, and West Coast Scottish fishermen, who put down creels in Highland lochs to catch Norway lobsters continue to be known as 'prawn' fishermen, their product still referred to as 'prawns'.

Norway lobsters continue to attract a gourmet following and are exported around the world. In the last five to ten years, however, they have been appearing more frequently on native Scottish menus as chefs follow the trend towards making more use of local and national foods. Several Highland restaurants now have arrangements with creel fishermen to purchase the entire catch directly from their boats and some have speciality seafood restaurants selling only freshly caught shellfish of this kind.

They are fished in clear waters with a hard mud seabed, where they are able to dig burrows, on both the East and West Coast, particularly in the Firth of Forth, the Moray Firth, the Minch and the Clyde. There are 1,607 creel fishing vessels and 387 fishing by nephrop trawl. Approximate annual catch is 19, 407 tonnes.

Season / buying:

They are most plentiful and in best condition from April to November. Creel-caught are considered superior since the shellfish remain alive after catching. Those trawled suffer damage and many die giving a flabbier, often crumbly, cotton-wool texture and less flavourful meat. They may be sold live (if creel-caught), frozen or processed.

King, Queen and Princess scallops: Great or King scallop (*Pecten maximus*); flat bottom shell and a concave upper shell — muscle diameter approximately, 5cm (2in); minimum legal carapace size 1cm (⅜in); Queen scallop, (*Chlamys opercularia*); top and bottom shells both concave — muscle diameter approximately. 3cm (1¼in); Princess scallop (an immature Queenie) — muscle diameter approximately 1cm (⅜in). Queen and Princess scallops may be smoked. The Great scallop and the Queen scallop have creamy shells, a creamy-white muscle surrounded by an orange roe. The Princess scallop has a reddish-pink shell, a creamy-white muscle but the roe, because of its age, has often not developed.

An important dredged and dived scallop industry developed in the 1950s and 60s, harvested from natural West Coast scallop beds. The development of the farmed scallop began in 1974 and its popularity has grown with the age of the scallop controlled to around five years, guaranteeing a tender muscle and regular size. (Scallops from natural scallop beds can live for up to 20 years, when the texture of their muscle becomes quite tough.)

Solway boats have around 155 square miles of Queen scallop fishing grounds stretching out into the Irish Sea. For a fisherman's favourite breakfast-at-sea, the small scallops are fried with bacon and served on toast with scrambled eggs.

In the wild, scallops spend most of their life on the seabed and spawn many millions of eggs each year. These go through a free swimming stage, during which time they are carried around on currents and tidal streams. After three or four weeks they settle on a suitable substrate such as seaweed.

Scallop farming produces a more uniform supply than wild scallops. The young 'spat' are carried by currents into 'spat collectors' where they attach themselves to the sides of the nets. As their shells begin to grow they fall off the nets and are gathered and put into free-floating 'lantern' nets suspended in the sea water where they feed and grow (Queen scallops for 1½-2 years; King scallops for 4-5 years). Princess scallops are harvested when they are about a year old.

Aquaculture is still a developing industry and methods are constantly undergoing change. Ranching or bottom culture is seen by some farmers as the way forward. This has always been a risky business because it is not possible to protect stocks from dredgers or divers. Recently, however, the first Several Fishery Order has been recommended by the Secretary of State for Scotland to be granted to scallops giving their stocks legal protection.

There are 109 shellfish farming sites producing shellfish for sale on the coastal waters on the West Coast from Dumfries and Galloway to the Shetlands which produce an annual 1,147,000 Queen scallops.

Season/buying:

In good quality all year except in November when they spawn. Farmed available all year. Scallops may be bought either live, in the shell, or shelled. Shelled scallops, to prevent them drying out, may have been soaked in water. 'Soaked' scallops are likely to have considerably less flavour than 'unsoaked' or live in the shell; they should also be cheaper since they will have absorbed added water. Soaked scallops are not suitable for frying or grilling though they can be used poached and in sauces.

SEAFOOD BROTH

EIGHTEENTH CENTURY

Mussel brose was a common dish, mentioned in a poem by Robert Fergusson (1750-74), and according to a traditional recipe (F M McNeill, 1929) it was made with cooked mussels and their liquor, plus fish stock and milk. The mussels and the liquid were then poured on top of a handful of oatmeal in a bowl, in the traditional method of making brose, and the mixture returned to the pan for a few minutes to cook through.

TWENTIETH CENTURY

WEST COAST SHELLFISH AND BREE

This was served at a Scottish dinner at the 1991 Oxford Symposium on Food and Cookery. The shellfish came from the Argyllshire coast and were transported live, overnight to Oxford in a refrigerated lorry. John MacMillan at the Sea Fish Authority research station at Ardtoe (Arnamurchan) dived for the razor fish. Hugh MacPherson, an Ardtoe fisherman, supplied the wild langoustines, squat lobster and farmed princess scallops. Norrie Etherson supplied the Loch Etive mussels and John MacMillan collected and packed all the shellfish before its journey south.

The shellfish was served unshelled, so there was a picking session, first with finger bowls and napkins. Then some guests lifted their soup plates to slurp the good flavoured bree and others copied.

INGREDIENTS

Quantities according to taste and availability:

mussels

Princess scallops

razor fish

squat lobster

Norway lobster (langoustines)

Accompaniments: lemon, brown bread and butter

METHOD

Cook the shellfish in half an inch of boiling water until the shells open for the molluscs (mussels, scallops, razor clams); the squat lobster for 1-2 minutes and the Norway lobster for 2-3 minutes depending on size.

Pile the shellfish into a large wide bowl while still hot. Adjust the flavour of the bree, adding more water if it is too salty. Pour over the shellfish to about half way up the shells. Serve hot with lemon, brown bread, finger bowls and napkins.

SEAWEED

A new way

While seaweeds were traditionally used in broths or eaten raw, the salty, iodine flavours are very good deep fried, says Julian Clokie, of the Sea Vegetable Company in Easter Ross.

Julian is a marine biologist who started seaweed gathering after working for the oil industry in the Moray Firth. He set up the Sea Vegetable Company in the early 1980s, using some of the outhouses of his little cottage in Fearn as giant drying ovens where he dries out and packages the seaweed.

To visit Julian is to get involved in tasting his latest seaweed invention. Some dulse which he is toasting on the hot-plate of his Aga to eat like crisps. A pressure-cooked concoction which he reckons is a brilliant version of a Japanese seaweed pickle. What do I think? I actually prefer this idea he has of coating dried sloke in tempura batter and deep-frying.

CLOKIE'S SLOKE

INGREDIENTS

15g (½oz) dried sloke
2-3 tablespoons flour for drying
oil for deep frying — preferably groundnut or soya plus
a few teaspoons of sesame oil
tempura batter (see p.181)

METHOD

Put the sloke into water and leave for half and hour or so to rehydrate.

Heat oil to 190C/375F. Remove sloke from the water, shake off excess water then dry off thoroughly in flour. Dip in batter twirling it round to coat thoroughly, lift out and allow excess batter to drip off.

Fry quickly in oil for about a minute, turning once, until a light gold. Do not overfill the pan. Remove, drain on kitchen paper and serve immediately. Skim off any debris from the oil and continue frying.

The Japanese serve it with a soy sauce and fresh ginger-flavoured dip.

OATS AND BARLEY

Grains of character

Historically they are humble everyday staples, yet nothing represents Scotland more than the food and drink traditions which have developed around oats and barley. While porridge, haggis and oatcakes use oats as their distinctive ingredient, it's barley which makes the whisky. Until the end of the 17th century both oats and barley were commonly used for cooking but it was around this time that barley's power as a malted grain for distilling began to develop.

It was the Highlander's enthusiasm for home-distilling, a useful method of preserving surplus barley, which gave cold northerners their attractive warming drink. The 'water of life' (Gaelic — *uisge beatha*, Scots — *usquebae, iskie bae*) was a staple drink, taken regularly with meals by both adults and children before tea became the everyday stimulant. In every Highland glen, sacks of barley would be soaked in the burn for a few days to soften the grain and begin germination. Then the grain would be spread out to allow it to sprout, which would be halted by drying over a peat fire. The now 'malted' grain would go into a large tub with boiling water and yeast to ferment. Once fermented, it would be passed twice through the pot still and the middle cut (the drinkable part) would be separated from the foreshots, and the aftercuts or feints.

It was a skilled operation, which produced a quality of product distinctly flavoured by local water and peat smoke. Because of this added character, it was more highly esteemed than whisky malted and distilled in the Lowlands. The Highlanders' distilling activities grew and developed, but in 1707 the tax on spirits was increased and they began, with great ingenuity, to smuggle their malted whisky illicitly. In 1742 taxes on spirits were lowered and legal whisky production increased. The passing of the Excise Act in 1823 signalled the beginning of a new era for the Highlander's malt whisky when old smugglers became 'legit', linking their considerable whisky-making skills to the business of large-scale whisky production.

By this time the whisky industry had become so sophisticated that pure crops were grown of carefully selected barley, geared entirely for whisky-distilling. It was only in the remote areas of the Hebrides, Orkney, Caithness, and in some parts of the North-East, that some barley continued to be used in the old way as a flour for making into porridge and for baking bannocks and scones. As a whole grain it has also survived in the national barley broth, where its gentle thickening powers and mellow flavour continues to add character.

The main preservers, however, of old barley as a staple grain for baking into bannocks are the Orcadians, who continue to grow the flavourful northern variety, now an endangered plant, known as 'bigg' (*Hordeum vulgare*), or 'bere' (pronounced 'bare' in the north). It's a variety of barley which has four ear rows, rather than the usual six, yielding a lower amount per acre but producing a grain of remarkable flavour. Between 12 and 15 tons are grown in Orkney each year, and every Orkney baker makes a daily supply of the bere bannock — a 15cm (6in) round, 1-2.5cm (½-1in) thick, flat, girdle-baked, soft scone.

The original beremeal bannock, before raising agents were developed in the late 19th century, was a very thin soft chapati-type pancake, like a modern potato scone. Though the old bannock is now extinct, it is still remembered by a generation whose mothers never knew chemical raising agents. At the Clatt village hall in Aberdeenshire, where farmers' wives supply traditional baking for an unusual tearoom operation, Jim Lumsden, an 80-year-old retired farmer and manager of the tearoom remembers:

'My mother made beremeal scones. My wife made them too. They used to boil up the meal in a pot first with water to make a stiff paste which they rolled out like oatcakes, very, very thin. It was cut into four and put on the girdle and baked on both sides. We spread them with butter and syrup and rolled them up very tight from one corner. Then we ate them like a stick of rock.'

Now the modern, leavened bannock appears on Orkney tea tables in the evening: a staple with home-made farmhouse cheese. Tasting the grey-brown, characterful old bannock in a farmhouse kitchen on the island of Shapinsay with tea and a slice of fortnight-old farmhouse cheese, it's difficult to understand why the rest of the country abandoned old barley. Less mellow than oats, more gentle than rye, it has its own robust earthy tang. The culinary treasure, which the Orcadians have preserved, is to add only a spread of their rich butter and a slice of creamy cheese.

OATS

Old millers and new mills

The MacDonalds of Montgarrie Mill in Alford, Aberdeenshire, have been grinding oatmeal for three generations. Unlike other water-powered mills, which have been renovated with the help of development grants, there are no tourist signs attracting attention to teas and guided tours. The three of us, who have come to visit the mill, have made our own arrangements with the present miller, Donald MacDonald, who is always happy to show round those interested in the mill's workings. We are: two redundant millwrights on a nostalgic visit to see the old belts and bearings still in operation, and myself, just curious to discover why the flavour of this oatmeal should be so much better than others.

As we look down from the platform into the huge silos of newly-harvested oats waiting to be milled, a heady scent of ripened grain fills the air. The grain is being dried or 'conditioned', where the moisture content is reduced to around 15 per cent. We climb down to the basement, to see the smokeless fuel furnace and the long, 30ft chimney which takes the heat up to the top storey of the mill. Then it's a long climb up steep stairs to where the oats are spread out for drying on a large floor of perforated metal sheets. They are turned by hand with large shovels until the moisture content is reduced to around four to five per cent, when the meal will take on its mild nutty flavour.

Donald gets hold of one of the shovels and starts turning the meal as we talk. The slow, gentle warmth, he explains, creates more aroma in the grain as it lies slowly toasting on the floor. He is a purist who follows the old, and some would say inconvenient, and time-consuming methods. But they have a purpose.

'Think of the difference,' he says, 'between a slice of toast, toasted slowly in front of an open fire, and toast from a modern toaster. What we do here is toast slowly, to develop the flavour. Factories which mill oats, using a blow-drying method, just drive out the moisture.

'What you get by slow-toasting is an entirely different flavour in the grain, when the moisture content is reduced in this way.'

The milling begins with shelling the husks, then the grains are ground between stone millwheels to the required 'cuts' or grades: pinhead (whole grain split into two) — used for haggis; rough — used for porridge, brose and sometimes oatcakes; medium/rough (sometimes known as coarse/medium) — used by butchers for mealie puddings; medium — used for porridge, brose, skirlie and baking; fine and super-fine — used in baking and for feeding to babies.

As we stand beside the milling stones, the noise is deafening. Donald gestures to us to pick up some of the meal, just as it comes out from between the millstones, and we savour the fresh nutty sweetness of newly milled grain. Donald explains later that despite the friction, the stone millwheels do not heat up, protecting the natural flavour of the oats.

All in all, we have been wandering around the toasting and milling grain for a couple of hours and are almost as dusty as the miller himself when we come out into the bright autumn sunshine, shaking the fine mealy dust from our hair and clothes. Beremeal is milled today, not on Orkney, but on the mainland at the Golspie Mill, by Fergus Morrison, a self-taught miller who discovered the mysteries of the belts and bearings at the water-powered Boardhouse Mill in Birsay, Orkney, in the 1970s. He milled there throughout the 80s, another milling enthusiast who, like Donald, is always willing to show interested visitors round the mill. He also mills peasemeal, the dustiest of all grains to mill. In the early 1990s he moved the milling operation to another old mill which he has renovated at Golspie where he continues to mill Orkney bere and peasemeal.

It was the roller-mill revolution (1872) which was responsible for making these old mills redundant. The first roller-milling plant in Glasgow introduced the factory mill and a more efficient milling process, but at the same time changing the character and the quality of the grain. From this time onwards, many of the old watermills became derelict and it is only in the last 30 years or so that there has been a valiant, and valuable, last ditch attempt to save some of them. Montgarrie and Golspie are just two of a handful in Scotland which belong to a movement which has gathered more momentum in England, where a strong literary and artistic image of milling has stimulated more public interest in preserving the lifestyle of the traditional miller and his unique product.

The English painter, Constable, claimed in 1822, when writing to a friend, that old mills were the main source of his inspiration:'The sound of water escaping from mill-dams, etc, old rotten planks, slimy posts and brickwork ... those scenes made me a painter.' Then George Eliot wrote *The Mill on the Floss* (1860), which evoked other emotions associated with the country miller.

The derelict mills in Scotland which have been brought back to life in the last decade or so by campaigning millers and preservationists are to be found at Aberfeldy and Blair Atholl in Perthshire and Drummuir in Morayshire and the Lower City Mill in Perth, while there are also some factory mills which stone-grind oatmeal in the traditional way.

Rolled oats or oatflakes: developed in America by the Quaker Oat company in 1877 are made by steaming and rolling pinhead oatmeal. Jumbo oatflakes are made by steaming and rolling the whole groat. Oatbran is the extracted bran.

BARLEY BANNOCKS

Recipes vary in the proportion of beremeal to wheat flour. Most printed Orkney recipes suggest about half and half, but some Orcadians make their bannocks with very little wheat flour preferring the stronger flavour of the beremeal. The flour is mixed with baking soda and buttermilk to make a springy, moist bannock.

BERE BANNOCKS WITH CHEESE

INGREDIENTS

Makes 1 large or 8 small bannocks:
175g (6oz) beremeal
50g (2oz) plain flour
pinch of salt
1 teaspoon bicarbonate of soda
1 teaspoon cream of tarter
buttermilk to mix (approximately 1 cup (250ml/8fl oz) or use
fresh milk soured with lemon juice

METHOD

Preparing the girdle:
Heat slowly till the surface is pleasantly hot when you hold your hand about 2.5cm (1in) from the surface. Grease lightly with some oil.

Mixing and baking:

Sift the dry ingredients into a bowl and make a well in the centre. Add the buttermilk and mix with a knife to a soft elastic dough. Divide into two and roll out on a floured board to make a round which will fit the girdle, from 1-2.5cm (½-1in) thick.

Sprinkle the girdle with some beremeal and bake on both sides till cooked — about two minutes each side. Cool on a rack and wrap in a cloth to keep soft.

MODERN METHOD

Small bannocks can be made by removing tablespoons of the dough, flouring the hands well with beremeal, and tossing the dough gently till it is well coated and dropping onto the girdle. Press down lightly to flatten surface. The advantage of this method is that it keeps the handling of the dough to a minimum thus preventing toughening. Finish as before.

HEATHER HONEY

Extracting liquid gold

Next to the shed where clucking hens laid eggs was the honey shed. For most of the year an unused storehouse of hives, combs, glass jars and beekeeping clamjamfrie where the powerful aroma of beeswax and honey always lingered. In late summer, as the combs filled with honey from the heather moors of the Angus glens, extracting began. Besides selling tea and coffee in the family shop in Castle Street in Dundee, my uncles, J and G were enthusiastic beekeepers. Their bees were moved to the heather moors of Glen Clova every summer, the honey sold — as my grandfather had done — in the shop first opened in 1868 and now run by my cousin, Allan Braithwaite.

'Your uncles are extracting,' my grandmother would say. And I would go to watch, inhaling the powerful honey aromas, while they de-capped the combs, fitted them into the extractor and waited while it spun round, and the honey ran down the sides of the drum where it was left to settle before being poured out of a tap and into jars.

When I was old enough, I was allowed to de-cap the combs, fill jars, and every now and again got rigged out in a white boiler suit and a bee-hat and veil and went to the hives as Assistant Puffer of the Smoker (a bellows-like box filled with smouldering hessian, which was used to clear away the bees while the beekeeper checked out how things were going on in the combs). It was some time later before I realized that putting honey into jars is a tad more complicated than my childhood experiences in the honey shed.

The natural sweetener

Before sugar, honey was the natural sweetener in the Scottish diet, often mixed with the distinctive flavours of oatmeal and whisky. Honey was collected from wild colonies of bees as Osgood Mackenzie, describes in *A Hundred Years in the Highlands* (1921):

'… the boys were able to collect large quantities of wild honey, which, by applying heat to it, was run into glass bottles and sold at the Stornoway markets. Hunting for wild-bees' nests was one of the great ploys for the boys in the autumn … . Cameron tells me that, as a young boy, before he left his home, there was an island in Loch Bhad a Chreamha … where there was no necessity for hunting for bees' nests, as the whole island seemed under bees, the nests almost touching each other in the moss at the roots of tall heather … My stalker, too, informs me that his home at Kernsary used to be quite famous for its wild bees, but they finally disappeared …'

Bee-keeping, which originated as a hobby, or as a sideline for people running other businesses, continues to attract an enthusiastic following and the flavour of heather honey is highly esteemed for its distinctive character. Atholl Brose and Drambuie depend on it. And it's an integral part of a Cranachan (the harvest home celebration dish of toasted oatmeal, cream, fresh soft fruits, whisky and honey). It's also used as a flavouring in cakes and biscuits and appears on the traditional breakfast table with Dundee marmalade and oatcakes.

It may come from three varieties of heather — ling, bell heather and cross-leaved heath — though it's seldom sold as solely from one type of heather. Pure ling honey can be distinguished from the others by its thick, jelly-like (thixotropic) consistency and strong, sharp flavour. Unlike other honeys it is pressed out of the comb rather than spun out by centrifugal force and may have air bubbles trapped in the gel. Bell is thinner with a more bitter edge while cross-leaved is also thin with a much lighter flavour.

To ensure purity, hives are filled with unused combs and 'flitted' each summer, to the heather as it comes into bloom around the middle of July allowing the bees to collect the maximum amount of nectar in the shortest possible time. A commercial beekeeper, extracting honey, will first shave off the outer caps. The combs will then be subjected to a Honey Loosener (nylon needles with a bulbous end which disturbs the honey). The combs are then put into a Tangential Swinging Basket Reversible which extracts by operating two slow swinging movements and two fast. Sieving and seeding is the next process when the honey is sieved into barrels and 'seeded' (mixed with about a tenth volume of honey of the correct texture from the previous year's honey) before it is poured into jars.

The production varies from year to year depending on the amount of rain and cold during the period the heather is flowering and also on the number of days/nights with perfect nectar-collecting conditions. The beekeeper may be unlucky one year, when the amount produced could average out at as little as 350g a hive which happened in 1985. In a luckier year, 1984, the average per hive was a record 69kg. In a normal year the average per hive is usually around 23-30 kg. A medium to large producer will have around 300-400 hives.

Season/buying:

If the yield is good, heather honey will be available all year. In a bad year, however, it may be sold out by Christmas. For authentic 'Scottish heather honey', check the label on the jar for the name and address (a legal requirement) of the beekeeper. Jars from this source are the most reliably authentic. Some honey comes from firms of honey blenders who may, or may not, be beekeepers. They may blend heather honey with other honeys.

Selected combs which are cut and boxed are more liable to crystallize therefore should be used as soon as possible. Jars which have a chunk of comb in the middle of a clear extracted honey are also less stable and may start to crystallize sooner. Comb honey should be eaten by starting with a hole in the centre, so that the honey from the cut edges runs into a pool in the centre. To judge the flavour of honey requires a sensitive palate. There is a natural flavour and freshness in good honey which is lost if it has been overheated. Honey which has been heated too much to prevent crystallization is a darker colour. Honey which contains honey-dew (a sticky secretion from insects which bees may gather) is also a dark colour and gives honey a strong treacly or molasses flavour.

The best way to judge is by the aroma. A 100 per cent heather honey will have a strong aroma. Pure ling can always be distinguished by its jelly-like set. If the water content is too high, the viscosity will be thin and the flavour poor. To test viscosity tilt the jar with the lid on; if it's a clear honey and runs quickly it will have less flavour, if it's thick it will run more slowly and have a stronger flavour.

Tasting honey is full of surprises. For beekeepers who do not specialize in a pure honey, there is always the chance of a spectacularly good, or a disappointingly bad, flavoured honey. My uncle G, who is a qualified honey judge, rates highly a honey which this year his bees have gathered from a mixture of bell heather and clover nectar; the strong, normally dominant heather flavour is mellowed by the sweeter more fragrant clover. It's a perfectly balanced honey. It would be much more interesting, he says, if an outstanding honey, like this, could be described on the label. Instead, because it's a mixture, it goes under the pedestrian 'blossom' label.

Both jars and combs should be kept at room temperature, or in a warm place in the room, since a gentle warmth will do no harm and slows crystallization.

The great intoxicater — Atholl Brose

To intoxicate: take oatmeal, whisky and heather honey. Mix together and use against your enemies. There will be no battle, no bloodshed, just an unconscious army which has succumbed to the powers of Atholl Brose. It's a technique which has reputedly worked very well for the Atholl family in Perthshire. So well, that their name has now become attached to the mixture, which uses three of Scotland's most distinctive ingredients.

The legend of the family's brose exploits emerges first in the 15th century when an Atholl earl is reputed to have used the great intoxicater to rid the Scottish king of a particularly troublesome Lord of the Isles. Another legend involves a young man who rids the district of a wild savage by employing the intoxicating liquor and claiming as his reward the hand in marriage of a young Atholl heiress.

In the way that charming legends can obscure the facts, it seems unlikely that the Atholl family actually invented the intoxicating brose. A mealy brose was daily fare for the people. Mixing it with the national drink of the Highlands and the natural sweetener, appears in other mixtures based on the three flavours, but combined in different ways. Sometimes cream was added. Coming in frozen from the hill, Highlanders mix themselves something which they call a *cromack* sometimes pronounced *gromack*. A *cromag's-fu* being the quantity of oatmeal which can be lifted when the fingers and thumb are brought together. The meal is put into a mug or bowl and whisky, honey and cream added according to need and taste. There is also a *stapag*, which can take many forms, but is sometimes made with cream, oatmeal, whisky and honey. Intoxicating mixes were as common as peat smoke, yet the Atholl legend lives on.

NINETEENTH CENTURY

This is a recipe published by the Atholl family and drunk by Queen Victoria when she visited Blair Atholl in 1844:

'To make a quart, take four dessertspoonfuls of run honey and four sherry glassfuls of prepared oatmeal; stir these well together and put in a quart bottle; fill up with whisky; shake well before serving.

To prepare the oatmeal, put it into a basin and mix with cold water to the consistency of thick paste. Leave for about half an hour, pass through a fine strainer, pressing with the back of a wooden spoon so as to leave the oatmeal as dry as possible. Discard the meal and use the creamy liquor for the brose.'

The Edinburgh version, without oatmeal from Meg Dods (1826):

'Put a pound of dripped honey into a basin and add sufficient cold water to dissolve it (about a teacupful). Stir with a silver spoon, and when the water and the honey are well mixed, add gradually one and a half pints of whisky, alias mountain dew. Stir briskly, till a froth begins to rise. Bottle and keep tightly corked. Sometimes the yolk of an egg is beat up in the brose.'

MID TWENTIETH CENTURY

'Mix half a pound of run honey and half a pound of fine oatmeal together with a little cold water, and then pour in very slowly a quart of well-flavoured malt whisky. Stir the whole vigorously (using a silver spoon) until a generous froth rises to the top; then bottle and cork tightly. Keep for two days and serve in a silver bowl.'

Or with cream:

'Beat one and a half teacups of double cream to a froth; stir in a teacup of very lightly toasted oatmeal; add half a teacup of dripped heather honey and just before serving two wine-glasses of whisky. Mix thoroughly and serve in shallow glasses.'

A version of Atholl Brose in *The Scots Cellar* by F M McNeill, (1956)

LATE TWENTIETH CENTURY

1 bottle Scotch whisky
300ml (10fl oz) double cream
450g (1lb) honey
whites of 6 eggs
1 handful of oatmeal

Soak the oatmeal in Scotch whisky. Beat the egg whites until stiff, then fold cream into them. Add the honey. Very slowly blend in the whisky and oatmeal. Pour into bottles and store for a week, shaking — and no doubt tasting! — occasionally.

A version of Atholl Brose in *The Hogmanay Companion* by Hugh Douglas, (1993)

QUICK AND EASY ATHOLL BROSE

Put one heaped tablespoon of finely ground oatmeal (grind medium oatmeal in a coffee grinder, if it's not available) in a bowl, add four tablespoons of whisky. Leave for five minutes, or longer. Stir through two tablespoons of thickly whipped cream and dribble a tablespoonful of runny honey on top.

MUSHROOMS

On display

Pushing through the door of Auchendean Lodge at Dulnain Bridge, near Granton-on-Spey, there is a waft of fungal, rotting autumn from a tray of shaggy ink caps. The hotel owners have displayed them in the same way that fishermen in fishing hotels proudly lay out their salmon catch for public inspection. The catch from the Rothiemurchus forests, however, is accompanied by a note which describes the ink cap's distinguishing features and draws attention to the fact that for this evening's dinner they will be made into a soup.

Ian Kirk and Eric Hart, who run this Edwardian shooting lodge, are among a growing band of hoteliers and restaurateurs who make use of native wild mushrooms, encouraging the wary with their original hallway display. Perhaps the time has come for chemists in mushroom-rich areas to provide a mushroom-identification service, filling their windows, as they do in France and Italy, with safe and unsafe specimens. For mushrooms are a rich source of natural flavouring, which Scotland has in abundance.

Considering the lack of pollution, the plentiful woodlands, and the long rotting season, it's surprising they have not featured more prominently in the national diet. The season may last from June through to the first frosts of winter, but there is no trace in old recipes of wild mushrooms being used in the diet.

Now there is a greater awareness of these natural flavourings and in Speyside they are being marketed commercially though mostly sold to Italy and France. Strathspey Mushrooms was set up by Duncan Riley who operates between Aviemore and Muir of Ord, collecting and marketing wild mushrooms. On a particularly good Sunday this autumn (1995) he reports that his volunteer mushroom gatherers (who have been carefully instructed how to pick without damaging the habitat) have collected 1,000kg of penny buns, *Boletus edulus*, from the Speyside woods. This was an unusually large amount — a record, he says.

The other most prolific, and good eating mushroom in Scottish woods is the chanterelle. Because of the unusually hot weather in July and August this has been a bad year (1995) for them. A summer mushroom, they need more dampness with warmth in the summer months. Both ceps and chanterelles are easy to recognize, the chanterelles by their bright orange colour and trumpet shape, the penny bun with its chestnut brown cap and tubes rather than gills. Riley is looking for Grade A specimens of boletus, rock solid, he says, and between the size of a golf ball and tennis ball, with no discolourations or soft patches.

FLAT MUSHROOM OMELETTE

Moist, firm and full of flavour, this is the kind of flat round Spanish-style omelette which is cut into square chunks and served as a tapa with chilled Fino.

INGREDIENTS

For a main course for 4/for 8-10 tapas:
½ cup (125ml/4fl oz) olive oil
500g (1lb) sweet onions, finely chopped
salt
500g (1lb) mushrooms, preferably wild, finely diced
2 tablespoons parsley, finely chopped
2 cloves garlic, crushed
freshly ground white pepper
4 medium eggs, beaten

METHOD

Heat about two tablespoons of the oil in a deep 23cm (9in) frying pan and add the onions and salt. Cook uncovered over a low heat for about 30 minutes until they are soft, but uncoloured. Remove and add another three tablespoons oil and then the mushrooms. Salt them and cook over a high heat for 2-3 minutes, tossing occasionally. Chop the parsley and garlic together and add to the mushrooms. Cook for a minute until their scent is released. Add the onions and mix through. Remove to a bowl and add the eggs and seasoning, mix well.

Meanwhile, put the remaining oil in the pan and heat. When hot, pour in the mixture. Leave on a low heat till set but still soft on top. Place a plate on top and invert and slide back into the pan. Cook for another few minutes, then slide out onto a board and cut into mouthful-sized squares and serve tepid or cold. Or serve in the pan as a main course with salad and crusty bread.

Variation — Black Pudding and Apple Omelette:

Glasgow's Gibson Street hosts one of the city's more adventurous eating-out establishments, appropriately named Stravaigin (in Scots meaning: having fun in a raffish and colourful way). The stravaigar in the kitchen is Colin Clydesdale, who can often be found cooking up unusual dishes like omelettes flavoured with black pudding and apples. Follow method above, substituting 250g(8oz) black pudding, previously fried and chopped roughly and two eating apples, grated, for the mushrooms. Omit the garlic. Alternatively, use black pudding and apples with four eggs and stir-fry quickly in a wok.

BARLEY AND MUSHROOM STEW
WITH AYRSHIRE BACON

An earthy, filling stew which should be served with a contrasting sharp, crisp texture such as baked garlic toasts. Vegetarians can omit the bacon.

INGREDIENTS

For 4-6 servings:

2 tablespoons oil

250g (8oz) Ayrshire bacon

1 onion, finely chopped

250g (8oz) pearl barley, washed

500 g (1lb) mushrooms, preferably wild

125ml (4fl oz) water

2 teaspoons miso paste (optional)

salt and pepper

4 slices of bread

2 tablespoons olive oil

METHOD

Chop the bacon, finely. Heat oil in a large pan and cook bacon till crisp. Remove bacon with a slotted spoon. Add the onion and cook gently till lightly browned. Add the barley and return the bacon to the pan. Cook for five minutes stirring occasionally.

Meanwhile, chop half the mushrooms very finely, or pulse in a food processor, and slice the remainder. Add the mushrooms and continue to cook, stirring occasionally. When all the mushrooms have softened, mix the water with the miso and add. Cover and cook for five minutes.

To serve: Brush the oil over the bread and bake in a hot oven until crisp. Serve with the barley.

PICKLED MUSHROOMS

This is a common method of preserving wild mushrooms in countries where they are gathered in large quantities.

INGREDIENTS

500g (1lb) mushrooms

50g (2oz) salt

300ml (10fl oz) dry white wine
300ml (10fl oz) white wine vinegar
1 teaspoon black peppercorns
1 teaspoon oregano
2 cloves garlic
4 tablespoons olive oil

METHOD

Trim stalks, if necessary and blanch in boiling salted water for about 2-3 minutes. Drain. When cold, pack into jars.

Boil white wine, vinegar and peppercorns for about five minutes. Add garlic and oregano. Cool. Pour over mushrooms. Cover with oil as a sealing layer. Cover and store for a month.

BREEDING BEEF

Converting rough grazing into premier beef

With thick coats and sturdy feet, beef breeds such as Galloway and Highland can be maintained on exposed hill and marginal land, which Scotland has in abundance. It's their natural habitat. They eat a natural diet, thrive and produce prime quality beef on low cost winter rations and in summer and on unimproved rough grazing which is otherwise useless as arable land. It makes sense to breed beef. The other native breeds, Aberdeen Angus and Beef Shorthorn, though wintered inside, are still fed a natural high-quality diet based on silage (preserved grass). This extensive system of husbandry, where calves are allowed to feed from their mothers until they are able to feed for themselves, has been the method for centuries earning Scotland the tag of a premier beef-breeding country. These native breeds have attracted the attention of environmentalists who are concerned about the disadvantages of intensive farming.

Around three-quarters of the beef produced in Scotland comes from beef-breeding herds, not all of which are pure-bred native breeds. Farmers describe them as 'beef-suckler herds' and the animals which produce this prime Scottish beef will reach the highest prices on the market. Cheaper beef comes from dairy cattle, past their age of useful production, or from herds which have been more intensively reared indoors, known as 'bull-beef' which are fed on a less natural diet.

In distinguishing the difference, when it comes to buying beef, the High Street butchers play a vital role, many working closely with farmers to get the best shape and size of the muscles and correct percentage of fat on the carcass (some butchers own their own herds and take the responsibility for 'finishing' the cattle themselves). It's the way to improve quality, but also a precaution since the unsavoury facts regarding the feed of intensively reared beef were first revealed in 1986. The butcher who can trace back to the source of his beef can confidently reassure his customer.

Aberdeen Angus or Angus beef

While this is the most widely known Scottish breed, it's also the most recently established. Pioneer breeder, Hugh Watson (1780-1865) from Keillor near Dundee, first showed his black polled cattle in 1820, and by 1829 was sending some of his stock from the Highland Show in Perth to Smithfield. While previously cattle had been transported on the hoof for fattening in Norfolk and Suffolk, the trade to London of prime beef in carcass (sending only the most expensive cuts) developed, alongside the success of Watson's herd. With the completion of the railway to London in 1850, this new, and more sophisticated, method became the norm.

Watson is regarded as having 'fixed' the type of the new breed and by the time his herd was dispersed, in 1861, it had been highly selected within itself. For the 50 years of its existence, it seems that he never bought in a bull. He sold stock to William McCombie (1805-1880) of Tillyfour, near Aberdeen, who carried on with the breeding, attaching the same importance to meeting the requirements of the London market.

The breed's main rival in Scotland was Amos Cruickshank's Scotch Shorthorn (established in the 1830s) which could be fattened more rapidly, but which did not milk so well and was less hardy. To overcome its problems, and introduce more rapid fattening in the Aberdeen Angus, the characteristics of the two breeds were combined by crossing them, and the Aberdeen-Angus cross Shorthorn became the source of most of the prime beef produced in Scotland.

The Polled Cattle Herd Book was started in 1862 and the Aberdeen-Angus Cattle Society inaugurated in 1879. In 1891, a separate class at the Smithfield Show was provided for the breed, and at the Perth bull sales in 1963 a single bull made history with a world record price of 60,000 guineas.

Changes have occurred in the breed in the last three decades. Firstly a peak demand developed in the 1960s for a small, thick bull with a lot of meat. A trend which was reversed with entry to the EU when a fashion developed in the 1970s and 80s for a taller, leaner animal with a minimum of fat. Now there has been a return to more fat marbling which has stimulated a new era in the history of the breed as breeders and retailers have established more effectively the importance its succulence and flavour. Quality rather than quantity has been the criterion, in the 90s established with the Certification Trade Mark registered by the Aberdeen Angus Cattle Society.

The breed has a special ability to thrive on low-quality pasture, rough grazing and natural rations, such as silage and arable by-products. For unknown reasons it converts these rations, more effectively than most other breeds, into high-quality, early maturing beef with a marbled fat, making it both economically and environmentally desirable. The number of pedigree registered bull calves born in Scotland is 627; total pedigree bulls in the UK, 500; commercial bulls in the UK, 4-5,000. Total commercial herd in the UK 500,000 (all figures 1994). There are 500 registered pedigree herds throughout the UK (1994). The season is best in late summer, after summer feeding, and autumn.

Galloway beef

Though the bloodlines of Galloway (Belted Galloway) and Aberdeen Angus eventually followed very different paths, these two modern Scottish breeds of black, hornless beef-cattle still have some superficial similarities, which reflect their descent from the same primitive stock. While the Angus has responded to intensive feeding, resulting in a rapidly maturing animal, in keeping with the farming practices in its native North-East, the Galloway has made the most of its native marginal and hill lands of the South-West by producing a slower maturing breed.

During the 18th century, South-West Scotland had been a major source of store cattle, which were taken south by drovers to be fattened in Norfolk and Suffolk for the London market. By the mid-19th century, however, the droving trade had ended. Cattle farmers in the South-West had turned to dairying, and the beef cattle were forced to live in the hills.

The Galloway Cattle Society was formed in 1877 in Castle Douglas, which is still the headquarters of the breed for administration and for the main sales. Until its inception, the polled Angus or Aberdeen cattle and the Galloways were entered in the same Herd Book, but with the founding of the society the copyright of the Galloway portion was purchased.

During World War II the value of the pure-bred Galloway for hill grazing was recognized and numbers were expanded under Government encouragement. While the breed has maintained its position, despite subsequent changes in Government policy, its most recent history has also been significantly affected, once again, by its practical ability to forage on rough ground without too much extra feeding expense, making it an attractive breed in a period of rising costs.

Out-wintered and maintained on exposed hill and marginal land, they survive on low-cost winter rations and in summer on unimproved rough grazing. They are particularly suited to more natural extensive husbandry. There were 1,600 pedigree females registered in 1994, the estimated pedigree breeding herd is 3,200. There are also around another 300 pure-bred animals which are not registered. Most herds are to be found in southern Scotland, with the greatest concentration in the South-West. There are some in Cumbria and other parts of the North of England plus a few in other parts of England and Ireland.

Highland beef

Native long-haired, black or dun coloured Highland cattle were an important part of the traditional clan-based economy. Used as a supply of milk, cheese and butter, the dairy cows were driven at the beginning of summer to the mountain pastures as the women and children moved with them to live in 'sheilings' (summer pastures and dwellings in the hills) where they made cheese and butter. Surplus cattle were herded south, along ancient drove roads, to markets in Falkirk and Crieff where they were bought for 'finishing' on more lush Lowland pastures on which specialist graziers fattened them for slaughter.

By the mid-19th century the trade had declined, partly as a result of the break-up of the clan system, followed by the Highland Clearances in the first half of the 19th century, but also because of a demand for a better quality of beef. The Highland cattle which were driven along the ancient drove roads were often four to five years old and their carcasses did not provide the kind of tender meat which could be obtained from young animals, reared and fattened on the new fodder crops nearer the market.

Although it suffered in popularity, the breed was encouraged by certain lairds, notably the Stewart brothers of Harris, MacNeil of Barra, the Duke of Hamilton and the Duke of Argyll. Stock seems to have been selected from island and mainland populations with no evidence of Lowland blood having been brought in. Hardiness has remained a key characteristic of the breed. Like the Aberdeen Angus, it is quite closely related to the Galloway with a common ancestry in primitive native stock, but influenced in its physical development by the more rugged and more severe weather conditions of the Highlands.

The breed society was founded in 1884 with 516 bulls listed in the first herd book, most of which were black or dun. Some went to Canada in 1882 and in the 1920s exports were made to the USA and South America. Today there has been a revival of interest in the breed, particularly for the quality of its meat, and some pioneering butchers have taken to specializing in pure Highland beef, attracting a loyal and growing following from both the domestic and catering market.

The animals can survive well on rough mountain pasture, with some additional feeding in winter. Because of their hardiness and very long thick coats they have a natural ability to withstand extreme cold and thrive outside during the winter. The registered stock bulls amount to 417, and there are 278 registered breeders (1994). Most herds are in Scotland, with many in the Highlands, but there are other herds throughout the UK.

Beef Shorthorn

The Beef Shorthorn or 'The Great Improver', as it has often been called, has a recorded history of over 200 years and has played a major part in the beef industry throughout the world. Though it is generally considered that the pure Shorthorn breed was first developed in Yorkshire in the late 18th century, the pioneering of the Scotch Shorthorn (later described as the Beef Shorthorn) began in the 1830s when Amos Cruickshank and his brother became tenants of an Aberdeenshire farm. By the 1870s, the Cruickshanks' bull calves were being sold to neighbours as crossing bulls. New herds were being built up and it was from this source of beef cattle that the Beef Shorthorn developed. The beefy type of Shorthorn was eventually treated as a separate breed from the Dairy Shorthorn.

By the 1940s and 50s, Beef Shorthorns were numbered in the thousands and considerable emphasis was placed on the export market. The fashion was for early maturing 'baby beef', short and dumpy by today's standards. Fat animals were the order of the day and in the following decades the breed suffered a decline.

As a result of some dedicated breeders, however, who have modernized the breed to ensure it meets the requirements of height and smooth fleshing, while still retaining the other qualities of flavour and character in the meat, the breed has now been experiencing a substantial revival.

It is used in regions where there is a need for extensive farming, where ease of calving and hardiness are essential. Their eyes, skin pigment and coat texture ensure a greater tolerance of excessive weather conditions and their excellent feet and legs make them ideal for range conditions. In the UK there is a population of 590 pedigree females; most are in Scotland and North Yorkshire with other small herds throughout the country.

Breeding for quality

In recent years the issue of flavour and succulence has become an important factor in beef breeding. Twenty years ago when supermarket policy was to provide lean, pink, fresh-looking beef the farmers were challenged to look, not to native breeds, but to Continental breeding stock, intermingling their native animals with French breeding stock, particularly Charolais. This policy produced a beef type which is not in the Scottish tradition but produces lean meat with no fat marbling. Some have suggested that this move was as damaging to the beef industry as mixing French brandy with Scotch whisky would have been to the whisky industry.

In 1994 Jim Jack, President of the Aberdeen-Angus Society, in his message to breeders admitted that: 'This meat [Continental crossed] does not have the succulence and flavour that the consumer requires. Thus, the aim now is to have meat that has a marbling of fat through it, to give a healthy product, that is succulent and tasty.'

The move back to producing beef with the native characteristics of good fat-marbling for flavour appears to be gathering momentum. Our friendly, High Street butchers, have always kept their eye on the native breed's ability to produce a quality flavour and they continue to be the best place to find this quality — rather than quantity-bred meat.

Now more farmers, like Michael Gibson of Forres, who is Chairman of the Agricultural Committee of the Scottish Landowners Association, are pioneering the quality of native breeds. 'In the 1980s,' says Gibson, who also owns MacBeth's butchers in Forres, 'we wanted to do a presentation on the quality image of pedigree Highland beef at a farming exhibition in Hyde Park and were warned-off because we were seen as old-fashioned.

'All we wanted to do was get across the point that, small native Scottish breeds, foraging naturally on Scottish mountains, produce top quality beef. But that was out of step with the official Meat and Livestock Commission (MLC) line.'

Besides the importance of breed, there is also the question of its treatment before and after slaughter. The MLC have conducted scientific research throughout the world, to establish a blueprint for treatment, before and after, slaughter which will produce the best eating quality. What the blueprint does not provide, however, is any sort of guide for farmers on the question of breeding.

'Quality differences between beef breeds,' says Basil Lowman, Senior Beef Specialist at the Scottish Agricultural College, 'cannot be supported by scientific evidence, so it's really up to the farmer to decide what to go for. The problem is that they have been confused by the messages which have been coming from consumers.

'Of course there are as many arguments as there are farmers, but it seems, that there has been some damage to the perceived quality image of Aberdeen Angus beef by the trend towards fresh, pink, lean beef. I think farmers need to take much more interest in the finished product and its eating quality.'

Hanging for quality

On the shelves of the leading multiples I can pick from a number of tags which suggest that this pack of sirloin steak might be worth treble the price of common mince. But which to choose? — Aberdeen Angus, Selected Aberdeenshire, Angus, or just Specially Selected Scotch Beef.

One is too pink with hardly any fat marbling, so that could be dodgy. Another looks too wet — why pay a premium price for water? There is only one which is well-marbled with fat and looks dark enough to have hung for longer than the minimum seven days which the MLC recommends will produce good eating quality in a steak.

Hanging for quality costs money. At a slaughterhouse in prime Scottish beef-rearing country, carcasses which have been sold to one of the supermarkets are hung for less than the minimum seven days before they are cut then packed into sealed plastic packs. Meanwhile, the meat which has been bought by several local butchers and one or two hotels continues to hang, with subsequent moisture loss, for at least two weeks. Seen side by side, the difference is startling: the well-hung carcass much smaller, the meat a firm looking deep-red while the other is a watery looking pinkish-red.

ROAST RIB OF SCOTCH BEEF

Choosing a rib roast cut:
Choose a cut at the top end of the sirloin but before the beginning of the neck. Too high up, near the neck end will have a thick layer of tougher meat, which is the start of the shoulder muscle and shoulderblade. This should be avoided since, apart from the inconvenience of removing the cartilage, the top layer of meat will take longer to cook than the tender rib muscle.

Buying a boned and rolled joint means that both the bone's flavour, and its useful protection of the meat during roasting, is lost.

Minimum size: 2-2.5kg (4-5lbs) to serve 8-10 with some left over.

Preparing:
Rub the whole joint with some dripping or butter and coat with salt and freshly ground black pepper, or sprinkle over a special seasoning mixture: one level tablespoon of dry mustard, mixed with two tablespoons of lightly browned flour and a generous grinding of black pepper. Leave for several hours, preferably overnight when the surface absorbs the flavours.

Roasting:
Heat the oven and roasting tin for at least fifteen minutes to gas mark 9/240C/475F.

Put the beef, fat side up, in the tin. The roast root vegetables (see below) can be put in the tin with the beef or roasted separately. Put into the oven.

After five minutes, reduce the heat to gas mark 6/200C/400F and from this point, time the roasting.

Allow: 15 minutes per 500g (llb) for medium rare. This produces a finished joint which will provide enough medium well-cooked meat at either end for about two or three who prefer it this way, but which is mainly rare.

Or allow: 20-25 minutes per 500g (llb) which will produce a result which is mostly well-cooked with very little rare meat.

Turn the roast root vegetables once during the roasting. If they are ready before the meat, remove and keep warm.

Remove the meat from the oven, put it on a serving ashet, and keep in a warm place to rest while making and serving the puddings.

Yorkshire puddings:

Use pouring batter (see p.). Put a knob of dripping or lard into Yorkshire pudding moulds, place in the oven and heat till almost smoking. Remove, pour in batter and cook for ten minutes gas mark 9/240C/475F. Remove and serve with gravy as a first course.

Gravy:

Decant excess fat. Put a large glass of robust red wine into the roasting pan and reduce over a high heat for a few minutes, scraping up bits of debris from the base of the tin. Season, strain and serve in a sauceboat.

Horseradish:

Use freshly grated horseradish which has been mixed with whipped cream.

Mustard:

Serve with English mustard.

ROAST ROOT VEGETABLES

Roasting in olive oil adds a special flavour to root vegetables in this dish which can be served before the beef course with the Yorkshire puddings and gravy.

They can either be roasted in the same tin with the roast beef or, for vegetarians, made as a main course with the puddings and served with a hot orange vinaigrette (see p.62)

INGREDIENTS

For 4 servings:
1 small turnip (swede)
4 medium parsnips
4 small carrots
4 medium potatoes
4 small onions
1 bulb fennel
100ml (3½fl oz) extra virgin olive oil
sea salt

2 sprigs rosemary
1 bulb garlic
1 tablespoon sesame seeds

METHOD

Preheat the oven to gas mark 8/230C/450F. Put the olive oil into a large roasting tin and place in the oven. Leave for 5-10 minutes until it becomes very hot. Meanwhile, peel the vegetables. Cut into large chunks about the same size. Remove the hot oil from the oven and add the vegetables. Turn well in the oil so that they are all coated. Add rosemary sprigs. Cut the top off the garlic bulb and add.

Roast until all the vegetables are tender, turning once or twice. They should take 40-45 minutes. Remove from the oven. Leave to rest for five minutes. Press the softened insides out of the garlic cloves and mix through the vegetables. Sprinkle over the sesame seeds and serve with Yorkshire puddings and hot orange vinaigrette.

LAMB OR MUTTON?

Until the mid-20th century, most people ate the strong-flavoured, mature sheep which had grazed on the rough heather hills for many years. A little would be eaten fresh, but most was saved for winter use in a salt pickle. Until a process of re-education by the meat industry took place, in the second half of the 20th century, tender, milder-tasting, and more quickly cooked lamb was a rarity. Mutton was the norm.

Embodying the meaty equivalent of wisdom which comes with age, the flavour of over-the-year-old mutton is more complex. More suitable for use in slow-cooked broths and stews. This may not be the most popular late 20th century style and mutton may be a rarity for most, but the old taste is not entirely forgotten.

In some northern areas of the Highlands, on the Hebrides, Orkney and Shetland, salting over-the-year-old sheep remains popular. In Shetland, the cure is known as *reestit mutton* and it continues to hang in butchers' shops in Lerwick while many Shetlanders still make their own at home. First salted and then hung on a wood or rope drying or smoking frame (*reest*), it was a plate of reestit mutton broth, served at the St Magnus Bay Hotel in Shetland, which first alerted me to its charms.

Besides its use in broths, the meat may also be removed and eaten separately with potatoes, or chopped finely and returned to the broth. It's also eaten sliced cold on a Shetland bannock or chopped finely and mixed into *milgrew*, a colloquial term for milk gruel, or porridge made with milk. It also takes its place on the festive table at Up-Helly-Aa in January (see p.29) when platters of the best cuts (saved for the occasion) are served with the traditional bannock, oatcakes and butter at festive tables throughout the town.

I bought my first reestit mutton from Jim Grunberg, a rugged Shetlander who (at that time) managed Smiths the butchers in Lerwick and canoed, winter and summer, back and forward across the narrow strip of water to his home on a nearby island. His cured mutton hung from hooks all about the shop and in the window he had the following notice: 'Reestit Mutton, What is it?' —

'Traditionally, it was salted lamb or mutton dried above a peat fire. It will keep for years if you keep it dry. Reestit mutton soup is an acquired taste that you acquire at the first taste. A small piece is enough to flavour a pot of soup which should include cabbage, carrots, neeps and tatties.'

Smiths in Lerwick make approximately 2,400kg each year, with production on the increase to supply demand. They also provide a mail-order service to remote areas and islands. To make reestit mutton the meat is cut up into fairly small pieces, always left on the bone. Sometimes whole legs or whole shoulders are used. The meat is put into the curer's 'secret' brine pickle: approximately 80 per cent salt to two per cent sugar. The meat is left for between ten days to three weeks, then removed and hung up on hooks to dry.

MID TWENTIETH CENTURY

REESTIT MUTTON

Three and a half pounds of Salt.

Four quarts of Water.

Six ounces of Sugar.

Two to three ounces of Saltpetre

About sixteen pounds of Mutton.

M Stout, *A Shetland Cookbook* (1968)

LATE TWENTIETH CENTURY

PICKLED LAMB OR MUTTON

This is a salt-and-sugar-flavoured pickle which adds a subtle character to meats and poultry. In three to four days new flavours will have developed. Only if the meat is left for too long will it become strongly salty. As with the smokers' modification of smoking cures, there is no need today to use a pickle for more than added flavour.

The meat can be used for flavouring broths and soups but joints which are to be pot-roasted, rather than boiled, can also be improved by a short 12-hour soak in the pickle.

Pork (leg, shoulder or loin), a duck or chicken will develop a good flavour in 36-48 hours and can be poached or pot roasted.

The thickness of the meat will always determine how quickly the pickling flavour is absorbed. Do not mix types of meat. Mutton is often available from Halal butchers in cosmopolitan areas of large cities.

INGREDIENTS

Flavouring pickle for a 2kg (4lb) leg of lamb with bone:

2 litres (3½ pints) water

625g (1¼lb) coarse sea salt

250g (8oz) brown muscovado sugar

1 sprig bay leaves

1 sprig of thyme

5 crushed juniper berries

5 crushed peppercorns

METHOD

Put everything into a pan and bring to the boil. Stir to dissolve the salt and sugar and boil hard for about five minutes. Leave to cool.

Pickling the meat:

Put the cold pickle into a well-washed earthenware crock or bucket with a lid. Immerse the meat and keep it below the surface by laying a heavy plate, or other weight, on top. Cover and keep in a dry cool place. Pickling time will always depend on the thickness of the meat, but for thick joints follow the rule: 3-4 days — mildly flavoured; 7-8 days: — medium flavoured; 10-14 days — very strongly flavoured.

To cook the meat after flavouring:

PICKLED LAMB-MUTTON BROTH

Pickle a 2kg (4lb) leg on the bone for three-four days, rinse. Put into a pan with 2 onions stuck with 3 cloves, 2 medium carrots, sliced. A bay leaf and 8 peppercorns. Cover with water and bring slowly to the boil. Skim. Simmer till the meat is just tender. Leave the meat to cool in the liquid. The next day skim off the fat. Taste for flavour. If too salty add water to dilute.

Slice the best meat and serve reheated in some of the stock with the carrots, chopped parsley and floury boiled potatoes, or serve cold with salad.

Use the remaining stock and meat scraps to make broth adding sliced potatoes, a finely sliced bulb of fennel or half a head of celery, or half a small cabbage. The broth should be thick with vegetables. Simmer gently until the vegetables are tender. Add the meat scraps, finely chopped, taste for seasoning and add freshly ground white pepper and 3-4 tablespoons of chopped parsley.

POT-ROASTED PICKLED CHICKEN

Remove from the pickle after about 48-60 hours for a 2-3kg (4-6lb) chicken. Rinse and leave to dry out thoroughly (3-4 hours or overnight). Heat 3 tablespoons of oil in a pan, add 250g (8oz) halved medium-sized mushrooms and half a head of celery, chopped roughly. Toss in the oil, cover and sweat for a few minutes. Add the chicken and brown lightly. Place on top of the vegetables. Add enough water to come half-way up the vegetables. Cover with a tight-fitting lid and cook very slowly for about 1-1½ hours, or until the chicken is tender. Remove the liquid, strain, season and serve in a sauceboat. Serve chicken on the bed of vegetables with floury mashed potatoes.

SEPTEMB:

Fallow, Trench, and level ground. Prepare pits and bordures for Trees. Gather plan feed, Almond, Peach, and white Plum Stones. Gather ripe Fruits. Plant furth Cabbage: Remove bulbs and plant them. Refresh, Trame, and House your tender Greens. Refresh and trim pots and cases with July-flowers and other fine Flowers and plants, Carrying them to pits, shelter, and covert, giving them Air, &c.

Towards the end gather Safron.

Make Cyder, Perry, and other Wines, &c,

Straiten the entrance to Bee-hives, destroy Wasps, &c.

Also you may now remove Bees.

Garden Dishes and drinks in season.

Varieties of Pot-herbes and Sallades, Cabbage, Cole-flower, Peas, Beans, and Kidnees, Artichocks, Beet-card, Beet-rave, Scorzonera, Carrots, Turneeps, Radish, Cucumbers, Aples, Pears, Apricocks, Peaches, Nectarines, Quince, Grapes, Barberries, Filbeards.

Cyder, Liquorish Ail, Metheglin, and Wine of Cherries, Rasps, Goolberries, Currans, &c.

John Reid, *The Scots Gard'ner*, (1683)

Smoking and Curing
Hot Suppers

Finnans, Smokies, Salt Cod and Ling, Salmon,
Ayrshire Bacon, Tripe Suppers, Scotch (mince)
Collops, Fish 'n Chips, Scotch Pies, Forfar Bridies

Cold, hot, real or artificial

What to do was salt first. That kept the bugs at bay, for a while. But long-term the idea was to hang food from smoke-blackened rafters for at least one winter, if not two. During which time the cool peat smoke wafting upwards from the open fire in the centre of house also smoke-blackened the food. Between the salt and the smoke there would be a lively appetite-rouser when the need arose.

Now food is salted and smoked for a shorter time and not from rafters. But modern methods have the same effect of producing new flavour compounds in food when the aromatic acetates and aldehydes in the cool smoke vapour combine with salt in the flesh. So long as the smoke is not too hot and the food does not 'cook', the new smoky flavour will travel gradually through the food, altering its colour and flavour. But if the smoke cooks the food, the flavour will settle mainly on the surface, as it does in an Arbroath Smokie, or a barbecued steak.

While primitive, cool, rafter-smoked food came from animals and fish which roamed freely and had firm flesh and well-developed muscles, the same may not always be the case today. Intensively farmed animals and fish, which have been poorly exercised and fed a concentrated diet which enables a fast weight gain in the shortest time possible, will have bulk but no muscle tone. If they have been starved before killing the tone will be a bit better, but attempting to smoke this kind of flesh is likely to produce a soft, wet, flabby piece of smoked food.

The alternative, of course, is not to attempt smoking at all. Such are the skills of the modern food industry that a smoked flavour can be obtained from a pot of liquid smoke, brushed on with a paint brush. A smoked colour can be obtained by dipping in artificial dyes, both well-established practices in the food industry. Dying kippers with a coal-tar dye, known as Brown F (for) K (kippers) was a wartime practice which is still in operation.

No labelling regulations currently exist which makes it crystal clear whether a real or artificial method is used. Besides kippers, smoked haddock (Finnans) have also been subjected to this process over the years, with manufacturers claiming that they are merely producing what the customer demands. One of the largest fish smokers in Aberdeen claims that 80 per cent of Scots prefer undyed fish, while 90 per cent of the English want theirs dyed. Americans will not buy any dyed fish at all, while the Irish and French want everything dyed.

SMOKIES

Hot off the barrel

As the row of fish, hanging in pairs over a wooden rod is removed from the fire, the smoker lifts off a pair of hot newly-smoked haddock. Splitting the fish open he takes out the central bone and inside is the pale creamy-coloured, succulent flesh. He passes me the filleted fish. The smokie aroma is intense yet the flavour is quite delicate and subtle. We eat the hot fish with our fingers and it tastes like no smokie, before or since.

Bob Spink cures smokies in a small square brick-walled pit about a couple of feet high with a fire at the bottom. The method of smoking over this hot fire has been handed down through many generations, and remains the same, though the brick pit has replaced the round whisky barrel it's still called the *barrel*.

Rows of fish hanging over rods are waiting to be smoked. Computerized kilns may make the process less labour intensive, says Bob, but no amount of careful button-pushing can produce the kind of smokie which comes hot-off-the-barrel.

Most smokies today are smoked in Arbroath, though the cure originated in Auchmithie a few miles north, once populated with fisher folk of Scandinavian origin (Spink is a Norse surname). The fishwives, smoking the fish on rods, originally put them onto halved whisky barrels with fires underneath and the smoke was contained under layers of coarse sacking, the finished product a darker, deeper copper colour than the modern version.

The tiny fishing village of Auchmithie is perched on the edge of a cliff with a harbour reached by a winding path down to the shore. Before the smokers moved to Arbroath, the reek of smoking fish, when the fires were going, was an unforgettable smell, which I remember from childhood day-trips to this favourite picnic venue. When Norse fisher-people settled here, they recognized the useful purpose of the upward draught of sea breezes, rising from the cliff face, and built their fish-smoking fires on grassy ledges. Old photographs of Auchmithie fishwives show them bending over the smoking barrel arranging the fish on rods with more fish hanging on a washing line to dry, beside the smoking barrels.

The museum in Arbroath is a good place to get the flavour of old smoking times.

It was about the beginning of the 20th century that the first Auchmithie fisher-folk began moving to Arbroath, and instead of using the old barrels started building the brick smoke-pits in their back gardens. When the output from Arbroath eventually exceeded the amount cured in Auchmithie the cure became known as an Arbroath smokie.

Today, the fisher-folk of Arbroath continue to smoke in their back-yards, selling their smokies from small shop counters in the house. When the 'barrels' are smoking the smell wafts through the streets. Though some prefer to remain small, with a single smoke-pit, selling to loyal and regular customers, others have developed large fish-processing plants though they continue, like Bob Spink, to smoke in the traditional way.

To make a smokie, the haddock is gutted, headed and dry-salted for a about two hours, depending on the size of the fish, to draw excess moisture from the skin and impart a mildly salty flavour. The fish are tied in pairs and hung over wooden rods, the salt washed off, and the fish left to dry for about five hours to harden the skin. Then they are placed in the smoke-pit and hot-smoked over a hardwood fire of oak or beech, covered with layers of hessian (the number of layers depends on the weather and may be adjusted throughout the smoking to prevent the fish either smoking too quickly and burning, or smoking too slowly and drying out). The smoking time is approximately 45 minutes.

To reheat

Baked:
Smokies can be split open and the bone removed, the fish spread with butter, closed up and heated through in the oven, preferably wrapped in foil to keep them moist.

Grilled:
They may be opened up, the bone removed, spread with butter and the open fish grilled for a brief minute just to melt the butter and heat the fish through, a grinding of white pepper to finish.

Poached in milk:
The skin and bone are removed first. If the fish is freshly smoked, the skin will peel off easily, but if not, cover with boiling water, leave for a few minutes, pour off the water and peel off the skin, open up and take out the bone. Leave the fish in large flakes, just cover with milk, and heat through. Serve with a poached egg and mashed potatoes, butter and freshly ground white pepper.

To make main-course smokie salad (see page 100): use flaked fish with boiled rice and chopped, crisply fried, streaky bacon.

EARLY TWENTIETH CENTURY

SMOKIE KEDGEREE

For her large family (seven children plus sundry holidaying relatives) my grandmother's favourite way with smokies was to use them as a flavouring for filling carbohydrate (rice) while eking out expensive protein with boiled eggs from her hens.

INGREDIENTS

For 4 servings:
4oz (125g) cooked fish
1 hard boiled egg
1oz (25g) butter
4oz (125g) boiled rice
seasoning
garnish: chopped parsley

METHOD

Remove skin and bone from the fish, and flake roughly. Chop the white of egg. Melt the butter, and add the rice, fish, white of egg, and seasoning.

Mix well, and stir over the fire until steaming hot. Pile on a hot ashet, and sieve the yoke of egg over. Garnish with parsley.

Plain Cookery Recipes, published by Aberdeen School of Domestic Science.

FINNANS

Check the colour

Finnans are the other East-Coast haddock cure which have, like smokies, survived the hi-tech developments of the late 20th century, more or less intact. While the smokie is still in its original form, as a beheaded haddock, unfilleted and hot-smoked, a number of variations are now made of the Finnan. In its original form it was a beheaded haddock, split open with the bone left in and cold-smoked. But now the cure has been altered, the bone and skin removed and artificial dyes added to substitute for proper smoking. This pseudo-Finnan is sometimes known as a *yellow fillet*. Another variation — but with more integrity — is the *Aberdeen fillet*, or *smoked fillet* which is made without colourings, as for a Finnan, but with the bone removed.

Aberdeen has been one of the main centres of the haddock fisheries since the 13th century when fishermen first started exploring the rich waters of northern seas, and it has now become established as the centre for all kinds of cured fish. Huge quantities of smoked salmon, salted herring, salted and smoked white fish were exported from here to the continent and beyond and it is still Aberdeen that supplies most High Street fish shops throughout Scotland.

The size of the Finnan depends on the size of the haddock but they are usually around 500g (1lb) in weight. The whole haddock has the head removed, it is then split open, the bone left in, then brined and smoked, usually to a pale straw colour through to golden brown. The flavour is light and delicate, only mildly salty. The original Finnan cure involved dry-salting overnight and smoking over soft 'grey' peat for 8-9 hours, then cooling and washing in warm salted water. Other original Finnan cures around the country included Eyemouth and Glasgow 'Pales' which was a milder, paler cure, smoked for only a half to two hours and split with the bone on the right hand side. A Moray Firth Finnan was split like a 'Pale' but smoked for about 12 hours making it much darker. Methods today vary, from commercially produced large-scale smoking in 'Torry' kilns to small independent smokers, using a more traditional type of smoker. There are five large-scale industrial smokers and many small smokehouses around the coast.

THE FISHWIFE'S READY-MADE DINNER

My grandmother's fishwife, Kate, came to the back door twice a week with a fish-filled creel on her back and two fish-laden baskets over her arms. A dark, curious, friendly woman in fisherman's navy, who smelt strongly of fish as she sat at the kitchen table with a cup of tea. Her fresh fish had come from boats in the harbour at Broughty Ferry, a short walk along the shore. It was dumped into the kitchen sink and her cup of tea and chat came after she had done some filleting. She would come to my grandmother first, with the pick of the catch, knowing that she would be relieved of a large portion of her burden.

Kate was the last of an intrepid breed of sturdy women whose unremitting toil makes the hassle of modern living appear timid. Many of the women of her generation, in addition to selling and filleting fish round the doors, baited lines, smoked fish and looked after large families. Fish-smoking would begin in the early morning, perhaps around 5am when the fire would be laid in the shed. Surplus piles of haddock, and other fish, from yesterday's catch would be gutted, split, washed and salted. With no help from freezer or microwave she also had to feed her family.

So half-a-dozen Finnans and a couple of sliced onions would go into the big black pot. This would be covered with water and left at the side of the fire to simmer gently. The bones and skin would be removed later and some leftover boiled potatoes mashed in with some milk. What Kate had made was neither a stew, nor a broth, but an old fashioned 'skink' (soup-stew).

Ever since this soup-stew first attracted the attention of food writer and folklorist, F M McNeill, which she describes in her book *The Scots Kitchen* (1929) as *Cullen Skink*, it has been known by that name though, of course, it was a universal habit throughout East-Coast fish-smoking communities who harvested their living from the sea.

EARLY TWENTIETH CENTURY

FISHWIFE'S STEW

INGREDIENTS

For 4-6 servings:
750g (1½lb) floury potatoes
1 onion, finely chopped
1 litre (2 pints) water
1 Finnan, or 250g (8oz) Aberdeen fillet
50g (2oz) butter
1 cup (250g/8 fl oz) milk
50g (2oz) butter
salt and pepper

METHOD

Cooking the potatoes and fish:
Wash potatoes and put into the pot with onion and water. Bring to a gentle simmer and cook until the potatoes are almost tender. Put smoked fish into the pot and cook until the fish is almost cooked through. Remove from the heat and leave to cool. It is best left overnight to extract the maximum flavour.

Finishing the skink:
Remove the fish and potatoes. Skin the potatoes and return to the pan. Mash into the fish stock, or cut into chunks. Reheat, and add butter. Remove the bones and skin from the fish, flake it roughly and return to the skink. Adjust to the desired consistency — thick stew-soup, or thinner soup — with milk. Check seasoning and serve.

LATE TWENTIETH CENTURY

CULLEN SKINK WITH MUSSELS

INGREDIENTS

For 4-6 servings:

1 onion, chopped

1 tablespoon oil

1 Finnan or 250g (8oz) Aberdeen fillet

water to cover

3 medium-sized waxy potatoes

1kg (2lb) mussels 1 tablespoon chopped parsley

METHOD

Cooking the fish and potatoes:

Heat the oil in a pan, add the onion and sweat until transparent and soft, but not coloured. Add the smoked haddock, cover with water and bring slowly to a simmer. Cover and simmer for two minutes. Turn off the heat and leave the fish in the hot water to finish cooking. Leave until cold enough to handle. Remove the fish. Wash the potatoes, chop roughly and put into the fish stock, cook gently until soft.

Cooking the mussels:

Wash the mussels well and discard any which have opened. Heat about 1cm (½in) of water in a wide pan with a tight-fitting lid. Bring to the boil and put in the mussels. Put on the lid and shake the pan. Leave for a minute when the shells should have opened.

Finishing the dish:

Check seasoning of mussel-cooking liquor and fish/potato stew. Add mussel liquor, some or all depending on saltiness. Put mussels on top of stew. Ladle into wide, deep soup plates or large bowls. Sprinkle with parsley and serve with a small jug of cream.

SALT COD AND LING

This is cured mainly in Aberdeen, though it is also cured in smaller quantities on Orkney and Shetland and on the islands. John MacCallum, fish merchant, of Troon, who comes from Islay, cures a supply for his customers in Troon and Glasgow.

With potatoes and garlic:

This is the piquant appetite-rouser (*brandade de morue*) which is sold in French charcuteries, looking deceptively like a mound of boring mashed potatoes, which makes its stunning flavour punch all the more surprising.

INGREDIENTS

For 6-8 servings:
1kg (2lb) salt cod or ling
water or milk to cover
2 sprigs thyme
2 bay leaves
3-4 large, floury, baking potatoes
1 cup (250ml/8fl oz) light olive oil
5 large garlic cloves
chopped parsley
lemon juice
freshly ground white pepper

METHOD

Soak the cod for 24 hours and discard the water. Put into a pan with water/milk to cover, add the thyme and bay leaves. Cover and simmer until the fish is tender and falling off the bones.

Meanwhile, rub potatoes with oil, pierce and bake till soft. Cut in half. Scoop out insides and mash in a bowl. Reserve shells.

Strain the fish, reserve the liquor. Remove the flakes of fish and put into a food processor, pulse until smooth. Heat the oil in a pan. Crush the garlic finely. Add the hot oil in spoonfuls to the fish in the processor, pulsing between each spoonful. Add garlic and parsley and pulse till smooth. Remove from the processor to a bowl and gradually beat in the potatoes. Use some of the fish stock to make a light creamy consistency, beating well. Add lemon juice to taste (optional), season with freshly ground white pepper and pile into potato shells.

SMOKED SALMON

Though this was originally a domestic procedure, since the mid-20th century smoking salmon at home has declined and large-scale commercial smoking has increased. It has created a huge variation in the quality and price of today's smoked salmon. The issue of less-than-wonderful smoked salmon has only developed in the last couple of decades, as farmed salmon has moved into mass-production, bringing with it not only availability for a wider market, but also the problems of maintaining quality with volume.

Those who both farm and smoke salmon opine that many of the problems come from the demand for a high-volume, low-price product. A policy which has been pursued by some multiples in their search for a gourmet product at an affordable price. The quality of smoked salmon has suffered. The solution is not simple.

To attempt to overcome the problem, some salmon farmers are now rearing their fish at relatively low-stocking densities in fast flowing water on a naturally balanced — not too high energy — diet. These salmon, the experts agree, are much more difficult to distinguish from the wild stock, and smoke better. They cost more to produce, but if there was more demand, more would be produced.

There are currently around 100 smokehouses in Scotland smoking approximately 14,000 tonnes of fish from Scottish waters in a year. Unlike other competing countries, such as Norway, Scotland has the advantage of a farming industry which has grown up in the last couple of decades alongside an old existing smoking industry. While Norway's salmon is transported to France or England for smoking, a close relationship has developed over the last couple of decades between Scottish fish farmers and smokers, some farmers moving into smoking, and vice versa, with benefit to the industry on both sides.

Smoking, of course, is essentially a craft-skill with a hands-on element which is difficult to automate successfully on a large scale. Comparing the difference in the methods of production between a small craft-smoker and a large industrial smoker highlights some of the reasons for the huge range of quality in the finished fish.

Small-scale traditional smokers will dry-salt for around 15 hours, wash and dry out the fillets overnight before cold-smoking at 20-30C, usually over smouldering oak chips, though some smokers still continue to use peat. During the process the temperature and moisture content are monitored and controlled. Some curers 'rest' or 'mature' the fish for a further 3-4 days at a chilled temperature before packaging. At every stage there is a need to control the process by the 'gut feeling and nose' of the smoker.

In the large-scale process an automatic smoker will be set by computer and the smoking process may proceed without personal judging of the progress of all the fish at different stages. Smokers, both craft and large-scale, may add flavouring ingredients — sugar, juniper berries, herbs, molasses, rum or whisky — at the salting stage to impart a distinctive cure. They may also use these flavourings to disguise a poor-quality fish. The purist, who flavours only with salt and smoke, maintains that additional flavourings should not be necessary if there is already a good flavour in the fish.

While establishing quality as an important issue for both farmer and smoker, Scotland has also had to protect its smoked salmon against a number of unscrupulous smokers producing bogus Scottish cures. Hijacking the Scottish tag for its prestige, some are labelled 'Scottish' which may use neither Scottish fish nor be smoked in Scotland.

There have been 13 convictions under the Trades Description Act against two companies and one individual.

Protection against this practice is difficult, but an attempt has been made with a guaranteed quality mark ensuring Scottish fish and smoking authenticity. One of its flaws, however, is that it cannot appear on all authentic fish since it does not apply to wild salmon, or to any genuine Scottish salmon which has been smoked in Scotland from companies not members of the quality-mark scheme.

Buying / preparing:
Smoked salmon is sold in whole trimmed sides (sliced or unsliced, by machine or by hand) or in small vacuum packs, sliced by hand or machine. Buying a whole side may be up to 30 per cent cheaper, but this includes the skin (which can be used for stock) and the scraps (which can be puréed with cream and pressed into pots).

The colour varies from pale pink through to dark pink depending on the cure and the original colour of the fish. The flavour also varies according to the cure and the quality of the fish. It can vary from intensely peaty to delicately sweet. A craft-smoked wild fish which has been smoked slowly over peat will be a very different product to a factory-smoked farmed salmon with a low salt content balanced by sugar-sweetness.

The cured salmon may be sliced by hand or chilled and machine sliced then packed in vacuum or modified atmosphere packages. To slice a whole side requires a very sharp, long, thin, pliable knife and a steady hand. If they have not already been removed, remove the 'pin' bones up the middle with pliers. To slice: start at the tail and work up, cutting the largest thinnest slices possible. Keep covered before serving and serve at room temperature.

Machines have now been developed which slice fish almost as expertly as hand-slicing. Buying hand-sliced is still the most expensive since it produces a wafer-thin slice.

Serve slightly chilled with tangy brown bread, fresh, good-flavoured, unsalted butter and a lemon.

CURING

Ayrshire Bacon

Scotland's only distinctive bacon cure developed in the richest and oldest dairying area as a cheese-making by-product, using excess whey to feed the pigs. In the last couple of decades, however, it has been under threat from a bacon industry which now relies on the power of polyphosphates to absorb and retain water in bacon. Those who continue to make old cures in the traditional way, without phosphates, have found it difficult to compete against cheap and watery bacon.

At one of the largest Ayrshire bacon curers, Ramsay's of Carluke, they cure around 140 pigs a week and most of the bacon is sold within a 20 mile radius of the factory. The pigs are delivered live from a farm in Perthshire and slaughtered after a night's rest. Their contract with the farm, which they have visited to see the management of the pigs, is for a fatter than normal pig, for which they pay a premium.

'Because it's better fed, and has a bit more fat on it,' says Andrew Ramsay, the fourth generation of Ramsay pig curers, 'the pig has a better flavour. That's half the battle. No point in having a pig that's half starved and so lean, that the meat's like rubber.

'Nobody's asking you to eat all the fat. Cut it off if necessary, but we need a pig with a wee bit fat on it then we know that it's got some flavour.'

This is particularly important for the Ayrshire cure because there are no other strong flavours added, and it's not smoked, so the taste of the pig matters more. When the meat is brined it loses water, about 2 per cent, and it is this weight loss which is recovered when phosphates are added turning the flesh into a sponge, which then re-absorbs the water. If there is 10 per cent added water it need not be shown on the label since according to the Government this is an acceptable level. Some cures can soak up as much as 20 per cent added water, in which case they will have a misleading 10 per cent stated on the label.

The use of the term 'ham' in Scotland loosely refers to any kind of bacon, and not just to the cured leg joint and meat from it, which is the usual English interpretation of the word. In Scotland this is usually called a 'cooked ham' or a 'gammon'.

While the Ayrshire cure is made by some other large traditional curers, like Ramsay's, some High Street butchers also make their own cure since it requires nothing more than a brining vat and a place to dry out. Pre-packs in supermarkets, which are described as Ayrshire-style bacon, look like the authentic cure, but they are not cured in the traditional way.

This involves removing the bones from the whole side of the pig, taking off the skin and wet brining for two days, with a small proportion of nitrates for preservation. When it's removed from the brine, it's dried out for two to three weeks before being cut up and rolled. Some may be lightly smoked over oak chips, though this is not traditional. The gigot (leg) is boned, rolled and tied, the shoulder cut into boiling joints. Whole hams on the bone are popular festive joints.

In late November, the cold room in Ramsay's Wellriggs factory is many hams deep with orders waiting for collection. Some have been treated with a spiced cure, which they make only to order from an old family recipe dating back to the days when the preservation often included spices as well as salt and smoke.

'Look for a short shank in a whole ham on the bone,'says Andrew Ramsay. 'Avoid the long one. The broad and plump joint with a good layer of fat is the best buy.'

For end-of-the-year festivities, I take home a chunky 15lb leg, wrapped in muslin, which sits in the centre of festive table. It's something worth celebrating, in its splendid entirety, and the leftovers are a welcome source of many hassle-free meals in the days to follow.

BAKED HAM ON THE BONE

INGREDIENTS

1 x 7-8 kg (15lb) ham on the bone
3 heaped tablespoons soft brown sugar
whole cloves

METHOD

Preparing the ham:
You will need two large pieces extra-width foil and one large roasting tin. Pre-heat the oven to gas mark 3/160C/325F.

Check with the curer whether it is very salty and will need a soak. (Ramsay's ham is mildly salted and does not need to be soaked.) Soak the ham in a large bucket or basin (or the bath if necessary) in cold water overnight. Remove from the water. Put two pieces of foil crosswise on the roasting tin. Place the ham on top and bring up each piece of foil to meet in the middle, making an enclosed tent over the ham and ensuring that there are no gaps. Do not wrap it too tightly since the ham should cook in some steam.

Baking the ham:
Put into the oven and cook for 30 minutes per 500g (1lb). Check near the end of the cooking time to see how tender the ham is. It may need less or more cooking. Slice off a bit to test. When it is ready, remove from the oven.

Glazing:
Turn up the oven to gas mark 7/220C/425F. Fold down the foil, lift the ham onto a board and remove the skin with a sharp knife taking care not to remove too much fat. Score the de-skinned surface fat into a diamond pattern and stud a clove into the centre of the diamonds. Rub the whole surface with sugar. Drain off all the cooking liquor from the foil and roasting tin (this can be used for soup) and return the ham to the oven for 30 minutes to brown. If it is to be served hot, leave for another half-hour in a warm place before carving.

BACON AND EGG PIE

This was my grandmother's picnic pie. With salad it can be served for high tea either hot or cold.

INGREDIENTS

For 4 servings:
350g (12oz) packet puff pastry
150g (6oz) Ayrshire bacon, chopped
4 eggs
freshly ground black or white pepper
18cm (7in) round tin or pie plate
egg or milk for brushing

METHOD

Pre-heat the oven to gas mark 8/230C/450F. Cut off two-thirds of the pastry and roll out to fit the base of the tin. Put in the chopped bacon and make four hollows. Break the eggs into the hollows.

Season eggs with pepper (there will be enough salt in the bacon). Roll out the remaining third of the pastry to make a lid for the top of the pie. Wet the edges and press together. Score in a diamond design on top, brush with egg or milk and bake for 20 minutes until puffed and golden on top.

Bacon rolls/baps

The convenient round shape of Ayrshire-cured bacon is grilled or fried and used as a filling for a bap or roll. Bacon rolls made with a hard-crusted, chewy, Glasgow rolls are popular hand-held fast foods, which may be eaten at any time of the day.

HOT SUPPERS

An Edinburgh speciality

For an end-of-the-day gastronomic treat (circa 1800) you might have followed the wafting aroma down a flight of stairs to the warm den of the tavern kitchen. At Douglas's, scotched (minced) collops are simmering in the pot on the fire. The cook makes the best in Edinburgh, everyone says so. Just as everyone agrees that the best puddings are at Lizzie's, the best sheep's heid at Duddingston, the best tripe suppers at the Guildford tavern ...

Supper, for the majority of those who earned their living in the town, was a one-pot affair, eaten during the evening. Dinner was in the afternoon. The late afternoon and early evening were for lounging in a coffee house, browsing over the two-day old news in the London papers, which had just arrived in the stagecoach. Gossiping with cronies in a tavern was another way of passing the time. If you were in the social class which could afford servants, the gossiping might have taken place over a newly fashionable cup of tea and game of cards. By mid-evening, everyone was in need of proper sustenance.

In a country where a popular national dish was made in a sheep's stomach from ingredients plucked from its insides, there was no squeamishness about consuming these 'pluck meats'. They were as valuable, if not more so, than those from the carcass. Unsentimental Scots realists had eschewed the unfortunate English term 'offal'. (What would they have thought of prissy modern America's 'variety meats'?) For them, 'pluck' was liver, heart, kidneys, lungs and stomach bag, not regarded as second-rate odds and ends, or only fit for the poor house, or the dogs, but raw materials for favourite dishes. It was this public approval for such ingredients plus the skill of the tavern cooks, who knew how to make a good meal out of them, which made them so popular.

Making a tripe supper was not a difficult operation, just a slow one. It started — according to the recipes which have survived — on the previous day, when a week's supply of cleaned, unbleached tripe had come from the fleshmarket.

Cut up into cutlet-sized pieces, it was put into a huge earthenware jar with a knuckle bone or some cow-heel. The jar was covered and put into a cauldron of hot water and left at the side of the fire, just simmering, for about a day, by which time the tough tripe had softened, and the knuckle bone released its goodness.

The bone was removed, and the stewed tripe left to cool and set into a firm jelly. Kept on a marble slab in a cool larder, it would stay good for a couple of weeks. To make a tripe supper, all that was required was a chunk of jellied tripe and the cook's skill at dishing it up.

Other than registering its popularity, no chronicler of the day reported the recipe for the good tripe at the Guildford tavern, so we will never know. Was it simmered it in its own jelly and served with salt, mustard and roasted onions? Or did the cook follow the 19th century gastronomic Cleikum Club's advice, and use the French thickening of butter rolled in flour to add to a milky sauce. Was the seasoning mustard, or mushroom-catsup, or just onions fried in butter?

MEG DOD'S TRIPE SUPPERS

MID NINETEENTH CENTURY

'In good, old French cookery, the tripe, when boiled and cut in bits, was stewed in cullis [its rich cooking liquor], with all sorts of herbs, onions, and chives, a glass of wine and a little tarragon. When the sauce was thickened, a little made mustard was added, and the whole strained, heated and poured over the tripe.'

or

'To Fry Tripe, Scottish fashion, make a batter with three eggs allowing a spoonful of flour to each egg, and as much milk as will make a thick batter. Season with ginger, onions or chives and parsley minced very fine. Cut the tripe in small cutlets and dip them in the batter, and fry in beef-dripping.'

Meg Dods (1826)

TWENTIETH CENTURY

Despite a rich tradition of tripe-cookery, today's surviving recipe is tripe and onions in a white sauce. Yet tripe works well with many flavours and textures: lemon, bay leaf, thyme, parsley, crisp fried bacon, hot buttered toast, floury potatoes …

TRIPE WITH BACON AND NUTMEG

INGREDIENTS

For 2-4 servings:

50g (2oz) butter

4 rashers of streaky bacon, diced

2 large onions, finely chopped

500g (1lb) prepared and cooked tripe, cut into very
thin strips the size of tagliatelli

125ml (4fl oz) meat stock or water

2-3 sprigs of thyme

zest ½ lemon

2-3 bay leaves

salt and freshly ground pepper

½ grated nutmeg

1 tablespoon chopped parsley

METHOD

Heat the oil in a pan and add the bacon. Cook over a low heat until lightly crisp. Add the onions. Cook gently until they are transparent and lightly brown. Add the tripe to the pan along with the stock or water. Wind some thread round the peel, thyme and bay leaf and add. Season with salt and pepper and grated nutmeg and simmer gently for 1-2 hours. Remove the bunch of flavourings, taste for seasoning, add parsley, and serve with hot buttered toast or a baked potato.

Tripe is the collective name for the four stomachs of ruminant, or cud-chewing animals. 'Thick-seam' tripe comes from the first stomach, its outer surface ridged into smooth seams and the rest of the stomach, with a rough texture, is known as 'blanket' tripe. Tripe from the second stomach is known as 'honeycomb' from the pattern formed by its raised texture. 'Bible' tripe from the third stomach is the most delicate texture and 'reed' tripe from the fourth stomach is soft and supple. 'Dressed' tripe has been cleaned, bleached and pre-cooked by the butcher. Sometimes it has been cooked until just tender so that it needs very little extra cooking.

'SCOTCH' COLLOPS

Mince and tatties

Before mincers were invented, meat was chopped finely, making incisions, lines or 'scotches' (as in a game of hopscotch). In the course of time, the verb to scotch was mistaken for the people, and things made with *scotched* meat were called *Scotch* though there was nothing particularly Scottish about them. Scotch(ed) egg and Scotch(ed) Collops, the forerunner of modern mince, were dishes which caused this confusion. The tavern's Scotched Collops had developed from a fast-cooked collops-in-the-pan which became scotch(ed) when the cook decided the meat was too tough for cooking in a piece and chopped it up.

When mechanical mincers appeared the confusion was removed and the old words for mince abandoned.

LATE TWENTIETH CENTURY

MINCE WITH HERB DOUGHBALLS

This quick meal-in-a-pot in less than 30 minutes, depends, first and foremost, on gristle-free, not too fatty, good quality steak. Scots, buying mince from High Street butchers, will have it minced-to-order, choosing their steak and watching it being minced.

The other necessity for a memorable-tasting mince is a thorough browning for flavour of both onions and meat.

INGREDIENTS

For 4-6 servings:
2 tablespoons oil
500g (1lb) beef steak, finely minced
1-2 onions, finely chopped
salt and pepper
1 teaspoon sugar
1 teaspoon lemon juice or wine vinegar
600ml (1 pint) water or beef stock

For the doughballs:
200g (6oz) fine self-raising flour
2 tablespoons olive oil (or 50g/2oz beef suet, traditional)
1 egg
1 tablespoon herbs (own choice), finely chopped
1 level tablespoon grated fresh ginger, unpeeled
2 cloves garlic, crushed
salt
freshly ground white pepper
½ cup (125ml/4fl oz) milk to mix

METHOD

For the mince:
Heat the oil in a pan and add the onions. Cook for about ten minutes until they begin to colour. They should be golden but not dark brown. Add the mince. Break up with a fork and fry for another ten minutes until the mince is lightly browned and the moisture driven off. Add salt, pepper, sugar, lemon juice and just cover with stock or water. Bring to a gentle simmer. Taste and adjust the seasoning.

For the doughballs (makes 8):
Sieve the flour into a bowl. Make a well in the centre and add all the other ingredients. Mix with a fork to a soft, but not too wet, dough. Drop in spoonfuls on top of the mince. Cover tightly with the lid and cook for 5-10 minutes or until they are well risen and cooked through.

FISH 'N CHIPS

The fried supper

As food marriages go, there are few which have given birth to quite such a proliferation of offspring as the union of Fish and Chip. 'Chippies' in Scotland and in some parts of Northern England, 'fish 'oles' in Yorkshire, and 'fish shops' to Londoners, they have bred and multiplied. There may be more serious things to discuss about the present generation, such as batter crispness, fish freshness, and the damage done by wrapping them in paper, but some attempt must first be made to discover where and when the remarkably successful marriage took place.

Scotland, Lancashire, Yorkshire and London have all made their claims which the late Gerald Priestland, the religious affairs broadcaster and author, investigated at some depth in his book *Frying Tonight: the Saga of Fish and Chips* (1972). His inquiry took him to several of the 'original' family shops where he discovered that there was little written evidence to back up anecdotal claims made by present-day owners. The story continues to roll, with other investigations following Priestland's, but the real truth remains elusive.

What has been established, however, is where and when the two became common in the diet. Fried fish had become an everyday food by the early 19th century. Before refrigeration and steam transport sorted out the distribution problems, gluts of North Sea fish were salted, dried and smoked, but they were also fried in batter.

It was often the less good quality surplus fish which was given a good salting, and fried in batter to camouflage its rotten taste. It went down particularly well in the gin-drinking areas of deprived inner cities and became a staple street food. The fish was deep fried in coal-fire heated cauldrons of fat in Fish Warehouses (first recorded in *Oliver Twist*, 1837-39). Itinerant street sellers (described in Henry Mayhew's *London Labour and the London Poor,* 1861) walked the streets with newspaper-lined trays — attached round their necks with a strap — which were filled with cold fried fish dusted with a sprinkling of salt.

While this fried fish may have been eaten with a baked potato, also a common street food at this time, the square plugs about the length and thickness of the little finger, also fried in deep fat, which became its lifelong partner, appear to have come from the French. My Dundonian father has always claimed that it was a Belgian immigrant, Eduard de Gernier, who invented the chip. It was claimed in the town that Mr de Gernier (who sold my father chips with hot peas and vinegar, known as a *buster* — of wind — on his way home from school) had introduced the chip to Britain when he set up his stall in Dundee's Grassmarket in 1874.

Far too late, says Priestland. The chipped potato 'à la mode', or just 'alamode' as it was first called, was definitely around in England by 1865. Old established families in the trade have fairly convincing oral traditions to prove it. But Mr de Gernier could still have been the first to street-sell chips in Scotland, a habit subsequently taken up with great enthusiasm by Italian immigrants who realised its potential as the perfect winter alternative to ice-cream. The fact that chips were first sold in Scotland without fried fish, perhaps explains why the Scots still refer to the 'chippie' not the 'fish shop'.

In order to place a plaque above the door, the *The Fish Traders Review* magazine set themselves the task of finding: The World's Oldest Fish and Chip Business. After much research in the 1960s, they gave the title to Malin's in London, putting the date at 1865, and causing much grumbling dissent in Northern fish 'oles.

Priestland is inclined to sympathize with the North on several counts. For a start, he points out that the potato was much more popular in the North than the South. It's a well-known fact that the Southern English, were not too keen on potatoes which they associated with the 'bog Irish'. There is also the fact that in the North, fish and chips filled a growing social need. In Lancashire, in particular, where women were employed in the cotton mills, the fish-and-chip supper filled the bill for a warming, cheap, ready-made dinner. It was also in Lancashire that positive proof exists of engineers creating and improving the first frying ranges. In addition, Priestland found some convincing anecdotal evidence from a frying family in Lancashire that they were actually ahead of Malin's. So until a more plausible story turns up, Fish and Chip did not meet in Scotland, though their Scottish offspring have been prolific.

The batterologist

In the world of batterology the Japanese take some beating. Much debate and rivalry exists among fish-and-chip fryers as to the best batter, but sit on a high stool at a Japanese tempura bar — and before you is the expert.

A carefully considered blend of oils first: ground-nut, olive, sesame seed, cotton-seed, peanut. The proportions are geared to provide the most delicate flavour. While he heats them to around 190C/375F, he prepares the ingredients: bite-sized pieces of fish and thin pieces of vegetables, not too wet, which will cook quickly. There are aubergines, mushrooms, peppers, asparagus, mange-tout.

He puts an egg into a bowl, and adds ice cold water from the fridge and a large pinch of baking soda. He sifts in enough flour to allow the liquid to run easily over the back of the spoon. He must work quickly now for the batter will only last about ten minutes before the flour particles soften and spoil the crispness of his finished result. The prepared food is coated and dropped into the oil.

As cold batter hits hot oil it puffs up. The moisture in the food turns to steam and makes it tender in minutes. Only a few pieces are cooked at a time, or the cold food will reduce the temperature of the oil and the food will become soggy.

A minute on one side and then he turns the food with his chopsticks to brown on the other. It's pale golden and puffy as he lifts it from the oil and places it on the little bowl, lined with a paper napkin, which sits at everyone's place. There is a bowl of warm sake, some dipping-sauce, and the deep-fried delicacies keep coming ...

There's nothing quite like it in any Western food culture, but there is no reason, it seems to me, why British fish and chips could not aspire to similar heights of gastronomic excellence by following some of the tempura rules; good flavoured oil, crisp light batter, and instant eating.

How you overcome the problem of the wrapped take-away is another matter. Flabby chips and soggy batter are one of the hazards we have come to accept as the price of convenience. But it would be good to see some of the restaurants who pride themselves on the quality of their cooking, making more of an art of the deep-fat frier. It would be good to sit again on a bar stool and look down on the sizzling food, carefully tended by a home-style version of the Japanese expert.

LIGHT TEMPURA BATTER

INGREDIENTS

To make enough to cook food for about 4 people:
1 egg yolk
250ml (8fl oz) bottled carbonated
water (Scottish), chilled
75g (3oz) fine, plain white flour
pinch of bicarbonate of soda

METHOD

Put the egg into the bowl and add about three-quarters of the water. Sift the flour and soda on top and whisk in. The consistency should just coat the back of a wooden spoon. Add more water if it is too thick. Use immediately.

Fish:
Use any filleted white fish, cut into small pieces, or prawns or scallops.

Chips:
While all potatoes will make chips, dry varieties like King Edward, Golden Wonder, Maris Piper or Kerrs Pinks will cook faster and make lighter chips than waxy varieties. Dry them well.

Frying:

Use oil in the proportions: 75 per cent ground-nut oil or other light-tasting vegetable oil; 20 per cent sesame seed oil; 5 per cent olive oil. More expensive, but also more highly favoured by the experts, is a blend of 70 per cent peanut oil to 30 per cent sesame oil.

Heat to 190C/375F and fry the food in small quantities at a time, removing any debris with a slotted spoon. Serve as the food is ready in bowls or plates lined with paper napkins.

FISH BATTER (TRADITIONAL)

INGREDIENTS

To make enough to cook fish for about 4 people:
125g (4oz) self-raising flour
1 teaspoon salt
250ml (8fl oz) milk
1 tablespoon oil

METHOD

Sift the dry ingredients into a bowl and gradually add the milk and then the oil. It should be a smooth consistency of thick cream, much thicker than tempura. Use immediately.

PIES AND BRIDIES

Scotch pies

'Delightful as were her pigeon and apple pies,' says a St Andrews professor, describing a favourite pie-wife, 'her chef-d'oeuvre … was a certain kind of mutton-pie. The mutton was minced to the smallest consistency, and was made up in a standing crust, which was strong enough to contain the most delicious gravy … There were no lumps of fat or grease in them at all … They always arrived piping hot … It makes my mouth water still when I think of those pies.'

On the West Coast the renowned pie-maker was also a woman, known as 'Granny Black' whose tavern in Glasgow's Candleriggs became Mecca for pie-lovers. Pie-wifes and tavern pie-makers, around the beginning of the 20th century, satisfied the demand for a hand-held meal for working people. Small Scotch pies are the forerunner of the modern hamburger or hot-dog. Though they are sold today from all bakeries on a daily basis, the 'hot-pie' trade moves into mass-production on Saturdays as they are delivered by the thousand to football grounds for eating at half-time — with a cup of hot Bovril. Not all pie bakers, however, regard the football pitch the best place to sell their pies.

Bill Strannigan of Short's Pies (Irvine and late of Glasgow) refuses to sell to football clubs, since he claims that they are looking for extra-cheap pies. If there is a fault in the Scotch pie, (any pie for that matter) it's the *cheap pie* made with too little meat, too much fat, lots of breadcrumb filler, and plenty of pepper to cover the defects. To check out Short's pies in the making, I arrive at 7.30am, as pie-baking is about to start for the day. The bakers are Alex and Logan Hall who keep the production line going during the day with hot-out-the-oven pies. The first thing to see are the pastry shells. Into the mixer goes flour, fat, salt and hot water to make the dough, which is then broken-up into small lumps. A heated metal disc moulds them into the pie shape, cooking the dough slightly as the hot metal presses out the dough. Then they are put onto a tray and left for three days to harden. Logan will shape around a 1,000 pie shells before the day is out.

Meanwhile, Alex has already mixed the pie filling for the day: 6kg (12lbs) of beef, including lean and fat. Around 40 per cent fat is required for a good pie. Too much, and it become too greasy, too little and the meat becomes tough. Into it goes a measured amount of salt and pepper, and pints and pints of water. It's very sloppy by the time he is finished. Dollops of it fill the now rock-hard pie shells to within half an inch (1cm) of the rim. The mix settles down and more water is added. If the mix is too dry, he explains, the meat will dry out and the pie will be unpleasant to eat. The lid goes on — a thin disc, which fits on top of the filling — and they are baked in a very hot oven (250C/500F) for 20 minutes.

On to the next batch. Soon there is the aroma of cooking pies in the bakehouse, and the browned, sizzling and bubbling pies are coming out of the oven.

'The best time to eat them,' says Alex, 'is when they are just off the boil. But if it's a good pie it should be just as good cold.'

It makes my mouth water still when I think of those pies.

Their history

The *Scotch pie* is a development of the early raised pie made with hot-water paste and 'raised' up the side of a mould, then left to set and harden before the filling is added. Though it's made in the same way, the Scots version is a small individual-portion size pie — 9cm (3½in) diameter by 4cm (1½in) deep, the top edge of the pie extends by about 1cm (½in) beyond the filling which makes its characteristic holding-space for fillings. Its popularity appears to have developed in the latter half of the 19th century as the industrial revolution brought large numbers of people into urban areas where wages were low and living (and cooking) conditions poor. Local bakers, itinerant pie-men or women, or tavern cooks made the 'hot-pie' ('het-pey' in Dundee) and it became a sustaining hand-held convenience food for working men, women and children.

They had to be eaten hot: either hot from the bakers, or reheated at home. Some bakers who provided the 'hot-pie' service also kept a jug of hot gravy for pouring into the centre of the pie. Tinned beans and mashed potatoes became popular 'fillers', piled up in the space above the meat filling. While the inside filling was originally minced mutton, making use of the tough mature meat unsuitable for other purposes, the mutton has largely been replaced by beef.

Small, half-size pies are made by a few bakers, they may be made with or without onion. Some use chopped beef steak rather than mince and call them 'steak' pies. Many bakers now make other pies, using their Scotch Pie moulds but with a wide range of other fillings; some of which are vegetarian, such as a savoury custard of cheese and tomato, macaroni cheese, vegetables in a savoury custard. These are mostly baked without the pastry lids but still with the space on top for adding sauce.

Forfar bridies

While the mutton pie was an everyday hand-held meal, the bridie was a treat. A flat, horseshoe-shaped meaty pastry, not filled with minced mutton, but the very best, finely chopped steak. They have become associated with Forfar though they are widely made today throughout Angus and Aberdeenshire by both bakers and butchers. So why Forfar? And why 'bridie'? Was it from a woman named Bridie, who hawked them about the town in the late 19th century? Or did they take their name from the fact that their lucky horseshoe shape made them popular fare at the bride's meal? Opinions differ.

The treat tag, however, is undisputed, with anecdotal evidence of late 19th century farm-hands congregating in Forfar on Saturdays for their day off and queuing up outside the bakers for a special carthorse-shoe-sized *het bradie*. The Forfar bridie was also a treat for those of us of a later generation, more familiar with a Glaswegian impostor (a dod of mediocre sausagemeat encased in a semicircle of puff-pastry).

Our bridie treat came once a year, when we went to the soft-fruit fields around Forfar to pick berries for a few hard-earned pennies. Each morning we hoped for rain, when we could escape the red berries and queue up for a *het bradie* treat. A favourite butcher, we reckoned, made the best. Clutching our hot bridies we would make for *the pictures* and sit eating the large flat horse-shoes, filled to the edge with meaty steak and onions, while watching the film, and wishing the rain would last forever.

Childhood nostalgia is all very well, but what has happened to the bridie today? Have they changed? And who makes the best now? I arrived in Forfar one morning to bridie-eat my way round the town.

First sample, to my mind, had too much pastry and not enough meat. The next had a taste of unnatural additives and pseudo meat-flavouring, that one was dropped into the nearest bin. Was I being too fussy? Then I found McLarens, a third-generation baker, with two shops in the town and one in Kirriemuir. William McLaren's grandfather started the business in 1893 and his bridie production for the day (around 300 a day during the week, rising to 3,000 at the weekend) was in full swing.

'Would you like to come into the bakehouse and see the bridies being made?'

Among the bustle of bakers baking, there was also a butcher butchering. Cutting up a shoulder of beef, removing the excess fat and sinew and preparing it for the mincer. To each shoulder of meat, he would add about 15kg (30lbs) of beef suet for flavour and to prevent the meat drying out and hardening. Salt, pepper and onions were the only other additives.

Like proper pasties in Cornwall, bridies in Forfar, made to the traditional recipe, use high-quality meat and have a high meat content, which makes them more expensive. This is, after all, as William points out, the very heart of Aberdeen Angus beef country where people are fussy about both the quality and quantity of beef in their bridies.

While our nostalgic best-butcher's-bridie relied on finely chopped steak, the modern method involves mincing the beef through a large plate on the mincer to give a coarser texture than for pies. This allows the addition of a bready-filler to eke out the expensive meat, a fault discovered on subsequent bridie-tastings further afield than Forfar. Robinson (butchers) of Arbroath produced the steak-bridie with the best flavour and most steak, though the pastry was puff rather than short. Wallace (bakers) of Dundee, like McLarens of Forfar, make an authentic all-meat minced-steak filling encased in short pastry. McLaren is the place to go for the widest range of sizes. Other notable bridies were from the Strathmore Bakery, Blairgowrie, Irvines (butchers) Blairgowrie and Goodfellows (bakers), Broughty Ferry.

At McLaren's, bridies have been in production for around a hundred years. The average production per week is now around 4-5,000. The founder of the business, James McLaren, served his apprenticeship with Jollys, generally regarded in the town to be the first baker to make the bridie. Of the bridie origins, William prefers his grandfather's story which links the pastry with lucky horseshoes and a bride's wedding breakfast.

The luck of the bridie, I am happy to report, continues to hold.

OCTOBER.

Gather Winter Fruits. Trench and fallow grounds (mixing with proper foil) to ly over the Winter. Prepare dungs and mannures, mixing and laying them in heaps bottom'd and covered with Earth. Plant Hawthorn Hedges, And all Trees that lofe their leaves ; Alfo lay their branches. Prun Rofes. Gather feeds of Haffell, Hawthorn, Plan, Afh, Beach, Oak, Aple, Pear, &c. Cut Strawberries, Artichocks, Afparagus, covering their beds with dung and Afhes. Earth up Winter Sallades, Herbes, and Flowers, a little. Plant Cabbage, &c. Plant Tulips, Anemonies, and other Bulbs. Sow the feed of Bairs-ears, Cowflips, Tulips, &c. Beat and Roll Gravel and Grafs. Finifh your laft weeding and mowing. Lay bair leopered Tree Roots and remove what harms them : alfo delve and dung fuch as require it. Drain exceffive moifture wherever it be. Pickle and conferve Fruits. Make Perry and Cyder.

You may now fafely remove Bees,

Garden Difhes and drinks in feafon.

Coleworts, Leeks, Cabbage, Cole-flowers, Onions, Shallot, Beans. Blanched Endive and Sellery. Pickled Afparagus, Purflain, &c.

Scorzonera, Beet-rave, Carrots, Turneeps, Parfneeps, Potatoes, Skirrets, Artichocks, Cucumbers, Aples, Pears, Plumes, Almond, &c.

Cyder, Perry, and Wine of Cherries, Currans, Goosberries, Rasberries, Ail of Liquorifh, Metheglin, &c.

F I N I S.

John Reid, *The Scots Gard'ner*, (1683)

Sources

This is a select bibliography with details of trade associations, academic organisations, commercial food producers and retailers who have provided much useful help and assistance on this project.

Baking and milling

Banfield, W T, *"Manna": A Comprehensive Treatise on Bread Manufacture* (2nd edition), Maclaren, London, 1947.
Gauldie, E, *The Scottish Country Miller 1700-1900*, John Donald, Edinburgh, 1981.
Kirkland, J, *The Modern Baker*, Gresham Publishing, London, 1931.

Trade associations and useful addresses:
Scottish Association of Master Bakers, Atholl House, 4 Torphichen Street, Edinburgh.
Contact: Ian Hay, Director.

Beremeal
Golspie Mill, Golspie, Sutherland.
Tel: 01408-633278. Contact: Fergus Morrison (miller).

Butteries
Aitkens Bakers, Glenbervie Road, Torry, Aberdeen.
Tel: 01224-877768.
Chalmers Bakers, 13 Auchmill Road, Bucksburn, Aberdeen.
Tel: 01224-712631. Contact: Ron Chalmers.

Dundee Cake
Goodfellow and Steven Bakers, 81-83 Gray Street, Broughty Ferry, Dundee, Angus.
Tel: 01382-730181. Contact: David or Inglis Goodfellow.

Oatmeal
Aberfeldy Water Mill, Mill Street, Aberfeldy.
Tel: 01887-820803.
Blair Atholl Water Mill, Ford Road, Blair Atholl.
Tel: 01796-481321.
Lower City Mills, West Mill Street, Perth.
Tel: 01738-627958. Contact: Stephen Page (miller).
Montgarrie Mills, Alford, Aberdeenshire.
Tel: 01975-562209. Contact: Donald MacDonald (miller).

Forfar bridies
McLaren Bakers, Market Street, Forfar.
Tel: 01307-463315. Contact: William McLaren.

Scotch pies
Bradford Bakers, 70 Spiersbridge Road, Thornliebank, Glasgow.
Tel: 0141-638 1118. Contact: Hugh Bradford.
Short's Bakers, 147 High Street, Irvine.
Tel: 01294-273198. Contact: Mathew Short, Alex Hall.

Selkirk Bannocks
Dalgetty Bakers, 6 Bank Street, Galashiels.
Tel: 01896-752508. Contact: Bill Murray.

Tearooms
Fisher and Donaldson Bakers, 12 Whitehall Street, Dundee.
Tel: 01382-223488. Contact: Eric Milne. (Branches also in St Andrews and Cupar)

Beef and lamb

Aberdeen Angus Review, Official Journal of the Aberdeen-Angus Cattle Society, October 1994.
Hall, S and Clutton-Brock, J, *Two Hundred Years of British Farm Livestock*, London, 1989.
Highland Breeders' Journal, July 1994.
The Highland Cattle Society Newsletter, Dec 1994/Jan 1995.
The Galloway Journal, Dec 1994, (official publication of the Galloway Cattle Society).
Information leaflet 994: Rare Breeds Facts and Figures, The Rare Breeds Survival Trust, National Agricultural Centre, Warwickshire.
Shorthorns: Two Centuries of Breed Development, The Shorthorn Society, 1993.

Trade associations and useful addresses:
The Aberdeen Angus Cattle Society, Pedigree House, 6 King's Place, Perth.
Tel: 01738-622477. Contact: R Anderson.
The Beef Shorthorn Society, 4th Street National Agricultural Centre, Kenilworth, Warwickshire.
Tel: 01203-696549. Contact: John Wood Roberts.
The Galloway Cattle Society, 15 New Market Street, Castle Douglas, Kirkcudbrightshire.
Contact: Alex McDonald.
The Highland Cattle Society, 59 Drumlanrig Street, Thornhill, Dumfriesshire.
Tel: 01848-330438. Contact: A Wilson.

Meat and Livestock Commission, Winterhill House, Snowden Drive, Milton Keynes.
Scotch Quality Beef and Lamb Association, Rural Centre, West Mains, Ingliston, Newbridge, Midlothian.
Tel: 0131-333 5335. Contact: Brian Simpson, Liz Welsh.

Ayrshire bacon curers

Ramsay of Carluke Butchers, Wellriggs Factory, 22 Mount Street, Carluke, Lanarkshire.
Tel: 01555-772277. Contact: Andrew Ramsay.

Haggis

Macsween Butchers, 130 Bruntsfield Place, Edinburgh.
Tel: 0131-229 1216.
Contact: Jo and James Macsween.

Highland beef

Macbeth Butchers, 20 High Street Forres, Morayshire.
Tel: 01309-672254. Contact: Michael Gibson.

Reestit mutton

Smith Butchers, 61 Commercial Street, Lerwick.
Tel: 01595-693306. Contact: Mark Anderson and Laurence Tulloch.

Sassermaet

Anderson Butchers, 49 Commercial Road, Lerwick.
Tel: 01595-692819. Contact: Peter Anderson.

Cheese

Cheke, V, *The Story of Cheesemaking in Britain,* Routledge, London, 1959.
Cultural Connections and Cheese in *Folk Life* Vol. 25, A Gailey, 1986-7.
The History of the Ayrshire Breed, Centenary Journal of the Ayrshire Cattle Society, 1977.
Rance, P, *The Great British Cheese Book*, Macmillan, London, 1982.
Smith, J, *Cheesemaking in Scotland*, Scottish Dairy Association, Glasgow, 1995.

Trade associations and useful addresses:

The Ayrshire Cattle Society, 1 Racecourse Road, Ayr.
Tel: 01292-267123. Contact: Stuart Thomson.
British Cheese Awards, Old Woolman's House, Hastings Hill, Churchill, Oxon.
Tel: 01608- 659325. Contact: Juliet Harbutt.
Handmade Cheeses of Scotland, Ogscastle, Carnwath, Lanarkshire.

Tel: 01899-810257. Contact: Humphrey Errington.
McLellands, New Cheese Market, Townhead, Glasgow.
Tel: 0141-552 2962.
Iain Mellis Cheesemonger, 30a Victoria Street, Edinburgh and 492 Great Western Road, Glasgow.
Tel: 0141-339 8998.

Fish, shellfish and seaweed

Cutting, C L, *The History of Fish Processing from Modern to Ancient Times*: Hill, London, 1955.
Davidson, A, *North Atlantic Seafood,* Macmillan, London, 1979.
Davidson, A, *Seafood,* Mitchell Beazley, London, 1989.
Holmyard, N, *Shellfish Farming in Scotland — from crofting to big business* in *Fish Trader Yearbook*, 1993.
Phillips, R, *Seaweeds and Seashells,* Hamilton, London, 1987.
Scottish Shellfish Farms, Annual Production Survey, 1995.
Marine Laboratory Aberdeen, report of The Scottish Office: Agriculture, Environment and Fisheries Department.

Trade associations and useful addresses:

Association of Scottish Shellfish Growers, Polfearn, Taynuilt, Argyll.
Tel: 01866-822454. Contact: Nicky Holmyard.
Loch Fyne Oysters, Clachan Farm, Cairndow, Argyll.
Tel: 01499-600217/264. Contact: Andrew Lane.
MacCallum's of Troon, Fish Merchant, 944 Argyle Street, Glasgow.
Tel: 0141-204 4456 Contact: John MacCallum.
The Scottish Office: Agriculture, Environment and Fisheries Department, Marine Laboratory, Fish Cultivation Building, PO Box 101, Victoria Road, Aberdeen.
Tel: 01224-876544. Contact: David Fraser.
Scottish Salmon Board, Drummond House, Scott Street, Perth.
Tel: 01738-635973.
Sea Fish Industry Authority, 18 Logie Mill, Logie Green Road, Edinburgh.
Tel: 0131-558 3331. Contact: Julie Edgar.
Shellfish Association of Great Britain, Fishmonger's Hall, London Bridge, London.

Food, festivals and cookery

Banks, M M, *British Calendar Customs Scotland*, Vol.1: *Moveable Festivals*. Vol.2: *The Seasons, The Quarters,*

Hogmanay, January to May. Vol.3: *June to December, Christmas, The Yules*. Folk-Lore Society, London and Glasgow, 1941.

Barz, B, *Festivals with Children,* Floris, Edinburgh, 1984.

Brown, C, *Scottish Regional Recipes,* Richard Drew, Glasgow, 1981; *Scottish Cookery,* Richard Drew, Glasgow, 1985; *Broths to Bannocks,* John Murray, London, 1990.

Burt, E, *Letters from the North of Scotland* (5th edition), London, 1822.

Carey, D and Large, J, *Festivals, Family and Food,* Hawthorn, Stroud, 1982.

Clark, Lady, *The Cookery Book of Lady Clark of Tillypronie,* Southover, 1909 (reprinted 1994).

Dods (Dods, 'Meg', of the Cleikum Inn, St Ronan's), *The Cook and Housewife's Manual,* Edinburgh, 1826.

Douglas, H, *The Hogmanay Companion,* Neil Wilson Publishing, Glasgow, 1993.

Hannan, B, (ed.) *The Flavour of Scotland,* Mainstream, Edinburgh, 1995.

Irvine, J, *Up-Helly-Aa,* Shetland Publishing, Lerwick, 1982.

Kinchin, P, *Tea and Taste: The Glasgow Tea Rooms 1875-1975,* White Cockade, Oxon, 1991.

McNeill, F M, *The Scots Kitchen,* Blackie, Glasgow, 1929; *The Silver Bough,* Vol.1: *Scottish Folk-Lore and Folk-Belief.* Vol.2: *A Calendar of Scottish National Festivals, Candlemas to Harvest Home.* Vol.3: *Hallowe'en to Yule.* Vol.4: *Scottish Local Festivals,* MacLellan, Glasgow.

Molyneux, J, *The Carved Angel Cookery Book,* Grafton, London, 1992.

Reid, J, *The Scots Gard'ner*: published for the *Climate of Scotland.* (facsimile, Mainstream, Edinburgh, 1988.) *Scottish National Dictionary*, Edinburgh, 1931-76.

Simmons, J, *A Shetland Cookbook,* Thuleprint, Shetland, 1978.

Stevenson, S, *The Magic of Saucery,* Mitchell Beazley, London, 1995.

Thomson, G, *The Other Orkney Book,* Edinburgh, 1980.

Fruit and vegetables

Bowen, S, *Scottish Potatoes — through the 20th Century,* (academic paper, undated).

MacLean, D, *Potato Varieties*, *a Factsheet on Special Properties*, undated.

Salaman, R, *The History and Social Influence of the Potato,* Cambridge University Press, 1970.

Soft Fruit Research Information, published by the Scottish Crop Research Institute, Invergowrie.

Wilson, A, *The Story of the Potato through illustrated varieties,* Alan Sutton, Fleet, Hants, 1993.

Trade associations and useful addresses:

British Potato Council, Broad Field House, 4 Between Towns Road, Oxford. Tel: 01865-714455. Perth office, tel: 01738-622305.

Leeks, turnip and kail

Scottish Agricultural College, Horticulture Department, SCRI, Invergowrie, Dundee. Tel: 01382-568362. Contact: Mark Sutton.

Potatoes

Scottish Agricultural College, Crop Systems, Bush Estate, Penicuik, Midlothian. Tel: 0131-535 3000. Contact: Simon Bowen.

Farm farm stalls, shops, pick-your-own

Arbuckles Fruit Farm, (just off the A90, a mile out of Dundee). Tel: 01382-360249. Contact: Peter Arbuckle

Ballinshoe, Kirriemuir (on the A926 between Forfar and Kirriemuir). Tel: 01575-573466. Contact: Brian Lilley.

Bankhead, Meigle (on the A94 between Coupar Angus and Meigle). Tel: 01828-640265. Contact: George MacLaren

Bramblebank Fruit Farm, Blairgowrie (on the A93 Balmoral road). Tel: 01250-872266. Contact: Peter Thomson

Broadslap, Dunning (on B9141, south of A9 between Auchterarder and Perth). Tel: 01738-730242. Contact: John or Vilma Kirk.

Cairnie Fruit Farm, Cupar, Fife. Tel: 01334-652384. Contact: John Laird.

Donauful, Keltney Burn, Coshieville, Aberfeldy. Tel: 01887-830371. Contact: Bill Scott.

Evanshen Fruit Farm, Dalhonzie, Comrie. Tel: 01764-670416.

Flocklones Fruit Farm, Longforgan, Perthshire (to the west of Dundee, off the A90 on the Benvie Fowlis road).

Newbigging Fruit Farm, Newbigging (off the Forfar road going north from Dundee at turn-off for Newbigging). Tel: 01382-380255. Contact: Ian Reid.

Ruthven Fruit Farm, Alyth, Perthshire (on the A936 Alyth to Kirriemuir road). Tel: 01575-530284. Contact: John Hamilton.

Scones of Lethendy Fruit Farm, Perth
(on the A93 north of Scone).
Tel: 01738-551135. Contact: David Leslie.
Stiellsmuir Fruit Farm and Shop, Woodland Road,
Rosemount, Blairgowrie, Perthshire.
Tel: 01225-872237.
Contact: Morag and David Rendall.
Slatefield Fruit Farm, Dundee Road, Forfar.
Tel: 01307-462466. Contact: Donald Morrison.

Soft fruits

Scottish Crop Research Institute, Invergowrie,
Dundee.
Tel: 01382-562731. Contact: Tim Heilbronn,
Rex Brennan.
Scottish Soft Fruit Growers Ltd, 45 Allan Street,
Blairgowrie, Perthshire.
Tel: 01250-875500. Contact: Michael Thomson,
Director.
The Scottish Office Economic Statistics Unit, Leith,
Edinburgh.
Tel: 0131-556-8400. Contact: Paul Gagan.

Food smoking

Walker, K, *Practical Food Smoking,* Neil Wilson
Publishing, Glasgow, 1995.

Trade associations and useful addresses:

Alba Smokehouse, Kilmory Industrial Estate,
Lochgilphead, Argyll.
Tel: 01546-606400. Contact: Mike Leng.

Equipment manufacturers

Innes Walker Food Smokers Ltd,
Midton of Fulwood, Stewarton, Ayrshire.
Tel: 01560-484869. Contact: Kate Walker.

Game and eels

Teviot Game Fare Smokery, Kirkbank House,
Eckford, Kelso, Roxburghshire.
Tel: 01835-850253. Contact: Denis Wilson.

Peat-smoked salmon

Mermaid Fish Supplies, Clachan, Locheport,
Lochmaddy, North Uist.
Tel: 01876-580209. Contact: George Jackson.

Salmon

Joseph Johnston, 3 America Street, Montrose.
Tel: 01674-672666. Contact: Marshall Halliday,
Ken Bruce.
Macdonald's Smoked Produce, Glenuig, Lochailort,
Inverness-shire.

Tel: 01687-470266. Contact: Simon Macdonald.

Smokies

R Spink, 33-35 Seagate, Arbroath, Angus.
Tel: 01241-872023. Contact: Bob Spink.

Solway salmon

Galloway Smokehouse, Creetown, Carsluith,
Newton Stewart.
Tel: 016771-820354. Contact: Alan Watson.

Game

Drysdale, J, *The Game Cookery Book,* Collins, Glasgow,
1975.
Eden, R, *The Sporting Epicure,* Kyle Cathie, London,
1991.
Little, C, *The Game Cookbook,* Crowood Press,
Wiltshire, 1988.
Stuart-Wortley, A, *Fur and Feather Series — The Grouse;
The Salmon,* Longmans Green, London, 1895.

Trade associations and useful addresses:

Game Fayre, Unit 1 Tayview Road, Perth.
Tel: 01738-443200. Contact: Alan Cory-Wright.
Red Deer Commission, Inverness.
Tel: 01463-231751.

Venison and game birds

Pitlochry Game Services, Ferry Road, Pitlochry,
Perthshire.
Tel: 01796-473254. Contact: Kenneth MacKay.

Honey, marmalade and preserves

Wilson, C A, *The Book of Marmalade,* Constable,
London, 1985.

Trade associations and useful addresses:

Bee Farmers Association, Newcastleton,
Roxburghshire.
Tel: 01387-376737. Contact: Brian Stenhouse.

Tea, coffee and honey

Braithwaites, 6 Castle Street, Dundee, Angus.
Tel: 01382-322693. Contact: Allan Braithwaite
(tea and coffee), George Braithwaite (honey).
Heather Hills Honey Farm, Bridge of Cally,
Blairgowrie, Perthshire.
Tel: 01250-886252. Contact: Ian Kirkwood.
Struan Apiaries, Burnside Lane, Conon Bridge,
Ross-shire.
Tel: 01349-861427. Contact: Hamish Robertson.

Ices

Liddle, C and Weir, R, *Ices: The Definitive Guide,* Hodder and Stoughton, London, 1993.

McKee, F, *Ice Cream and Immortality: Oxford Symposium on Food and Cookery, Public Eating*, Prospect Books, London, 1991.

Useful addresses:

Boni Ices, Lochran Buildings, Edinburgh.
Tel: 0131-229 2740. Contact: Mr S Boni.

Nardini, 8 Greenock Road, Largs, Ayrshire.
Tel: 01475-674555. Contact: Pete Nardini.

Rizza's, 16 Gordon Street, Huntly, Aberdeenshire.
Tel: 01466-793907. Contact: Phillip Morrison.

Mushrooms

Phillips, R, *Mushrooms,* Pan Books, London, 1981; *Wild Foods*, Pan Books, London, 1983.

Useful addresses:

Strathspey Mushrooms, Seaforth Road, Muir of Ord, Ross-shire, or Kila, Grampian Road, Aviemore, Inverness-shire.
Tel: 01479-810573. Contact: Duncan Riley.

Whisky

Brown, G, *The Whisky Trails,* Prion, London, 1993.

Bruce Lockhart, R, *Scotch — The Whisky of Scotland in Fact and Story* (7th edition), Neil Wilson Publishing, Glasgow, 1995.

Jackson, M, *Malt Whisky Companion,* Dorling Kindersley, London, 1989.

Milroy, W, *The Original Malt Whisky Almanac* (7th edition), Neil Wilson Publishing, Glasgow, 1998.

Shaw, C, *Whisky,* (Collins Gem series), Harper Collins, Glasgow, 1993.

Trade associations and useful addresses:

Morrison Bowmore Distillers Ltd.,
Springburn Bond, Carlisle Street, Glasgow.
Tel: 0141-558 9011 Contact: James McEwan

The Scotch Malt Whisky Society, 87 Giles Street, Leith, Edinburgh.
Tel: 0131-554-3451. Contact: Richard Gordon

The Scotch Whisky Association,
20 Atholl Crescent, Edinburgh.
Tel: 0131-229 4383. Contact: Campbell Evans.

Index of recipes

Main index